The Handbook of
World Transport

The Handbook of World Transport

by
Yvan du Jonchay

translated by
Loren Goldner

Facts On File, Inc.,
119 West 57th Street, New York, N.Y. 10019

The Handbook of World Transport

Copyright, 1978 by Bordas

Published by Facts On File, Inc., 119 West 57th Street, New York, N.Y. 10019

Library of Congress Cataloging in Publication Data

Du Jonchay, Ivan, 1899-
    The Handbook of World Transport.

    Translation of Les grands transports mondiaux, by Ivan du Jonchay, with the collaboration of Michel Murphy and Francois Serraz.
    Includes bibliographical references and index.
    1. Merchant marine.   2. Aeronautics, Commercial.
    3. Transportation.   I. Murphy, Michel, joint author.
    II. Serraz, Francois, joint author.   III. Title.
HE735.D8313   387.5   79-27413
ISBN 0-87196-393-0

9 8 7 6 5 4 3 2 1
PRINTED IN THE UNITED STATES OF AMERICA

Contents

Introduction

Transportation has always played an important role throughout the long history of the human race, favoring seafaring nations to the detriment of others. All great civilizations were trading nations. Control of trade routes has always been an important aspect of power and the quality, low cost and safety of transportation networks have been the basis for a civilization's dominance. Japan is the best contemporary example of this. Lacking oil, gas and iron, Japan has been able to obtain all its energy and raw materials by means of its transport systems.

At various times since earliest antiquity, there have always been countries—or empires—that were more advanced and powerful than their neighbors and that were able to obtain the dominant proportion of the available wealth. This was true of Egypt, of Phoenicia and of Alexander the Great's empire. The most recent case was the British empire, which dominated the 19th and 20th centuries through the world's most important fleet and its coal reserves, the energy source of the era. Two consecutive world wars and the growing importance of oil changed this. Now the world is dominated by the "Big Eight," made up of the United States and Canada, the USSR, Japan and the four European powers: West Germany, France, the United Kingdom and Italy. With 20% of the world's population, these countries, according to the World Bank, have 65% of the world's per capita income and consume 80% of the world's energy.[1]

The disparity between the Big Eight and the world's other 195 countries is obvious. It is also clear that this accumulation of wealth is a result of the development of elaborate transport systems.

1. "Population, per Capita Product, and Growth Rates," *World Bank Atlas*, Washington, D.C. 1976.

RANK OF "BIG EIGHT" IN MAJOR ENERGY INDICATORS (1975 - 1976)

	Population (millions of inhabitants)		GNP* (millions of U.S. $)		GNP* per capita (U.S. $)		Electricity twh* (% of World)			Automobiles (millions)	
	(World rank listed to right of each column)											
United States	214	(2)	1,508	(1)	7,060	(1)	1,947	33.0%	(1)	101	(1)
Canada	22	(8)	152	(7)	6,650	(2)	262	4.4%	(6)	7	(7)
U.S.S.R.	254	(1)	666	(2)	2,620	(8)	914	15.0%	(2)	1.8	(8)
Japan	111	(3)	495	(3)	4,460	(5)	470	8.0%	(3)	14.5	(4)
West Germany	62	(4)	409	(4)	6,660	(3)	300	5.0%	(4)	17	(2)
France	53	(7)	304	(5)	5,700	(4)	174	3.0%	(7)	14.6	(3)
Great Britain	56	(5)	215	(6)	3,800	(6)	282	4.7%	(5)	13.5	(6)
Italy	56	(5)	164	(8)	2,950	(7)	145	2.4%	(8)	13.6	(5)
	828	20%	3,913	64%			4,494	75.5%		186.4	90%
World							6,042			207.4	

Source: World Bank, Washington, D.C., 1976.

Note: The People's Republic of China, with a GNP of $286 billion, has already surpassed the level of Great Britain, but its income per capita is much lower ($350).

*GNP: gross national product
**twh: tetrawatt hour

Transport involves two procedures. The first consists of taking inventory of resources, analyzing their content and locating their sources and their destination. This is a commercial operation of weighing prospects and selecting resources worth shipping. A century ago an economist wrote: "The history of trade is inseparable from the history of geography because it is the desire to obtain precious or useful items which was the stimulus for the boldest enterprises both in antiquity and in modern times." The other procedure involves carrying, in the widest sense of the term, these resources from one point to another. It depends, in the most general sense, on the "sailor" and the "ship."

The Handbook of World Transport studies the two major modes of international transportation, maritime and airborne, with these two procedures in mind. The study begins with maritime shipping. It first gives an overview of oil tanker fleets and the bulk carriers handling other goods. Then it turns to containerized ships, "roll-on/roll-off" ships (vessels with flat decks where cargo, e.g., vehicles, is rolled on and rolled off) and barge carriers. Finally, it deals with the increasing number of liquefied natural gas (LNG) carriers. Then the study looks at production and shipment of major cargoes. It deals first with oil—the "lion's share" of such shipping. The study gives an overall picture of production and of existing reserves, tonnage per country and its uses; the important role of the major refiners; the use of huge ships and the more recent developments in oil transport. Then it looks at the transporting of iron ore, coal, cereals, bauxite, phosphates, liquefied gas and other goods, and passengers. *The Handbook of World Transport* then turns to the fleet's adaptation to changing trade patterns, its organization and finally to the industry's infrastructure.

I have adopted an analogous procedure for air freight. After a review of aviation history, the study looks at the evolution of airplanes, helicopters and VTOLs (vertical takeoff and landing planes), dirigibles and hydroplanes. After this breakdown, the study focuses on the transportation of passengers and the shipment of freight. Finally, it analyzes the industry's infrastructure. The third section deals with pipelines, river traffic, railroads and roads. The book concludes with a look at the transportation of energy.

I have included in the appendix three studies that will clarify and elaborate everything presented in this work: a history of oil and the search for new reserves and refining; an analysis of the oil crisis and the future of electricity; and a discussion of uranium and the new energy sources.

Finally, the reader can consult a series of 20 full-color maps. Throughout the work, specific references permit him to make concrete use of these documents. Map 1 is not directly related to the text, but it serves to remind us that problems of transportation are not new.

Maritime Transport

Introduction

It is not necessary to go back to the "flood" to present a study of maritime transport, although the flood did give rise to the first specialized ship. A rapid survey of the last 30 years will allow us to evaluate industry trends.

Under the headline "Thirty Years of Triumphant Expansion," the French *Journal of the Merchant Marine* presented the history of the world fleet from the end of World War II to July 1, 1975, the date on which *Lloyd's List* published its semiannual ship inventory. The headline's optimistic tone reflected both the mood in the postwar period and the subsequent lively expansion that accompanied or was facilitated by the development of the oil industry.

It was precisely because of oil that production boomed. This is seen in the geometric expansion of the number of ships, the growth in their size, the corresponding gigantic dimension of the shipyards that built and repaired them, and the growth of ports that received them. Industry expansion peaked roughly in 1970. At that point signs of malaise were already appearing in the Western economies. There was a slowdown in the expansion of international maritime transport and a significant fall in the volume of order for new ships. The overheated world economy of 1972-73 permitted a last burst of production in 1973 when 74 million gross register tons were ordered. This figure represented nearly two and one half times the volume of tonnage in service in 1973, which itself set a record.[2]

The considerable increase in oil prices—which quadrupled and even sextupled—prompted a downturn in the world economy, gradually affecting various sectors of maritime transport: first oil, then bulk cargo, then dry merchandise. Shipowners suffered a falloff in demand, but they took some time before canceling orders. Thus the fleet at hand, although not

2. Edouard Recolle, *Journal of the Merchant Marine (JMM)*, 1975.

necessarily in service on July 1, 1976, had grown still larger because of the earlier orders, particularly for oil tankers.[3]

WORLD SHIPPING TONNAGE
(millions of metric tons)

1937-38:	490
1952 :	660
1960 :	1,100
1964 :	1,507
1970 :	2,481
1974 :	3,277
1976 :	3,277

The evolution of the world merchant fleet during the last 30 years was characterized by two tendencies: growth in size and what might be called the search for fluidity. Some figures illustrate the growth of the basic size of ships:

SHIP SIZE 1920 - 1976

	1920	1939	1948	1960	1968	July 1976
Capacity (millions of gross register tons)	53.900	68.510	80.290	129.770	194.150	372.000
Number of ships	26,513	29,763	29,340	36,311	47,444	65,887
Average size (gross register tons)	30,330	37,365	27,365	35,738	40,922	56,460

Source: Fearnley-Egers, a Norwegian shipper and shipbroker.

This growth improved the productivity of maritime transportation because only a small part of the costs for investment and usage were proportional to the size. Moreover, it was thought that size meant safety, both by avoiding the excessive proliferation of ships and by justifying the installation of navigational equipment on large ships.

Oil tankers have grown tremendously while carriers of miscellaneous cargoes, which are often called on to make stops in small ports, have remained the same size. Similarly, a sizable number of ore haulers have had to face the limitations of the Panama Canal, which restricts weight to 70,000 dead weight tons (dwt), or one-eighth that of the largest oil tanker in service in mid-1976.

This progressive growth in ship size has gone hand in hand with the growth of transport firms. The French *Journal of the Merchant Marine*, in the Jan. 8, 1976 issue, quoted from a recent doctoral dissertation:

> Because of the capital that it requires, maritime transport is more than a service; it is in effect an industry. Moreover, it is an industry in more ways than one. In addition to the capital intensity coefficient, its structure on a world scale is quite close to the structure of our vital industries. The concentration of an activity that is an important portion of GNP and of the

3. *JMM* 1975.

final cost of goods (on the order of 10%) in the hands of the shippers of a few countries provides another example that it is an industry. Liberia, Japan, the United Kingdom, Norway and Greece by themselves effectively control 60% of the world's supply of ships.[4]

A member of the Central Committee of French Shippers explained this tendency in a 1975 study entitled *The Economic Utilization of Ships:*

These characteristics of a heavy industry in maritime transport are clearly shown by an analysis of the capital intensity ratio.[5] Based on the figures of the French national accounts dealing with various sectors, one can see that in maritime investment gross financial assets are slowly transformed into balance sheets: 1 franc in investment per year produces 0.40 francs on the balance sheet. This ratio of 0.40 is the same order as that for electricity and railroads, but much lower than the same ratio for other sectors considered to be part of heavy industry such as steel (0.7) or oil; air transport, which is also characterized by investments of a considerable sum, has a ratio two times as high (0.85).

If one moreover considers the structure of the balance sheet, one sees that the characterization of maritime transport as a heavy industry is well founded, since the net financial assets make up a very important part of the assets of shipping companies (on the order of 75% for French shipping as a whole). Here again comparisons with related sectors (oil 60%, steel 55%, iron ore extraction) demonstrate the exceptional weight of maritime investment.

MAJOR HEAVY INDUSTRIES, ASSETS AND LIABILITIES

	Bulk Goods Shipping*	Oil Tankers*	Total Shipping	Oil	Steel	Ship-building, Aerospace and Shipping	Machine-Tool Industry	Textiles
(1973)								
ASSETS								
Net capital	71.6	81.8	74.1	59.5	55.3	19.2	26.5	34.4
assets	(73.0)	(84.8)						
Inventory	1.1	1.1	1.1	9.5	17.8	10.1	30.4	29.0
	(0.9)	(0.6)						
Short-Term	27.3	17.1	24.8	31.0	6.9	40.7	43.1	36.6
Liquidity	(16.1)	(14.6)						
Total	100.0	100.0	100.0	100.0	100.0	100.0	100.0	100.0
LIABILITIES								
Capital Reserves	43.3	40.3	42.6	40.7	33.2	15.3	28.8	43.5
	(35.1)	(25.3)						
Medium- and Long-	33.5	40.3	35.2	21.4	35.0	12.5	10.4	7.7
Term	(40.6)	(51.0)						

4. B. Francou, "Cost Structure of Maritime Transport and International Economic Relations" (doctoral dissertation).

5. This ratio is obtained by dividing the balance sheet by the gross capital assets.

MAJOR HEAVY INDUSTRIES, ASSETS AND LIABILITIES

	Bulk Goods Shipping*	Oil Tankers*	Total Shipping	Oil	Steel	Ship-building, Aerospace and Shipping	Machine-Tool Industry	Textiles
Indebtedness	23.2	19.4	22.2	37.9	31.8	72.2	60.8	48.8
Short-Term Indebtedness	(24.3)	(23.7)						
Total	100.0	100.0	100.0	100.0	100.0	100.0	100.0	100.0

Note: Figures given in percentages.
*Most recent figures in parentheses.

As a result, capital charges weigh heavily on the working account of the ship. On the basis of a normal economic repayment schedule (12 years for oil tankers, 16 years for other kinds of ships), the financial annuity payment of capital and financial charges, based on a minimum interest rate similar to export credits, represents 60% or more of the cost of a time charter for a heavy tonnage oil tanker of between 80,000 and 250,000 metric tons, as well as for bulk cargo transports of more than 100,000 metric tons.[6] It is a bit less than 50% for bulk carriers of less than 10,000 metric tons: 75% for LNG carriers and carriers of gasoil of more than 70,000 cubic meters; 45% for common freighters on regular lines; 60% for heavy-tonnage container ships and about 40% for roll-on/roll-off ships.

In 1970 and 1973 inflation pushed up costs and increased demand pushed up prices, but the downturn of 1974 pushed them back to the level of several years earlier. The following table gives three examples of this:

CONTRACT PRICES FOR NEW SHIP CONSTRUCTION
(in millions of dollars)

	1968	1969	1970	1971	1972	1973	1974	1975	1976
Oil tanker (for finished products) 30,000 dead weight tons	6.0	7.0	10.0	11.2	11.4	17.5	20.0	18.0	15.0
Crude oil hauler, 210,000 register tons	16.6	19.0	31.0	33.5	31.0	47.0	42.0	38.0	34.0
Bulk carrier, 70,000 dead weight tons	8.7	10.2	11.9	12.3	15.0	20.5	25.0	20.0	16.0

Source: Fearnley-Egers.

The comparison of the ratios of price and size underlines the increased progress in productivity. The rise in construction prices was also slowed by standardization (hull, outfitting, propulsion). Utilization costs were reduced by the decline in the average age of the fleets, and

6. Charter expenses for ship only; crew not included.

capacity coefficients have been improved by specialization and greater rotation speed. Flexibility is increased when a ship has several specialties. This is true for multiple-use freighters built for dry cargoes and for ships carrying both oil and ores for bulk transport.

The large-scale ship has lowered shipping costs and attracted primary process industries out of interior areas, where they process domestic minerals, to locations on the coasts, where they process, at cheaper cost, imported minerals.

While a heavy industry, maritime transport is also fragile and subject to the hazards of the sea. In 1976 shipping losses due to shipwrecks, engine failures, collisions and other accidents topped all records. They surpassed one million tons of net register tonnage: 1,021,133 as opposed to 802,693 in 1975. It should also be noted that 56% of the lost tonnage was flying a flag of convenience (see p. 57).

The industry is dependent on the business cycle as illustrated by the slowdown of 1975. Its role in the world economy is therefore much more determined than determining. It exists primarily to respond to a demand for transport. Only in a few cases, as we shall see later, does it create, if not needs, at least a new way of meeting needs.

Maritime transport is international, a characteristic well known to those in the tramp shipping business, i.e., those who work from one job to the next, as well as those who feed into the regular lines. Customers can freely choose their port—Dunkirk or Antwerp, for example—as well as their shipper, whatever flag he may fly. The shippers, for their part, are free to have their ship built in the shipyard of their choice and can take on any cargo in any port for any destination.

There is an element of chance in the relations between the three main partners: builders, shippers and customers. Shippers know that the market for maritime transport is cyclical, and because of this, they can afford to lose money for years in order to make it at a later date. But, in the last analysis, anticyclical measures are much less the doing of shippers than of nations. International maritime transport is primarily limited by nation-states. A national fleet is a guarantee of independence. This strategic consideration justifies tax allowances given nationally based shipping companies and domestic shipyards to protect a nation's fleet against the advantages of foreign fleets. As the 1975 report of the Committee of French Shippers states, "The liability and the strength of the shipping company as an exporter of services is not only to be at the mercy of international exchange rates, but also in the service of the balance of payments." A shipping company only partly performs this service when it registers ships in a "free-registration country" under a flag of convenience.

Compelled by its very nature to open itself to the world, the maritime transport industry at the same time attempts to cover itself against risks, primarily through "conferences," long-term contracts between customers and shippers, or by registration under a flag of convenience. In addition, nations have always made an effort to shield the industry directly, as we have seen, or indirectly. But the president of the Hamburg Shipbrokers Association recently stated:

> "The freedom of maritime transport is threatened on every side: by the conference on the law of the sea, the conduct code of the long-term contracts, and by the development of the Comecon fleet. . . .[7] It appears today that after the decolonization of the continents, the world is moving toward the colonization of the oceans and the Balkanization of the seas, which are going to be distributed between the countries that border on them. With the extension of territorial waters to 12 miles and the creation of economic zones of 200 miles, the straits of Gibraltar, the Pas-de-Calais, the Grand Belt, the approaches to the Red Sea and the Persian Gulf will no longer be in free waters and there will no longer be a single square centimeter of free waters in the Baltic or in the Mediterranean."[8]

The Fleet

The world fleet consisted on July 1, 1977, of 67,945 ships, according to the statistics of *Lloyd's Register of Shipping.* These 67,945 units represented 393,678,369 register tons. Tons are a unit of weight and are generally expressed in metric terms. The register ton is a unit of volume equivalent to 100 cubic feet, or roughly 2.83 cubic meters, and is used to gauge the volume of a ship. The gross register ton (grt) is defined as the total capacity minus the motor compartment, fuel tanks, the crew's quarters and so forth. These deductions are often given in a single lump figure. The displacement ton is the weight of the volume of water displaced by the ship at a certain depth and at a certain density of water (sea water, in the summertime). A distinction is made between the ship's displacement when it is empty and when it is loaded. The dead weight ton (dwt) represents the loading capacity of a ship, including fuel, water and supplies. One must deduct these items to arrive at the weight of the cargo.

Because statistics are expressed, depending on the situation, in grt or dwt, it is important to know that in 1974 the average ratio of dwt to grt was 1.84 for tankers and 1.71 for bulk carriers, as opposed to 1.58 and 1.53 respectively in 1965. This indicates a productivity increase in the form of an augmentation of the dead weight relative to volume.

The distinction between weight and volume is very important in the design of each ship, which must be adapted to the nature of the cargo for which it is planned, as well as in the calculation of charges (by the metric ton or by the cubic foot) to the customers.

7. Comecon: Council of Mutual Economic Assistance, which includes, along with the USSR and Mongolia, most of the European Communist nations.
8. *JMM*, Feb. 26, 1976.

The world fleet is quite diverse. It includes fishing vessels of at least 100 gross register tons, the minimum size requirement for other ships listed, and additional vessels such as hydrofoils.

WORLD FLEET BY TYPE OF SHIP
July 1, 1977

	World		France	
	Number	**Register Tons**	**Number**	**Register Tons**
Oil tankers................	6,912	174,124,444	112	7,512,825
LNG carriers..............	493	4,410,727	7	211,485
Carriers of chemical products...	492	1,755,050	14	80,581
Other tankers.............	106	168,331	13	23,303
Oil tankers equipped for bulk transport (including tankers carrying ores).............	426	26,089,373	7	659,569
Ore haulers and bulk carriers...	3,887	74,832,253	46	971,104
Carriers of miscellaneous merchandise (single-bridge).............	10,671	16,798,598	64	95,885
(multibridge)..............	11,010	53,452,620	205	1,255,301
Multipurpose ships with passenger facilities..........	380	1,836,782	1	500
Container ships (entirely cellular)............	507	7,543,242	13	253,332
Barge carriers.............	27	794,419	—	—
Vehicle carriers............	114	633,323	1	1,600
Livestock carriers..........	65	177,137	—	—
Factory ships and fish transports.	762	3,535,660	3	6,119
Fishing ships (including trawler/fisheries)...........	19,178	8,626,375	561	189,479
Car ferries and other passenger ships...........	2,903	7,091,020	46	206,374
Supply ships...............	1,057	699,047	21	13,636
Tugs.....................	5,816	1,730,642	129	28,882
Dredgers..................	616	1,081,209	19	29,525
Icebreakers...............	88	342,339	—	—
Research ships.............	429	485,551	19	14,346
Miscellaneous.............	2,006	2,470,227	46	60,013
Total....................	67,945	393,678,369	1,327	11,613,859

Source: *Lloyd's Register; Journal of the Merchant Marine*, Dec. 8, 1977.

Three major classes of ships represent 70% of those listed. The 6,912 oil tankers represent 174,124,444 grt; the 426 oil tankers also used for bulk transport 26,089,373 grt; and the 3,887 ore haulers and bulk transports 74,832,253 grt. Their percentage of the total is as follows:

	% in number	% in volume
Oil tankers	10.1	44.2
Oil tankers/bulk carriers	0.6	6.6
Ore haulers	5.7	10.0
	16.4	69.8

Oil Tankers

Oil was the sole cause of the economic downturn of 1974. To the extent that this downturn is a crisis of civilization, the role of oil was less that of a detonator than a sign of the real situation. Similarly, in the boom period from 1950 to 1974, oil was both a cause and a sign of progress. During that period oil contributed to economic progress because its price fell in constant terms. From 1950 to 1970 the fob (free on board) price of typical crude oil from the Persian Gulf slipped from roughly $2 to $1.50 a barrel. The Teheran agreements of 1971 and, above all, the decisions of OPEC in 1973 raised the price by a considerable amount. The development of the enormous wells in the Mideast lowered the cost of oil on the production side, and competition among oil companies lowered the sale price on the consumption side. The effect of mass and scale lowered the costs of maritime transport and particularly of refinement.

The decline of the price of oil combined with the ease with which it can be used (relative to coal) explains why the consumption of oil grew more rapidly than the consumption of goods and services of energy in general. An additional factor contributing to the increasing need for maritime oil shipment has been the lengthening of delivery time. From 1965 to 1975 the need for maritime transport, expressed in metric tons, nearly doubled, and expressed in the ratio of metric tons to miles, it increased nearly two and a half times. The lengthening of delivery time after 1945 is in part the result of the growing importance of the Middle East, and more precisely of the Persian Gulf, in supplying the two major rapid-growth consumption centers, Europe and Japan—considerably distant from the Gulf. The introduction of large oil tankers shortly before the 1967 Middle East war also contributed to this development because their draft made it impossible for them to use the Suez Canal and thus increased travel time.

These factors provide the necessary background for understanding the development of the gigantic oil tankers. This surge in growth did not result from a race for records or for prestige but flowed from the desire for economies of scale. It also had implications for safety. In responding to the increasing demand for transportation, three solutions were possible: to increase the number, the speed or the size of the ships. In 1973, the last virtually normal year for oil, there were 3,500 ships used to transport petroleum. If the T2s (the 16,000 metric ton "giants" of the last war) had been used, 18,000 of them would have been necessary! Size was necessary to avoid a strangulation of capacity and to reduce the possibility of accidents (the same phenomenon that occurs in air transport).

Speed has had a tendency to peak, or even diminish, in recent years, not because of OPEC's 1973 decisions, which more than tripled the price of fuel (the consumption of which increases roughly exponentially relative to speed), but because it is only one of the elements taken into account in the design of a ship. Speed has to some extent been sacrificed to size. Size has been maintained simply because of the economy of scale.

Savings occur because the elements of cost are not all proportional to the dead weight and because their combination reduces the cost of each ton carried with the increase in the size of the ship.

The main elements of cost are investment, capital charges and utilization costs. We will see later how each of these influences the development of a ship. But it is obvious that if we multiply the length, width and height of a parallelogram by 2, we are multiplying the volume by 2^3, or in other words by 8, at the same time the weight is being multiplied, in effect, by only 2. For an oil tanker, the relationship between the weight of the steel hull and its dead weight varies as follows: 10,000 metric tons and 33,000 dwt; 20,000 metric tons and 120,000 dwt; 34,000 metric tons and 240,000 dwt. The light displacement ton, and therefore the price, consequently varies between ½ and ⅔ power of the dead weight. The hull, which represents a third of the weight and of the price of a 33,000 dwt, is no more than an eighth of a 240,000 dwt. The propulsive apparatus makes up 30% of the cost of a large ship. Its cost varies less than that of the dead weight because it is related to propulsive power. The latter, at a given speed, grows only to the ⅔ power of the total weight of the ship, which varies at roughly the ⅔ power of the dead weight. Assuming that 30%-40% of the rest of the ship is proportional to the weight of the cargo, the savings realized on 60%-70% of the two preceding items make it possible to use the classical law of economies of scale on ship construction.

Backing up this law is the improvement of the "block coefficient." This expresses the relationship between the volume of the hull and that of the parallelogram made up by the length, width and height of the ship. This ratio has shifted in a few years from 0.77 to 0.85, an increase in volume of roughly 10%, so that the ship is shaped like a soap dish having a coefficient of one. It is precisely here that speed again plays a role. Speed is an expensive factor in construction; given identical form and volume, power increases at low speeds at a little less than a third of the speed described and at high speeds at a little more than the cube. Improvements in the output of the propulsive apparatus are not enough to compensate for the increase in price.

This explains why the size factor has taken precedence over the speed factor in solving the problem of growing demands for transport. But the oil tanker is not free to grow in all three dimensions. The draft was the first of the three to reach its limits because of the depth of ports, channels and drydocks. The trade-off between length and width results from very simple mathematical and physical realities: the greatest resistance to forward motion, and therefore the power necessary to overcome it, results from the friction of the water on the hull. In arithmetic terms it is necessary to reduce this surface as much as possible. The cylinder represents the least surface, at a given volume, relative to a parallelogram. Therefore the width of the ship was proportionally stretched the most, making the ship resemble an iron. The evolution to giant vessels began prior to the Middle East war of 1967, which, of course, accelerated it.

The capital charges tied to investment currently represent well over half of the utilization costs of large oil tankers. It is risky to give figures on this phenomenon: a new 210,000 metric ton ship, delivered in 1972, was worth $31 million at the time and $47 million a year later. The conditions for loans vary considerably; they may cover as much as 75% to 80% of the value of the purchase. As of 1976, an annual capital charge of 12%, with a depreciation in constant segments over 13 years, and a financial charge of 6.5% to 7.0% per year over eight years on 80% of the purchase value is typical. On a 200,000 metric ton ship costing $48 million at purchase and carrying 1.5 million metric tons of crude oil per year from the Persian Gulf to Europe, the charge would amount to $5.76 million a year or $3.84 per ton carried.

There are two types of utilization costs: fixed and variable. Fixed costs include insurance and wages and payments for the crew. Insurance runs up to 4.5% of the insured value. At 2.5%, this represents a premium of $1.2 million a year on the above risk. Economies of scale play a role in wages and payments to the crew. For example, there were 50 men on a T2 weighing 16,000 metric tons and 29 men on the *Batillus*, a ship owned by Shell in 1976, weighing 554,000 metric tons.

Variable costs include maintenance costs, fees, port access and tolls and fuels and lubricants. Maintenance costs grow more slowly than tonnage. Fees, port access and tolls vary. However it should be noted that because of the toll, the round trip through Suez may be more costly than going around the Cape of Good Hope; it adds roughly $2 to the cost of a metric ton of crude oil shipped on a medium-sized vessel used in both directions. It penalizes such a ship about $1 to the ton, relative to a very large crude carrier (VLCC) going around the Cape.[9]

Fuels and lubricants are important given the total weight of combustibles in the "false freight" and above all in their consumption. The latter is proportional to the square of the speed: for a ship weighing 270,000 dwt, it is 80 metric tons a day at 11 knots, 125 at 14 knots and 170 at 16 knots. Companies try to save on marine fuel oil, whose price has increased enormously since the fall of 1973.

But a balance sheet of operating costs must make use of the tonnage transported annually, which is also proportional to speed. The table below shows the relationship between speed and fuel consumption and their impact on shipping costs:

9. The VLCC is an oil tanker weighing more than 160,000 dwt. The ultra-large crude carrier (ULCC) begins at 300,000 dwt.

OIL TANKER, 270,000 dwt

Speed (knots)	Fuel Consumption (tons)		Average cost of fuel consumption ($ millions)	Tonnage transported annually (million tons)	Fuel costs $ per ton transported
	Per 24 hours at sea	Annual			
11	80	26,000	2.3	1.0	2.3
14	125	41,000	3.7	1.3	2.8
16	170	56,000	5.5	1.5	3.7

Size limits have in effect been reached because there are practically no more orders for higher-tonnage oil tankers. At the beginning of 1977, the record was 554,000 dwt, the weight of the *Batillus* built by the Chantiers de l'Atlantique. The ship's other dimensions are:

overall length 352 feet
overall width 207 feet
draft 94 feet

It has two main engines producing 32,500 hp at 86 rpm. Size has its limits and also its risks. In case of engine failure or collision, the stakes increase with size. But, on the other hand, the number of risks diminishes because the number of ships diminishes as well. The equipment used on oil tankers not only makes them safer but also less of a risk to the environment. Explosions and fires occur less frequently because of improvements in the ventilation of the holds, a permanent check on their gas content and other safety features. Full or empty, the holds are covered with a "coat" of inert gases designed to prevent explosions.

The "load on top" is now a well-known procedure that consists of cleaning the holds while they are sealed and disposing of the water used for these purposes only after decantation or separation. The residue, kept on board, is then covered with the newly loaded crude, hence the term "load on top." British Petroleum has recently perfected the system by recycling the crude to give the tanks a vigorous cleaning with fixed washing installation as they are unloaded.

As a precaution against accidents, recent rulings of the Intergovernmental Maritime Consultative Organization (IMCO), a group with ties to the U.N., have imposed limits not on the size of ships, but on the volume of their tanks. Currently whatever the dimensions of any ship, up to and including 500,000 metric tons, the quantity of cargo liable to be discharged in the event of a disaster will not exceed 98,425 cubic feet under any circumstances. This translates into an increase in steel weight and a reduction in carrying capacity. It is here that the limitations of size are reached. To deal with possible accidents, the oil companies established two insurance systems, Tovalop in 1969 and Cristal in 1971. As a result, the owners of the ship and the owners of the cargo take responsibility for cleaning up any pollution attributable to them or else pay cleanup costs, with a limit of $10 million per ship, a ceiling that can be extended to $30 million. These systems have just been expanded to include maritime research and production operations, under the name of Opol.[10]

The quick survey above shows that in oil transport, growth has not been a question of multiplying the dead weight of ships by two or by 10 in order to increase it, for example, to 540,000 metric tons, but that growth resulted in different oil tankers—different in construction, design, kinds of structures and even the materials used. These ships are also different in form (e.g., the bulb-shaped stem, which reduces water resistance); in propulsion (e.g., improved output resulting from a decrease in the weight of the engine equipment); in engine automation; and in the preservation of the petroleum products en route. There are additional variations in instrumentation and navigation aids—radar, Decca, director indicator, gyrocompass, gyrocompass recorder, automatic pilot, sonar, "transit" systems (which give the position of the ship relative to satellites); and in the apparatus for monitoring temperature, fumes, gas etc. in the cargo areas.

Under these conditions, the typical oil tanker in service (and on order) is the 200,000 dwt expanded to a capacity of 250,000-270,000 dwt, just as an earlier generation of ships had been expanded to a capacity of 80,000-120,000 dwt. The 500,000 metric ton ship, in turn, which included such innovations as two lines of shafting with two propellers and two engines, constitutes another generation, which under normal conditions would have been succeeded by ships of 700,000-1,000,000 metric tons, already in existence—on paper.

A 270,000 dwt of the British Petroleum group, for example, built in the Mitsubishi Heavy Industries shipyards in Japan, has the following characteristics: overall length 1,111 feet, overall width 176 feet, draft 28 feet. Its propulsion system consists of a group of Mitsubishi double-effect steam turbines (high pressure, low pressure) capable of producing 34,000 hp with a service speed of 16 knots. It can make the round trip from the Persian Gulf to continental Europe in 63 days and transport 1.5 million metric tons of oil per year. The stay in port is usually 24 hours because the power of the pump is proportional to the cargo. In the case of this ship, there are four pumps with a combined output of 4,500 metric tons an hour for delivery (loading is done by gravity). The volume of the ship's 21 tanks (five central and 16 lateral, in keeping with IMCO standards) is 12,145,000 cubic feet. Its dead weight is 270,000 metric tons and its displacement when fully loaded is 307,328 metric tons. The ship has a crew of 33.

---

10. Tovalop: Tanker owner voluntary agreement concerning liability for oil pollution.
    Cristal: Contract regarding an interim supplement to tanker liability for oil pollution.
    Opol: Offshore pollution liability agreement.

Bulk Carriers

Bulk carriers have evolved in a process similar to that of oil tankers. A product of this process is the "mixed-bulk" carrier, three of which were introduced in 1964. These ships can carry crude oil, with a density of between 0.8 and 0.9; various mineral cargoes, e.g., coal and iron ore; and lighter bulk goods such as grains, fertilizers, phosphates and so forth. This versatility has earned them the designation OBO (oil-bulk-ore). Like oil tankers, bulk carriers have also grown in size but on a much smaller scale. While oil tankers have increased to 554,000 dwt (the *Batillus*), the largest ore hauler in service is 128,000 dwt.

Based on past experience this growth will continue. Over a decade the average tonnage of the existing ore haulers, including mixed carriers, almost doubled, going from 23,000 dwt on Jan. 1, 1966 (1,168 ships totaling 27.6 million dwt) to 42,000 dwt on Jan. 1, 1977 (3,872 ships totaling 163.3 million dwt). At the end of 1976, 55% of the tonnage of the ore haulers and mixed-cargo ships on order were vessels of more than 100,000 dwt (15.2 million dwt out of a total of 27.5 million dwt). However, during this time the rise in basic tonnages slowed, in part because of the limits of the Panama Canal.

Bulk cargo shippers, like those of oil, gas, containers etc., are constantly searching for continuous processes. Oil refineries have worked on such a basis since the beginning of the century. A refinery may even be continuously fed by a pipeline connected directly to a well and may, in turn, transport part of its production, again continuously, through a pipeline for refined products. But unlike a pipeline, a ship normally undergoes a period of inactivity, equal to that of its productivity, on the return trip after dropping off its cargo. The idea of the multipurpose ship is to reduce this period of dead time, e.g., by taking on ore in Brazil for Japan and, en route, picking up oil in the Persian Gulf for delivery in Europe. Another way of approaching continuous processing is to transform solids into liquids. Pipelines in the United States can transport coal after it has been pulverized and mixed with water into the fluid form of slurry. Coal slurry, or that of another mineral, can then be pumped onto or off of a ship, thereby reducing the time and the trouble spent on handling the solid.

Again like the oil tanker, the bulk transport ship assumes the form of a soap dish divided into seven, eight or nine holds, separated by watertight bulkheads. The engines and the bridge house are aft. This type of ship generally has one continuous bridge and often lacks a poop. The latter may be replaced by a pronounced curve. The hatches are as wide as structural capacity and safety regulations will permit. On two ships built by Burnmeister and Wain (B and W) and recently enlarged from 52,000 dwt to 60,000 dwt, sidetanks extend the hatches up to the plating, thereby forming lateral ballast. These ships have seven hull panels, each measuring 47 feet by 49 feet, and sliding hydraulic hatchcovers. Like all large bulk carriers, they carry little cargo-handling equipment because loading and unloading is done by port facilities. Their dimensions are: overall length 74 feet; width 113 feet; draft 41 feet; depth of holds 59 feet; and gross register tonnage 34,600. They have an excellent dwt/grt ratio of roughly 47 square feet per dead weight ton, corresponding to 30,800 cubic feet of total grain volume. These ships are in the "Panamax" class because the dimensions of the hull, particularly the draft, have been pushed to the maximum limit that will still allow them to utilize the Panama Canal. With 16,800 hp turning 112 rpm, the main B and W engine can produce a speed of 16 knots in normal service.

Container Ships, Roll-on/Roll-off Ships and Barge Carriers

Containerization is another process that is aimed at introducing continuity into the shipping process. The container unit is a receptacle or flexible covering in the shape of a large parallelogram made of steel, an alloy or plywood. Its size is standardized at 10, 20, 30 or 40 feet long. Two containers 10 feet long fit into a 20-foot container, and two 20-foot containers fit into a 40-foot container.

The loads are thus adapted to ships, railway cars or trucks and to the loading equipment. Although it is not necesssary to break down cargo during the loading process, the container does require handling and poses the problem of integrating land and ocean transport. This technique, introduced by an American trucker, became generally used in just 10 years. It was successful only because important investments were made to ensure the shipper of the main service expected—quick delivery. Speed is achieved by eliminating the breakdown of cargo in port and by added engine power at sea. Optimization studies estimate that such power can produce speeds of 23-24 knots under certain circumstances. But in providing rapid service, container ships are subject to two constraints similar to those of oil tankers: fuel consumption and its skyrocketing costs, and the loss of capacity resulting from tapered hulls.[11] Its speed continues to attract new kinds of cargo, such as the refrigerated containers that require many different compartments. The container ship is a specialized carrier, but its specialization has multiple uses: containers or pallets, frozen goods, minerals, cars, bulk shipments of sugar and other items.

To achieve rapid cargo turnover, the container ship is generally unloaded vertically through wide hatches by dockside equipment. Freight movement is accelerated by guide rails, forklifts and the cellular structure of the holds. Certain types of containers can also be handled by the

11. Fuel use can be as high as 300 metric tons a day on the faster container ships.

ship's own rigging: various derricks and cranes.

The *Ville de Strasbourg* is somewhat typical of the multicargo container ship. Its 16,570 dwt corresponds to the average tonnage of ships of this kind currently on order. Its overall length is 565 feet; width 76 feet; and hold depth from the upper bridge 41 feet. It has two bridges and a total capacity of 770,000 cubic feet with four major holds. Cargo-handling equipment includes four cranes, three derricks and an 80-ton mast-crane. The main engine with 17,400 hp can produce a speed of 20.6 knots carrying the kinds of cargo for which the ship was designed, but it can generally exceed that speed with other types of freight.

The polythermal freighter, which replaced the old "banana boat," falls into this category because of its speed, specialization and capacity to take on containers for the return trip. This ship carries bananas in its refrigerated holds (at a temperature of between -25 °C and 10 °C) and rum in its tanks. On the return trip it can deliver various goods in containers or on pallets as well as vehicles, which are brought aboard through loading doors and fixed in place by a moving bridge.

Vessels equipped for horizontal loading and unloading are called roll-on/roll-off ships. The process is accomplished with the use of dock ramps that are connected to the various decks of the ship through enormous plated doors. The decks usually number as many as half a dozen and are as continuous as possible in order to make them accessible to tugs. Their capacity is expressed in container feet of 20 inches and in the length of the tugs that service them.

A well-known version of the roll-on/roll-off ship is the carrier or car ferry, which is widely used for short distances. The car ferry is different from the ships used to transport new cars, such as the *Jinyo Maru*, launched in 1976, which has 16,109 register tons and a capacity of 6,015 vehicles. The ferry is designed to accommodate various kinds of goods and passengers. It is different from another, earlier type of freighter that carried goods on routes which appealed to travelers. These vessels carried tourists, but their major purpose was still the delivery of cargo. When carrying 12 or more passengers, these ships were required by regulatory agencies and insurance companies to provide a certain level of amenities and personnel, including a doctor. The cost of such services meant that the ship had to maintain a significant volume of travelers at all times. These ships lost business both to air travel for long distances and to the car ferry for short trips. They also lost business to cruise ships, which were often reconverted steamers, and increasingly to specialized ships. Thus two different needs, the business trip and the leisure trip, resulted in the creation of specific services.

Barge carriers transport nonself-propelled barges to locations outside of crowded harbors, where they are offloaded by shipboard equipment and towed ashore by tugs. There are currently two types of barge carriers used in long-distance transport. One type employs the Lash system, which has been installed on 24 out of 27 ships as of July 31, 1975. On this type of ship, barges are placed on a sliding beam that runs on guide rails along the entire length of the ship to the stern, where two overhanging horizontal arms lower the barges individually into the water.

The competing system is the Seabee, which is based on a technique developed by the military. A huge lift at the stern of the ship puts the barges, which carry up to 800 metric tons of freight and weigh up to 1,300 metric tons when fully loaded, into the water. The barges are kept on loading decks in transit. The difference between these two techniques is one of capacity: the moving beam of the Lash system is capable of raising 500 metric tons and the fixed lift of the Seabee more than 2,000 metric tons.

Because of the importance of multiple uses, 17 of the 27 barge carriers currently in service are outfitted to carry a large number of containers. But their principal task is to transport and offload barges, which can be integrated into river transportation because of their shallow draft.

This type of transport should not be confused with a new idea developed at the beginning of 1977 by the Chantiers de l'Atlantique, in which factories are mounted on barges and towed to their destination. The barges are not really considered part of "transportation" because in principle they are moved only once—at the time of delivery. The small refinery of Marsa El-Brega, in Libya, which began operation in 1967, was built on floats in Europe and then towed to Libya. Conceivably this technique will one day be applied generally. For example, nuclear reactors could be towed to permanent offshore locations, where they would have an unlimited supply of cooling water. A similar concept involves the construction of an industrial complex on barges. At the beginning of 1977 the Chantiers de France in Dunkirk, part of the Empain-Schneider group, proposed the construction on two barges of chemical and fertilizer factories, alcohol and oil refineries, an ore-treatment facility, a desalination plant and even a rolling mill weighing 22,000 metric tons.

The incinerator ship is another maritime innovation. The recently launched *Vulcanus* resembles a small bulk carrier, weighing 4,768 dwt. It is distinguished by two small cylindrical smoke stacks behind a main stack. The ship's purpose is to destroy, without causing harm to marine life, the halogenic hydrocarbons resulting from the production of such petrochemical products as vinyl chloride, epichlorohydrine, glycerine and epoxy resins. Burning these potentially harmful substances at sea is considered an economical and ecological alternative to burning or burying them on land or dumping them at sea. The ship's incinerators burn compounds and convert them to carbonic gas, which is not dangerous, and to hydrochloric acid, whose vapors dissolve into the sea and are neutralized by the alkaline components of water. The process, which can dispose of 4,200 metric tons of waste per trip, has no known adverse effect on birds or plankton and is in wide demand.

Miscellaneous Cargo Carriers

Traditional freighters are generally counted in statistics after the specialized ships—from oil tankers to dredgers, cable ships, tugs and icebreakers—all of which must be at least 100 register tons. Although in decline, they still represent a considerable proportion of the worlds fleet: 19.6% (77,088,000 grt) in July 1977 (including multipurpose ships with passenger facilities), as opposed to 22.1% in 1974 and 24% in 1975. However, despite the fact that it is decreasing as a percentage of the world's fleet, its absolute tonnage is increasing. The largest freighter fleets are those of the USSR (7.7 million grt), Greece (seven million grt), Panama (5.5 million grt), Japan (4.6 million grt) and the United Kingdom (4.5 million grt). The ships of these nations are part of the all-purpose category vessels, used mostly in tramp shipping.

Liquefied Gas Carriers

At the end of 1976, the fleet of ships carrying liquefied gas had a capacity of 199.5 million cubic feet, of which 73.5 million cubic feet were accounted for by haulers of liquefied natural gas and 126 million cubic feet by haulers of liquefied petroleum gas.

The main component of liquefied natural gas (LNG) is methane, which is transported at very low temperatures (-160° C). The liquefied petroleum gases (LPG), propane and butane, are carried at temperatures below zero in ships transporting other liquefied gases, such as alefin, ethylene, isopropene and ammonia.

The LNG hauler is both a complement to and a competitor of the pipeline. The ships that now provide gas to Spain, Great Britain, France and Italy will be rivaled by gas pipelines (most of which are under construction) that will cross the Mediterranean at the Strait of Gibraltar or of Messina. But in this area the LNG carrier complements the gas pipeline. For example, the shoreline plant for gas liquefaction in Algeria is supplied by pipelines from the Sahara and in turn the shoreline regasification plants in Europe transfer the gas into a pipeline distribution network.

The pipeline has the advantage of continuous functioning, and the LNG carrier, like the oil tanker, has the advantage of a flexibility that allows it to load and unload at different points, in keeping with market fluctuations or political shifts. The carrier's other advantage over the pipeline is that it reduces volume and thus saves on transport-related investment. Liquefied at -160° C, a cubic foot of LNG equals 600 cubic feet of gas in its natural state. In its liquid form, gas has a density approaching 0.45 and a heating power 20% higher than crude oil. However, because of the equipment needed to carry methane, the LNG carrier requires a much higher investment than the oil tanker. The value of an oil tanker weighing 120,000 dwt, ordered at the end of 1975, is estimated at $32 million, and a LNG carrier with a capacity of 4,375 million cubic feet—or less than 60,000 metric tons—at $125 million. The LNG carrier can be compared to other ships, such as the container ship, that fit into a transport system which emphasizes speed and frequency (similar to air transport).

World trade in LNG dates from 1964, when the *Methane Princess* and the *Methane Progress*, each with 945,000 cubic feet capacities, began carrying 35 billion cubic feet a year between Algeria and Great Britain. These two ships were followed in 1965 by the *Jules Verne*, with a 892,500 cubic foot capacity, which unloaded at Le Havre. All three vessels were equipped with transportable gas tanks. Thereafter the basic methane hauler expanded its capacity five times in roughly 10 years, and current orders call for ships carrying 4,375,000 cubic feet.

The special characteristics of liquefied natural gas impose rigid requirements on the material used in the tanks and their insulation. The oldest type of LNG carrier uses transportable tanks and the second type uses membrane or integrated tanks. In the first type the gas container is the tank, and in the second the gas container is the ship itself. In both cases the cryogenic materials used must resist low temperatures and prevent thermal leaks that could dangerously cool the hull of the LNG carrier causing it to become brittle. Transportable tanks are essentially vast receptacles in the form of a parallelogram, a sphere or a cylinder. Placed in the ship, these tanks are capable of resisting the hydrostatic charge of the cargo, which in turn is complicated by the static and dynamic effects of the ship's movement. The tanks, which are made of steel, with 9% nickel, or an aluminum alloy, must be able to contract freely, and the transmission of strains to the hull demands a relatively heavy structure. An insulator is inserted in the space between the tanks and the hull, which plays the role of a secondary or safety barrier in the event of leakages.

This technique was first used on the *Euclides*, a ship weighing 4,000 metric tons, but it began to lose ground with the introduction of integrated tanks. Recently transportable tanks have made a comeback with the *Norman Lady*, launched in mid-1977. With two other ships of the same type, this vessel has started transporting up to 3.6 million metric tons a year from Abu Dhabi to Japan. These ships are equipped with five tanks 99 cubic feet in diameter, each one sealed in a cylindrical skirt. Rigorous calculations of the effect of structural stress enable a considerable reduction of the secondary barrier, but there is still a considerable loss of space on LNG carriers equipped with cylindrical tanks.

Integrated or membrane tanks are flexible, watertight envelopes made of Invar with a 36% nickel component (the Gaz-Transport technique) or steel with a very low carbon content in the form of embossed plates (the Technigas technique). These envelopes have a flexibility that permits them to absorb thermal stress. The only pressures transmitted to the ship through a rigid secondary barrier (made of plywood or balsa) are those caused by the weight of the tanks and the movements of the ship.

Gaz-Transport of France has announced the development, with the American firm McDonnell-Douglas, of a new technique that combines the Invar membrane with a reinforced plastic insulation produced by McDonnell-Douglas for the space program. This technique is used to insulate tanks that carry liquid hydrogen used in propulsion.

Cargo

The total world tonnage transported by ship (dry cargo and petroleum products) increased from roughly 200 million metric tons in 1900 to 525 million metric tons in 1950—two and one-half times in 50 years. From 1950 to 1976 the total grew more than six times. This rise took place at an annual average rate of 7.5% during the 1950s and then accelerated to reach approximately 9% in the 1960s. It then fluctuated noticeably: 4% in 1971, 6% in 1972, 11% in 1973, 4% in 1974, an exceptional -6% in 1975, and 7.5% in 1976.

Oil

Production (See Map 3)

The following table shows that the USSR and the United States use a billion metric tons of oil in a single year. We will later discuss the current distribution of world oil production and reserves on a country-by-country basis.

WORLD PETROLEUM PRODUCTION, 1976 (Mt-millions of tons)

Rank/Country	Wells Drilled *	Demand per Wells Mt/day	Production Mt/Year **	Reserves Tonnage (Mt)	Reserves Number of Years
North America	514,000	2.97	526	5,700	14
3. United States	495,000	2.63	458	4,700	12
Canada	18,500	12.00	68	1,000	16

WORLD PETROLEUM PRODUCTION, 1976 (Mt-millions of tons)

Rank/Country	Wells Drilled *	Demand per Wells Mt/day	Production Mt/Year **	Reserves Tonnage (Mt)	Reserves Number of Years
Latin America	28,000	22.0	227	5,000	22
5. Venezuela	10,700	32.2	118	2,530	21
Mexico	3,000	31.2	46	1,350	27
Argentina	4,100	13.5	20	400	20
Near East	3,900	700	1,100	53,200	50
2. Saudi Arabia	711	1,316	429	21,200	48
4. Iran	425	1,764	293	9,200	33
6. Kuwait	592	373	108	9.700	88
7. Iraq	155	1,961	107	4,900	47
Abu Dhabi	215	839	76	4,200	55
Qatar	–	–	23	–	–
Oman	–	–	18	–	–
Dubai	–	–	16	–	–
Egypt	–	–	16	–	–
Far East					
Oceania	7,150	75.0	207		
10. China	–	–	87	2,900	35
Indonesia	3,020	57.9	75	2,000	27
Australia	350	15.0	20	1,000	100
1. USSR	–	–	520	11,900	25
Rumania	–	–	15	–	–
Western Europe	620	150	38	3,640	100
Great Britain	172	160	14	2,300	–
Norway	48	500	12	–	–
Africa			267	8,740	35
8. Nigeria			101	2,900	29
9. Libya			92	3,700	40
Algeria			50	1,050	22
Gabon			11	–	25
World			2,915	65,200	

Sources: *The Oil and Gas Journal*, January 22, 1975.
         **Committee of Petroleum Professionals*, February 1977.

Production by Area

At the end of World War I, the conversion from coal power to oil on ships resulted in an increase in world petroleum production to 200 million metric tons. The U.S. produced 123 million metric tons and the USSR produced 18 million metric tons—a ratio of about 6 to 1. The proportion remained the same until 1960, when the U.S. produced 350 million metric tons to the Soviet Union's 150 million metric tons. The U.S. growth then slowed and began to decrease, while the Soviet Union's production continued to rise. The pace of growth is summarized below:

ANNUAL VARIATION IN MILLIONS OF METRIC TONS

Year	United States	USSR
1967	0	15
1973	-15	27
1975	-23	38
1976	-10	29

By 1976 the USSR had become the world's number one producer of oil and number two producer of natural gas, with 11,200 billion cubic feet.

The USSR

For a long time Soviet production was limited to the Caspian Sea area on the Aspheron peninsula, opposite Baku. When it began to slow in this region, the Soviets prospected in many other areas, and began numbering the discoveries that followed. The Caspian area, called Baku I, eventually accounting for only 5% of Soviet production, was followed by Baku II, a large basin extending from Volgograd to the western flanks of the Urals, a distance of nearly 1,200 miles. This region is still the main source of Soviet production, constituting nearly 200 million metric tons of oil. The search for oil then crossed the Urals and moved toward Siberia and the estuaries of three important rivers. Baku III was founded at the juncture of the Ob and the Irtysh in Tyumen province.

The area's fossil fuel deposits extend over a distance of 120 miles from east to west, with the gas drillings farther to the north on both sides of the Arctic circle. This sparsely inhabited region stretches over 574 square miles from the Trans-Siberian railway to the Arctic Sea. The region's winter makes navigation on the Ob possible only between June and October. Beginning with Novy Port, there are numerous well-equipped ports, particularly Tyumen and Tobolsk, all along the river moving south. The development of this immense region, which had no manpower and no transport other than rivers that freeze over, required enormous resources. The airplane played an indispensable role in this process. The results were worth the effort; fossil fuel production reached the level of 120 million metric tons.

Because of the success of Baku III, a second Siberian zone may be developed in the same way. There is already talk of a Baku IV located between the industrial cities of Novosibirsk on the Ob and Krasnoyarsk on the Yenisey, where gas was recently discovered. The large dam at Brask on the Angara and the Trans-Siberian railway would play a major role in any such development.

The United States

The 458 million metric tons of oil and the 19,460 billion cubic feet of natural gas produced by the United States in 1976 came from about 500,000 wells whose output is in many cases declining. However, recent discoveries on Alaska's North Slope have stemmed absolute decline in production to some extent. More than two-thirds of the nation's wells are in three states, with 36% in Texas, 24% in Louisiana and 12% in California. The principal sources of natural gas are found in Texas (40%), Louisiana (30%) and Oklahoma (8%). Thus four states produce three-quarters of America's gas and oil. But this huge asset, equivalent to nearly a billion metric tons of oil, is located far from the big consumers in the Midwest and the Northeast. Energy use in the Northeast is particularly high because of the heavy concentration of people and industry. The length of pipelines transporting gas and oil to this and other parts of the country constitutes about a third of the world's total.

Because of its declining production and increasing consumption in recent years, the U.S. has had to import a growing quantity of its crude oil from the Middle East and Africa. Venezuela and Canada have also been contributing to the supply for some time. To reduce energy waste and dependence on foreign oil, President Carter has tried, with limited success, to enact an energy plan that would lower the consumption of petroleum products, particularly gasoline; greatly expand the production of coal; and encourage the development and use of solar energy and other alternative sources. Through various tax incentives and penalties, industries are being encouraged to switch from oil and gas to coal. Large corporations are also investing capital in coal mining operations. The goal of the U.S. energy program is to tax domestic energy resources, thus stemming the rising tide of imported oil and helping the nation's economy and balance of payments.

The nation's energy supplies have received some help from the recent development of oil reserves on the North Slope of Alaska, an area of 580,000 square miles, with less than 400,000 inhabitants. Current fossil fuel reserves are estimated at 10 million metric tons of oil at Prudhoe Bay and natural gas at Cook Inlet, which is ice-free all year round.

In 1954 the Navy began exploring for oil in one of its reserves at the extreme western end of the Beaufort Sea. After 75 unsuccessful drillings at a cost of $54 million, the operation was finally abandoned. Secretly oil companies then took up where the Navy left off. In 1963 an exploration team declared that "more than ever before in the search for fossil fuels, the Arctic is of major interest." Four years later two American companies struck oil at Prudhoe Bay in northern Alaska, which became the focus of future development. Announcement of the discovery the following year brought a rush of oil companies to the area, including British Petroleum, Shell, Texaco, Exxon, Standard Oil of California,

Mobil and French Petroleum, a subsidiary of the Compagnie Francaise des Petroles. Operations started quickly and $100 million worth of 48-inch pipe was purchased from Japan to build a pipeline for transporting the oil across Alaska for eventual delivery to the lower 48 states. The pipe arrived in 1969, but development was soon stymied by a protracted court suit launched by environmentalists concerned about the pipeline's effects on Alaska's natural resources, including 40,000 caribou. The dispute was resolved after the oil companies agreed to institute strict procedures to protect the tundra and wildlife along the route of the 780-mile pipeline linking Prudhoe Bay to the ice-free port of Valdez in southwestern Alaska. The pipeline cost more than $7 billion, but was considered vital because of the oil and gas shortage.

Recently the seven American companies financing the project agreed to raise the pipeline's future output from 60 million metric tons to 100 million metric tons of crude oil annually, which would increase U.S. production by 12% a year. There is even speculation that production could reach 140 million metric tons per year.

Canada

With almost six million square miles, Canada is second in size only to the USSR. Yet its relatively small population of 23 million makes it one of the least densely populated countries in the world. Oil production, which began roughly around 1860, accelerated significantly beginning in 1950, increasing at an average of 10% per year until it reached 100 million metric tons in 1973. But three years later production declined to 68 million metric tons. Canada, nevertheless, continued to export a portion of its oil to the United States. It is the world's fourth leading natural gas producer, with 3,115 billion cubic feet.

As in the past, oil exploration and development continues in the Northwest Territories and the Yukon despite its vastness and the severe climate of the region, which covers almost 1.5 million square miles inhabited by only about 60,000 people. Exploration is particularly intense in the western sectors, the Mackenzie River basin and the Arctic islands of the Beaufort Sea up to the 80th parallel, above the Arctic Circle.

The Middle East (See Map 7)

Out of 15 countries producing more than 50 million metric tons of oil in 1976, five Middle Eastern nations accounted for more than a billion metric tons, a figure they had almost reached in the two preceding years. In this area only Iran produces natural gas—740 billion cubic feet—at output levels unparalleled anywhere in the world. What is particularly striking is the rapid growth in oil production. In 1934, while the two large producers, the U.S. and the USSR, were producing 70% of the world's oil and gas (the equivalent of 147 million metric tons of oil), the Middle East had only two producer countries, Iran and Iraq, accounting for 5% of world production with nine million metric tons. In 1944 Saudi

Arabia's wells produced a million metric tons. By 1960 the Middle East already accounted for a fourth of the world's total oil output, while the U.S. and the USSR provided one-half. Ten years later the latter's share fell to 38% while that of eight Persian Gulf producers reached 30%. In 1975 11 Gulf producers accounted for more than a third of the world's oil, overtaking the U.S. and the USSR.

Such enormous success was possible because of the Persian Gulf's unparalleled advantages:
— more than half of the world's oil reserves;
— a sea that is almost completely bound by land (and thus free from swells), yet is only half the size of California;
— drillings less than 26 feet deep, which make exploration and production operations easy and relatively inexpensive;
— unequaled output: 1,430 metric tons per day per well, compared to six metric tons per day per well in the United States;
— the arrangement of the 11 producers in an unbroken line starting from the Strait of Hormuz: Iraq, Kuwait, the Neutral Zone, Saudi Arabia, Bahrein, Qatar, Abu Dhabi, Dubai, Sharjah, Oman and Iran, occupying the entire eastern shore and controlling access to the Gulf;
— the total cooperation of the largest international oil companies, which continued even after their facilities were nationalized;
— and most importantly, the enormous tanker terminals evenly distributed around the Gulf, including nine, out of the 12 in the world, that are accessible to tankers weighing from 300,000 to 500,000 metric tons.

With all of their wealth, the Gulf countries have only 50 million inhabitants, of which 30 million are in Iran, 10 million in Iraq, eight million in Saudi Arabia, and the other two million spread over the remaining eight states. Four of these eight states have less than 100,000 inhabitants. Because the average population density is only 26 inhabitants per square mile, most of the crude oil is exported to Western Europe, Japan, and the United States, as well as to large refineries in the Caribbean, which until recently had not brought oil from the Gulf.

Mexico

Although many countries saw their oil production decline from 1974 to 1976, Mexico's output increased from 30 to 46 million metric tons. New reserves are continuing to be discovered. Mexico took advantage of this situation to request admission to OPEC, but its candidacy was not accepted as a result of pressure from American oil companies. Its gas production was 770 billion cubic feet and still increasing.

Venezuela

Oil production in this country dates back to 1917. Venezuela is currently the world's fifth highest producer, and its proximity to the United States makes it an important oil exporter. For 50 years foreign companies controlled the extraction of Venezuelan oil, which fell to 118 million metric tons in 1976, a drop that coincided with a serious downward reappraisal of estimated reserves. These two factors led the Venezuelan government, after much hesitation, to push through a law that, in effect, nationalized all foreign oil companies, as of Jan. 1, 1976. At the same time, new fields were discovered in the Orinoco basin. Figures given for this "elephant tusk" (so-called because of the shape of the new reserve) were implicitly confirmed by OPEC, of which Venezuela is a member. Some now claim that Venezuela will become the world's number two oil producer after the Middle East.

Other Latin American producers are, in descending order, Argentina, with 20 million metric tons of oil per year; Trinidad, expanding at a rate of 17%, with 10 million metric tons; followed by Ecuador, a recent member of OPEC, and Brazil, both producing eight million metric tons. Petrobras, the Brazilian state oil company, after its failure to find oil, particularly in the Amazon region between Manaus and Belem, radically changed its methods and began drilling 200 miles off the coast. This search was successful.

China (See Map 13)

In 1907 the Chinese government dug its first oil well in Yentchag, in Chensi province. Later the government hired foreign engineers who searched unsuccessfully for three years. They abandoned exploration willingly because they were afraid of breaking the Anglo-Saxon oil companies' monopoly on the sale of oil if the search proved successful. In 1945, after years of inactivity, drilling was secretly resumed during the civil war with no equipment other than what was left from the past, and the first oil tonnage of any importance was produced and refined in China. When the People's Republic was established in 1949, there were 45 wells producing 100,000 metric tons, after more than 40 years during which only 123 exploratory wells had been dug in all of China. Discarding the old wells, the new government began exploration in several directions. Productive wells were started at the extreme western end of Sinkiang province, 2,400 miles from the China Sea on the old Silk Route. Halfway between Sinkiang and the sea, large reserves were discovered at Yumen, stimulating further explorations. By 1960 China was producing five million metric tons of oil per year, which prompted the construction of a large refinery at Lanchow, in the midst of the oil deposits.

During this period the only advisers were Soviet technicians, who proposed using heavy equipment and trucks for construction shortly before the break with China. The Chinese refused because, as they put it, their tens of thousands of men with their picks and baskets "would move faster." Eventually a 4,000-mile network linked the far western oil regions by railway, road and pipeline to the Pacific coast. Explorations using modern techniques continued at a high rate in Manchuria, and important discoveries were made at Taking and Skingli. The Chinese also built a road from the Yumen base to Kansu, which opened up an area of potentially rich oil deposits.

In 1975 *World Oil* reported that seismic investigations, carried out under the auspices of the United Nations, revealed an abundance of sedimentary deposits left by two of the three major rivers, the Yellow and the Yangtze. The study estimated these deposits contained "billions of barrels" of oil. In addition, the entire coast from Vietnam to Manchuria, including the Spartly archipelago and the Paracel Islands (annexed by China), holds oil reserves less than 330 feet from the surface. It is an ideal area for offshore drilling. Oil production increased from five million metric tons in 1960 to 53 million in 1973 and 87 million in 1976. During this period natural gas production reached 40 billion cubic feet.

On Oct. 24, 1975 an article in *Le Monde* predicted that China would become a "petroleum giant" in 1980, with an annual production of between 200 million and 300 million metric tons of crude oil, of which at least 20% would be exported.

Indonesia (See Map 13)

For a long time it was thought that Southeast Asia would become one of the major sources of world petroleum. Everything pointed to it: the geological configuration; shallow offshore deposits; the size of the area known to contain reserves (three times as large as France); the high number of oil companies (more than 40) that had obtained drilling concessions and the proximity to the Japanese import market. But there is now some doubt about the value of these reserves and as a result the euphoria has subsided. In fact, the only significant producer remains Indonesia, where oil was discovered in 1893. The oil industry there was originally controlled by Royal-Dutch Shell before its nationalization. Between 1952 and 1976 production rose from 10 million to 75 million metric tons, of which 52 million were exported, generally to Japan. The rest was consumed locally after processing in the nation's eight refineries. Gas production is 245 million cubic feet.

Australia (See Map 13)

After some small discoveries in 1933, drilling developed slowly, beginning in the country's interior and continuing in the Bass Strait. Oil was first sold commercially in 1967, and the country was able to free itself from imported oil. By 1976 Australia was producing more than 20 million metric tons of oil and 210 billion cubic feet of natural gas.

Nigeria

Africa's major oil producer is Nigeria, followed by Libya and Algeria (see Map 13). The output per well of these three nations puts them directly behind the Middle Eastern nations and all three, like the Mideast producers, are located on a coastline.

Commerical production in Nigeria began in 1957, but development was slowed by the Biafran war. Its output of 13 million metric tons in 1965 trailed that of both Libya and Algeria. But thereafter it grew quickly, reaching 112 million metric tons in 1974. In 1976 output dropped to 101 million metric tons, but Nigeria still ranks first among the 13 African producers and fifth in the world.

Nigeria's success is due primarily to the rapid pace of exploration and the quality of its crude, which has a low sulfur content. In 1974 there were 1,100 wells in operation, a fourth of which were offshore (almost exclusively producing oil) extending 30 miles on both sides of the Niger delta. Current production is about 300 metric tons per day per well, 90% of which is exported through four tanker terminals. Two of the terminals are among the 15 in the world accessible to oil tankers of 350,000 metric tons. Nigeria's oil shipments (primarily to Europe and, increasingly, the United States) have made it the world's fourth largest exporter. Since it is by far the most densely populated country in Africa, with 70 million inhabitants, and its industry, which includes Volkswagen and Peugeot factories, is developing, the domestic market has become relatively important.

Libya

Libya produced its first oil in 1961, five years after Algeria, whose production it has completely surpassed. After 1973 Libya's output reached a plateau of 105 million metric tons, fell to 71 million in 1975 and moved back up to 92 million in 1976. Because of this production and its small population—roughly two million inhabitants with a density of about three per square mile—Libya ranks ninth in the world in oil exports. Two of its well-equipped terminals are accessible to oil tankers of 300,000 metric tons.

Algeria

Algeria's oil production was the same in 1976 as it was in 1974—50 million metric tons. But since it is the sole producer of natural gas in Africa, aside from a small volume coming from Libya, its energy production is oriented toward the production and transportation of gas. LNG carriers make their way from Arzew to Le Havre, the Thames, the Rhone Valley and Spain. Algeria is already the leader of liquefied gas exports and the LNG tanker fleet supplies Europe, the United States and perhaps one day Japan. Its production, currently at a level of 245 billion cubic feet, continues to grow.

Angola (Cabinda)

A few years before independence, the Congo ceded to Angola a small territory called Cabinda, an enclave between Pointe-Noire and the mouth of the Congo river. After several favorable exploratory drillings, the Cabinda Oil Co., whose headquarters are in Delaware, obtained a concession of 50 years in this new Angolan territory. Cabinda's reserves are considerable, and Gulf Oil's production today stands at 10 million metric tons a year. According to its agreement, Gulf could earn a profit from this operation until the year 2007.

Gabon

The Societe Elf Gabon began its drillings in 1955 and struck oil in Anguille in 1960 and then in Gamba in 1968. Current production is 11 million metric tons a year. The loading terminal in Gamba has been equipped for oil tankers weighing 80,000 metric tons, with an extension planned to handle ships of 250,000 metric tons.

The North Sea

Beginning in 1959 a Dutch company, in collaboration with Esso and Shell, began oil explorations near Groningen in the Netherlands close to the German border. Ten years later the search for oil was dropped because of natural gas discoveries, which yielded 770 billion cubic feet per year. By 1976 gas output totaled 3,500 billion cubic feet. Over the same period, the Netherlands became the world's third largest producer of natural gas.

This rapid success spurred the British government to begin explorations within its territorial waters. At the beginning of 1967 British Petroleum made its first strike—West Sole—which would eventually produce 350 billion cubic feet of natural gas. Exploration was extended to the entire North Sea after the five countries bordering these waters divided the area into zones on both sides of a meridian passing through the Strait of Dover and extending to the Shetland Islands, 720 miles to the North.

An estimate of reserves shows 2.5 billion metric tons of oil in the British zone and 0.6 billion in the Norwegian sector. Condensates (liquids mixed with the gas and separated out on the drilling platforms) amount to 350 million metric tons. Natural gas totals 84,000 billion cubic feet, or the equivalent of 2.4 million metric tons of oil, half of which is in the British sector. Production estimates for the years 1982 to 1985 show roughly 250 million metric tons of oil and 7,000 billion cubic feet of natural gas per year, or about 25% of European consumption. Nevertheless, these estimates remain a matter of dispute; oil companies have a tendency to underestimate and economists a tendency to overestimate them.

In 1976 Britain's production represented 14 million metric tons of oil and 1,330 billion cubic feet of natural gas, or the equivalent of 52 million metric tons of oil.

However despite its potential, the exploitation of North Sea oil has run into three difficulties. The first is opposition from Britain's coal miners, whom the British goverment has feared for two centuries. Beneficiaries of Britain's monopoly on world energy at a time when coal had no competition, they fought to prevent the conversion to oil on ships in order to preserve the network of coal depots that covered the entire coast. Another problem is the development of offshore drilling procedures capable of resisting the fierce winds and cold temperatures of the North Sea. A third difficulty is the financing of a gigantic operation that involves all the multinational oil companies, the shipbuilding industry and all aspects of advanced technology.

Some claim that oil from the Persian Gulf or Nigeria, transported cheaply by large oil tankers, would be more economical in the long run than North Sea crude beset with financial problems. However, since 1974 the total price of OPEC crude has risen so steeply that it has made North Sea oil economically viable despite its higher production cost. The same is undoubtedly true for the crude oil from the Irish Sea and the Celtic Sea.

The Uses of Oil

Unlike coal and gas, oil has to be refined before it can be used. This process was not always necessary. The heavy oil of the Caucasus, known by its Russian name *mazout*, required only a double heating before being used to run ship boilers. But demand for oil soon focused on products such as gasoline, kerosene and gasoil, which required relatively simple refining processes. Crude oil was treated at the place of extraction and the products, whether Texas gasoline, *mazout* or Venezuelan lamp oil, were delivered to purchasers around the world. Of the total 363 million metric tons of oil produced in 1939, 64% was refined in the United States, 12% in the USSR, 11% in Latin America and only 4% in Europe.

Today demand is oriented toward complex products that require more and more costly refineries. Such refineries must have access to ports equipped to receive the large oil tankers that provide the crude, often from the other side of the world. Due to the growth of oil production in desert areas (the Persian Gulf or Libya) or in zones with difficult access (the Niger delta), it is now more economical to transport crude oil to the refineries of the major European and Japanese consumers as well as the large Caribbean refiners supplying the United States rather than to refine it at the point of extraction. The ease with which it can be transported—almost without human intervention—has always been one of the most important qualities of oil.

The utilization of oil, therefore, poses enormous problems at the international level. In 1939 only 35 countries—with about 50 refineries—were able to refine 363 million metric tons of crude. In 1976, 103 countries—with 800 refineries—refined 3.5 billion metric tons of crude oil, providing the world market with 10 times as many products as 45 years ago.

Oil is not a simple substance but a mixture of substances that give it different properties. There are several types of oils: heavy, light, high sulfur, low sulfur. The choice of which oil to refine generally centers on two considerations. The first is density, measured in American Petroleum Institute (API) international units of zero for the heaviest crude oil up to 100 for the lightest. The heaviest oils are Venezuelan, with 26 API, or a decimal density of 0.9 (seven barrels to the metric ton), while the lightest register 44 API, or a decimal density of 0.8 (7.8 barrels to the metric ton). This type of oil is found in Qatar or Libya. Between these two limits fall, in descending order of density, California, Iran "heavy," Kuwait, Iran "light," Iraq and Abu Dhabi. An oil tanker of 300,000 dwt could load either 11,725,000 cubic feet of 0.9 density oil in Venezuela, or 13,125,000 cubic feet of density 0.81 in Qatar, which represents a gain of 1.4 million cubic feet.

Sulfur content is the other important consideration in the choice of oil. Once thought a handicap, the sulfur is now recovered in the refinement process and sold. The oils with the least sulfur are found in Algeria (0.1%), Libya and Nigeria (0.2%), while those with the highest sulfur content are in Iran (1.5%), Saudi Arabia (1.6%), Iraq (2%) and Kuwait (2.5%).

Density and sulfur content are so important both for the loading and safe operation of the tankers as well as the refineries that they are measured at the embarkation point with extremely high-precision instruments, sometimes to three decimal points.

The Major Refiners

At the beginning of World War II, tonnage of refined oil reached 363 million metric tons, 65% of which was produced in the United States, 12% in the USSR, 11% in Latin America and 4% in Europe. In 1965 the United States was still first, but Europe had moved into second place with 22%, ahead of the Soviet Union's 5%. Six years later, Europe, which until recently had no oil production, took over first place in refining and has kept that position.

In 1976 world refining reached 3,528 million metric tons and the five regions listed below accounted for about 82% of the total:

| | WORLD REFINING | |
	(Millions of tons)	(% of World Total)
Western Europe	982	29
United States	754	22
USSR	451	13
Latin America	374	11
Japan	271	7

Source: *Committee of Petroleum Professionals*, 1977.

That year 730 refineries in 130 countries handled 2.8 billion metric tons of oil.

World refining is divided among three distinct groups, each processing roughly a billion metric tons:

—the USSR and the United States, both producers and refiners, refining 1.1 billion metric tons with about 400 refineries, some of them quite old;

—the major nonoil-producing countries (Japan, Italy, France, Germany and the Caribbean group) and Britain, a former nonproducer, refining 1.1

billion metric tons with 170 modern refineries; and

—the rest of the world, refining 1.1 billion metric tons with 170 refineries.

The annual average amount of petroleum products produced per refinery in the U.S. and the USSR is about 2.8 million metric tons, but yearly output ranges from four million metric tons per refinery in West Germany to seven million metric tons in the United Kingdom and France. The five refineries of the Caribbean group (the Netherlands Antilles, the Bahamas, the Virgin Islands and Trinidad), which are the largest in the world, turn out an annual average of 24 million metric tons per refinery.

The vastness of the two countries in the first group, the USSR and the United States, makes it difficult for them to refine oil efficiently. Both these nations resemble continents more than countries and sources of oil are spread over great distances, increasing the cost of refining. Both must also import oil. The United States (the world's second largest importer after Japan) buys 170 million metric tons of crude and 140 million metric tons of finished petroleum products (of which it is the world's leading importer). The USSR imports only 80 million metric tons of oil and exports 50 million of finished products. Access and climate present additional problems in certain petroleum-rich areas, such as western Siberia and the North Slope of Alaska. Another drawback for the United States is the very low output of its numerous active wells—494,352 compared to a combined total of 67,000 for all other countries.

The second group, made up of major refiners with no oil resources, include Japan (the second leading refiner in the world with 245 million metric tons), West Germany (145 million metric tons), the Netherlands (91 million metric tons) and the Caribbean group (120 million metric tons). Singapore, which also has no oil of its own, uses its strategic geographic position to process 42 million metric tons in five refineries. The United Kingdom, which has recently become a producer of North Sea oil, also belongs to this group, refining 148 million metric tons. Through their modern and well-equipped ports and refineries, these countries have fully exploited world maritime transport to obtain and refine a raw material that is essential to their economies.

World Trade in Oil

The world maritime oil trade has increased considerably since World War II. It totaled about 100 million metric tons in 1938, 285 million in 1952, 652 million in 1964 and 1,624 million in 1974. After the downturn of 1975 (1,492 million metric tons), world oil trade regained the 1974 level with 1,650 million metric tons.

As the volume of this trade increased, the centers of supply and demand began to shift with the emergence of the Middle East as a major producer and the decline of the U.S. output. Originally the Americas (the

United States and Venezuela) and the USSR constituted the two principal areas of oil production and refinement, and they exported a large part of their finished products. In 1938, 57 million out of the 89 million metric tons exported globally came from North and South America and six million came from the Soviet Union. In 1964 the respective figures, out of a total of 652 million metric tons, were 281 million and 38 million (part of the USSR's exports undoubtedly moved through pipelines). Europe, with imports of 336 million metric tons, of which a small part (about 10 million metric tons) came by pipeline, represents half of the world oil imports. At the end of World War II, the Middle East began a steady climb. Its share, which was 13 million out of a total 89 million metric tons in 1938, was 340 million out of 652 million metric tons in 1964, increasing from one-seventh to one-half of world oil exports.

WORLD OIL TRADE 1974

	Imports (millions of tons)	Exports (millions of tons)
United States	315 (172 in crude, 143 in finished products)	10
Caribbean and Venezuela	119 (116 in crude)	218 (122 in finished products)
Black and North Africa	32	249
Middle East	16	992
Western Europe	734	22
Japan	268	—
USSR, Eastern Europe, China	21	73
Others	151	92
Total	1,656	1,656

The bulk of trade in crude oil and finished products is conducted by ship (with the exception of several million metric tons of crude exported from Canada to the United States and from the USSR to Western Europe). The two major directions are toward Japan and toward Europe by way of the Cape of Good Hope. The volume of traffic bound for Europe is three times that headed for Japan. Europe's sizable imports are supplied essentially by the Middle East, primarily from the Persian Gulf. Some comes from Africa and a small amount from the Caribbean. These imports effectively equal the output of the main exporters in value. The exports of Venezuela and the Caribbean are directed primarily to the United States, which absorbs two-thirds of their output.

The need for transportation, as expressed in a ratio of tons to miles (tons/miles), has grown even faster than the need for goods. Japan's oil imports, which come mainly from the Middle East, have increased more rapidly than those of other countries. Europe's imports from the same region were already making the long detour around the Cape of Good Hope before 1967, when the Middle East war closed the Suez Canal to shipping for 10 years. The United States has been importing a growing portion of its oil, of which an increasing amount comes from the Persian Gulf, while less and less is obtained from closer sources such as Venezuela.

The United States, moreover, is the greatest unknown factor in any assessment of future world transportation needs. Those needs will be affected by the development of American oil production. Alaskan oil has been arriving on the West Coast from the ice-free port of Valdez since 1977. Some of this oil is being sent to the East Coast by ship via the Panama Canal. However, plans to funnel a large quantity through pipelines to the Midwest have been abandoned because of delays in gaining government approval. The nation's determination to achieve energy independence remains questionable, and in any case, the world will continue to be dependent for a long time on the production of the predominantly Middle Eastern OPEC countries. That region's share of OPEC production was 75% in 1976, or 1,102 million out of a total of 1,506 million metric tons.

The 1973-74 oil price increases caused an abrupt contraction in world oil trade. As already noted, the dollar price of oil at the port of embarkation increased sixfold between October 1973 and July 1977. In response consuming nations attempted to cut back on oil use. The effects of this will continue to be felt if these nations rigorously adhere to their decision to cut back on energy usage to reduce their currency outflows, and if users remain sensitive to the impact of energy prices on their economies. On the other hand, energy consumption and the need for maritime transport will increase with economic recovery.

The capacity of the world oil tanker fleet seriously exceeds current needs and will continue to do so for a long time. This situation is a direct effect of the 1973 oil price increase. Another effect, less widely perceived, is the end of an era during which increases in maritime transport productivity contributed appreciably to the lowering of oil prices in the consumer countries. This productivity increase is not easy to evaluate because of the upward effect of inflation on transportation costs per ton relative to ship size. Ten years ago, the cost of shipping oil was $4.32 per metric ton on a ship weighing 100,000 dwt going from the Persian Gulf to Le Havre by way of Suez and returning by the Cape of Good Hope. A 250,000 dwt ship making the same journey, using the Cape route in both directions, charged $2.88 per metric ton. For the larger ship, the curve has risen to roughly Worldscale 70 (W 70), a theoretical method of measuring oil transportation costs. It exceeds W 100 for the 100,000 dwt ship, which is no longer competitive and which still costs 50% more than the 250,000 dwt ship. The current gap is no longer $4.32 to $2.88, or $1.44 per metric ton, but 70 to 50, or $4.80 per metric ton, still to the advantage of the larger ship.

The escalation of costs was very rapid after 1974, particularly because of price increases for combustible fuels. On the Ras Tanura (Saudi Arabia) -Rotterdam route, the scale of W 100 has risen from $9.77 per metric ton (long), or $1.31 per barrel, in 1973 to $16.50 per ton, or $2.21 per barrel, in January 1977.

Iron Ore

Production and Use

Iron ore ranks behind coal as the most important commodity utilizing large-scale maritime transport. It is not a finished product but a raw material of which only a portion will be used. The grade of ore deposits varies from 20-30% for poorer sources to as much as 60-70% for the higher-grade sources sought today. Until 1935 iron ore was mined exclusively in the northern hemisphere, often in proximity to coal mines. That year the *Statistical Yearbook of the League of Nations* published the first data on the world production, showing an annual total of 63 million metric tons. Four countries accounted for 85% of production: the United States with 16 million metric tons; the USSR with 13 million; France with 10 million and Sweden with five million. The remaining 15% was divided among 22 countries. Steel production totaled 100 million metric tons, spread mostly among six countries: the United States with 35 million; Germany with 16 million; the Soviet Union with 13 million; the United Kingdom with 10 million; France with six million and Japan with five million.

In the 40 years from 1935 to 1975, the production of both iron and steel has increased sevenfold, in proportions similar to those of 1935, to 550 million metric tons of iron and 700 million metric tons of steel. The countries dominating steel production are roughly the same as in 1935. The USSR, the United States, Japan and Germany alone produce two-thirds of the world's steel, and, with the addition of the United Kingdom, the People's Republic of China, France and Italy, eight countries produce 82%. The distribution of iron producers, however, has begun to shift to the countries of the southern hemisphere, which have very rich ore deposits and often considerable reserves. Thus during the same 40-year period Australia has increased production from one to 45 million metric tons per year, Brazil from zero to 30 million, Liberia from zero to 23 million, Venezuela from zero to 12 million and both Peru and Chile from zero to six million. The grades of these ores are as high as 60% in Peru and Chile, 65% in Liberia and Australia and 68% in Brazil.

The steel-producing countries of the northern hemisphere are naturally very interested in developing these high-grade ores and have contributed both financial and technical aid, which has permitted the development of modern production techniques. Today's mines are almost all open-pit operations, which displace enormous layers of earth, thereby avoiding the traditional mine shafts and requiring much less manpower. The mines are generally linked by rail to a busy embarkation port. New diggings are underway, such as the operation at Sishen in South Africa, 420 miles inland. It is linked by rail to Saldanha, a new port under construction north of Capetown. Another, even more important mine, is planned for Sierra de Sarajas in the Amazon basin, separated from the sea by 540 miles of jungle. After mining the ore is stripped of its gangue and prepared in the form of small pellets. This operation, known as "pelletization," makes it possible to load semifinished products onto ships for direct delivery to the foundries of Europe and Japan.

As an example of modernized production, the iron ore of Itabira in Brazil (68% grade) is hauled daily 330 miles to the port of embarkation by trains 4,921 feet long, made up of 160 cars. In Vitoria the ore is simultaneously loaded onto ships at the rate of 14,000 metric tons an hour, a process that can fill six ships in 24 hours. Iron ore from Mount Waleback in Australia is transported 240 miles to Port Hedland by a railroad built in a record 15 months. Each train has three 3,600 hp locomotives and 136 cars with a capacity of 16,000 metric tons. Such equipment has enabled Australia to tap its extensive reserves, including Mount Tom Price with an estimated 600 million metric tons of 62% grade, to the point that it has become the world's third largest ore producer, after the U.S. and the USSR.

IRON PRODUCTION
(in millions of metric tons)

	1971-72	1975		1971-72	1975
USSR	113,000	129,600	Sweden	21,000	20,500
Australia	39,000	64,000	France	16,000	16,572
United States	46,000	48,558	Liberia	23,000	16,000
Brazil	29,000	41,600	Venezuela	11,000	13,600
China	26,000	33,000	South Africa	5,000	7,600
India	22,000	41,600	Peru	6,000	5,900
Canada	24,000	20,000	Chile	5,700	5,700
			Mauritania	5,000	5,400

Trade (See Maps 5, 14 and 15)

In 1975 iron ore represented nearly 50% of the tonnage of the five major categories of commodities transported in bulk cargo ships, and its share of the tons/mile ratio was also nearly 50%, compared to 42% of the tonnage and 46% of the tons/miles ratio in 1965. This increase shows that the demand for iron ore transport in the world increased slightly more rapidly over 10 years than that of the four major categories of freight (coal, grains, bauxite and phosphate) and that the trips have lengthened in order to transport high-grade ore from locations in the southern hemisphere to steel factories built on the coasts of Europe and Japan. This imported ore is now more economical to use than domestic resources. For this reason, regional shipments, between Sweden and other European countries, for example, have declined, giving an advantage to the large exporters.

The total exports of iron ore in 1975 were 340 million metric tons, of which 292 million were transported by ship. That year, the two largest exporting countries were Australia and Brazil, with 82.9 million and 61.8 million metric tons respectively. The two major importing zones were on roughly equal footing in 1975: Europe (121.8 million metric tons) and Japan (131.6 million metric tons). But Japan, supplied to a great extent by Africa and America, accounted for 814 billion metric tons/miles compared to 556 billion metric tons/miles for Europe, which is nearer to both sources. Australia among the exporting countries and Japan among the importers are the two areas whose growth has been the most significant in recent years.

The share of world transport held by bulk carriers and mixed-ore carriers has increased considerably in the course of the last few years because of excess oil transport capacity. In 1973, 81% of the fleet was carrying oil, whereas in 1976 that figure had fallen to 53%. However world trade in iron is not integrated in the same way as oil trade. FOB purchase contracts are negotiated every year and the ships are chartered less on the basis of long-term agreements and more through "spot" or per trip agreements. FOB prices vary considerably throughout the world and, more specifically, with respect to grade of the ore. They vary over time as well. Stable for an extended period, prices almost doubled in a few years after having reached $20 per metric ton (for a high-quality ore), but in 1976 they fell back to roughly $10 under the impact of the world recession. Shipping costs also fluctuate. They surpassed $11 per metric ton in 1973, but in 1976 costs between America and Europe had dropped to around $4 per metric ton. Shipping costs, as noted before, are approximately one-tenth of the cif (cost, insurance and freight) price of oil transported from the Persian Gulf to Europe. But they constitute between one-sixth and one-half of the cif price of ore imported to Europe from overseas.

Coal

Production and Use (See Map 3)

The United States, currently the world's largest coal producer, was still using wood for 90% of its energy needs in the middle of the last century, at a time when Europe, and particularly Britain, was already using coal. Until World War I Britain maintained a monopoly not only on coal production but also on its shipment and distribution to hundreds of "coal depots" from one end of the globe to the other. For 100 years coal fired the engines of ships, locomotives and almost all industry. In this century coal production remained predominantly centered in the northern hemisphere—the U.S., the USSR, China and Western Europe—but beginning around World War I, Australia and South America began to emerge as major producers. In 1938 production reached 1.5 billion metric tons, of which two-thirds was accounted for by four countries: the United States, the United Kingdom, Germany and the USSR. By 1967 world oil production nearly surpassed that of coal. The "oil rush" was causing a shift away from coal. It had become too expensive by comparison with this new and remarkably inexpensive product, which was easily shipped in huge quantities and, it seemed, inexhaustible. Until quite recently, the production of coal grew at less than 2% per year. In fact, it took coal 50 years, from 1920 to 1970, to double its production tonnage during a period when oil production increased by 20 times and reached every continent.

After a long plateau, coal production seemed to turn upward in 1976. In fact coal, whose reserves are enormous, may eventually win back its preeminence from oil and gas. According to a 1976 report by the International Labor Office in Geneva: "Coal potentially offers an energy source capable of satisfying the world's needs for centuries and assumes this role at a time when the reserves of other fossil fuels are being exhausted. When the techniques of gasification and liquefaction have been perfected, coal may very well become the primary energy source for all current uses."[12] This same study points out that many countries which had slowed down their coal production in favor of larger oil imports have already returned to greater development of coal or are preparing to do so.

COAL PRODUCTION
(in millions of metric tons)

	1940 (U.N.)	1976
United States	465	590
USSR	165	500
China	35	460
Three major producers:	665	1,550
Poland	40	173
United Kingdom	227	126
West Germany	120	95
India	26	83
South Africa	17	69
Australia	12	64
Japan	55	19
Canada	12	21
Indonesia	—	1
Latin America	4	10
World	1,230	2,300

Today, coal is used primarily by central heating stations, electric

12. A form of coal liquefaction, used successfully in Germany during World War II, has been adopted in South Africa by the SASOL Co., which provides an important part of South Africa's fuels and fertilizers.

utilities and steel mills. Even though it has been displaced in many areas by oil and natural gas, which are easier to transport and use, coal remains indispensable to the steel industry. In fact, iron ore and coal are so closely related that both are transported internationally by the same ore haulers.

The U.S. is the world's largest producer of coal, with 590 million metric tons. For years the nation's industrial policy depended on the availability of inexpensive coal to run its factories, fuel its railroads and heat its homes. Downgraded in the era of cheap oil, coal is beginning to reacquire its earlier importance to U.S. industry, particularly chemical production, and may one day be transformed into liquefied forms that can be funneled into the same pipelines used to transport gas and oil today.

The United States has surrendered its position as the world's leading oil producer to the USSR; second place has gone to Saudi Arabia. But the U.S. continues to retain its primacy in coal, which is becoming increasingly important. What counts henceforth is not so much the production of energy as access to a long-term supply. The U.S. government is pushing the development of coal by granting tax incentives to industries that convert from oil and gas to coal. Furthermore large oil companies appear to support such a conversion.

The coal reserves of the Donbass basin in the Urals were known for a long time. The discovery of coal during World War II in the Kuzbass basin, in the industrial zone extending from Novosibirsk to Krasnoiarsk and to Lake Baikal, was a veritable boon since it enabled the Soviets to tap an enormous source of energy at the time of the German invasion of the Ukraine. In this large and intensely active industrial zone, coal is mined in open pits from seams 33 feet (10 meters) thick, with some seams as much as 131 feet (40 meters) thick. Extraction has become child's play in this region. The coal is hauled away by the trans-Siberian railroad in long trains, but coal from the Kuzbass basin also fuels many heating terminals in western Siberia. Soviet coal production—500 million metric tons—is now second in the world.

The world's third largest coal producer is China, with 460 million metric tons in 1976. Virtually none of its production is for export but is used to power the nation's heavy industry. Currently the industrial zones of Manchuria, the upper Yangtze and the modern port of Chen-Kiang are linked by a new railroad to Chungking and its coal mines, the oldest in the world (see Map 13).

The fourth largest coal mining center is Europe. But Europe's production is encumbered by the highest operating costs of its old mines, compared with the cheaper costs of coal production in the United States, South Africa and Australia. Therefore, the real hope for the future economic survival of European coal lies in its conversion to oil or gas, which is now under study.

In summary, the distribution of the large coal mines in the northern hemisphere is spread over an axis starting in China and running from Szechuan (Yangtze) up to Manchuria and into the Soviet Union along Lake Baikal, the Siberian Kuznets, the Donbass and the Black Sea; and an axis in northern Europe beginning with the Polish mines, extending through the Ruhr in Germany, over to Britain and beyond the Altantic to North America.

The relatively recent development of the mines in the southern hemisphere (Australia and South Africa in particular), utilizing extraction and production techniques already proven, makes it possible for these countries to specialize in the export of coke to the steelworks of northern Europe and Japan.

Reserves

Like oil and natural gas, coal is a fossil fuel and therefore nonrenewable, but coal's exhaustibility, instead of lying a few decades in the future, extends over millenia. The following table is taken from an article by the assistant director of the Charbonnages de France, J-C Sore, entitled "World Coal Resources and the Place of Coal in Energy Economics in the Year 2000."[13]

WORLD COAL RESOURCES

	Proven resources in billions of coal ton equivalents (metric)	Proven resources in years of consumption at the current rate	Total resources in billions of coal ton equivalents (metric)	Percentage	Percentage consumed
Oil	150	20	300-400	4-8	95-100
Natural gas	80	20-25	150-200	2-4	70-80
Shales	(40-50)		(150-300)	2-4	
Coal	400-1,000	70-100	5-10,000	80-90	1-2
Uranium	50	25	150-200(?)	2-4	70-80

A study by two American experts, Ferry D. Teitelbaum and Jaroslav G. Pulak, published in 1972 by the European Office of Coal Information, concluded that there were 8,610 billion metric tons of proven reserves, based on the total number of seams 98 feet thick lying at a depth of less than 3,937 feet. More recent studies, such as those of *Coal Age* in 1973, give slightly higher figures. Leading the list is the Soviet Union with its Yakut and northwest Siberian reserves, equal to those of the United States and China. Thereafter comes Central Europe, followed by newcomers such as Australia and South Africa. Reserves of easily accessible solid fuels, listed in billions of metric tons, break down as follows:

13. *Sciences et Techniques*, no. 38, Paris, January 1977.

COAL RESERVES BY REGION

	Proven (billion tons)	Probable reserves in regions still unexplored (billion tons)
USSR	5,900	2,720
North America	1,540	2,520
Europe	560	190
Africa	70	910
Oceania	50	70
South America	20	10
	8,610	6,570

Total estimated reserves: 15,180 billion metric tons.

Shipment (See Maps 5, 14 and 15)

The problems of oil are refurbishing coal's image. The latter, however, represents no more than one-sixth of the world shipment of the five main products listed earlier. But it continues to play a major role in the world, both as a fuel, in the form of boiler or stoking coal, and as a catalyst, in the form of coke. The development of steel factories accessible to water transport favors the utilization of high-quality imported coal, which is now more economical to use than low-grade domestic coal, a situation similar to that of iron ore. Stoking coal is not as much of a factor in international shipping as coke. Less than 5% of its total production is transported by sea: 122 million metric tons in 1975, or 7% of the total coal, oil and natural gas transported by ship—about 1.6 billion metric tons.

As in the case of iron ore, coal's largest importer is Japan with 62.8 million of the 127.4 million metric tons imported in 1975, trailed distantly by Europe with 57.7 million. The largest exporter is North America with 56.1 million metric tons, accounted for by the United States with 44.5 million and Canada with 11.6 million. North America is followed by Eastern Europe and Australia, whose outputs have been roughly equal over recent years: 28.2 million and 30.5 million metric tons respectively in 1975. Of the 62.8 million metric tons imported in that year by Japan, 56.8 million (or more than 90%) came from North America and Australia.

Western Europe follows Japan in total coal imports. Among its most important suppliers are the Communist nations to the east: the USSR and increasingly Poland. However, since the decline of Britain as a major coal producer, the United States, which accounts for 25% of world resources, has become the leading exporter of coal. North America exports almost twice as much coal as Eastern Europe and the market impact of this coal is backed up by the weight of the U.S. in the world economy.

Coke, a product of destructive distillation of coal, is imported by steel companies on the basis of relatively short-term commercial contracts, comparable to those for iron ore. Stoking coal is imported by central heating stations for the production of steam and by electric utilities. Coke is more expensive than stoking coal; the respective fob prices for coke and coal in the United States are $50 per metric ton and $30 per metric ton, in addition to shipping costs. The latter vary with the length of shipment and represent roughly twice as much from the East Coast of the United States to Japan, via the Panama Canal, as for a transatlantic crossing to Europe. But prices fluctuate even more over time. The shipping costs per trip between Hampton Roads, Va. and Japan rose from less than $20 to nearly $30 per metric ton between the spring and summer of 1974, but the economic slowdown of 1975 has since reduced them from $7 to $9 per metric ton on the same route.

Grains

Production

During an average year world grain production might be broken down in millions of metric tons as follows:

wheat	362	soybeans	65
rice	342	oats	48
corn	321	millet	48
barley	154	rye	25

The Food and Agriculture Organization (FAO) provides a clear breakdown of the leading producers, exporters and importers of wheat, the key to the grain markets:

FOOD PRODUCERS
(in millions of metric tons)

Producers (1975)		Exporters (1974)		Importers (1974)	
USSR	75	United States	26	China	6
United States	58	Canada	11	Japan	5.5
China	40	France	8	India	5
India	26				
Canada	17				
France	15				

It is interesting to note that the total production of Europe, all of which in theory is consumed domestically, comes to 80 million tons, or more than the United States and Canada combined and more than the USSR.

Large-scale producers use highly automated equipment to prepare the major grains (wheat and corn) for export. This replacement of men by machines is taking place throughout the food production process. The transfer of the grain from gigantic silos to ships is also mechanized. The unloading procedures do not always work as smoothly, however, particularly in underdeveloped countries with poorly equipped ports where, in place of cargo-handling equipment, hundreds of laborers dump loose grain onto the piers.

Shipment (See Maps 6, 14 and 15)

World maritime shipment of grains is uneven because it is dependent not on economic cycles but on the climatic conditions and fluctuations that determine which countries are in surplus and which are in deficit. World grain transport is roughly comparable to that of coal, both in tonnage and in the tons/mile ratio. The respective figures for coal and grains are 127 million metric tons and 137 million metric tons in 1975, 122 million metric tons and 140 million metric tons in 1976, and 621/734 billion metric tons/mile in 1975 and 595/750 billion metric tons/mile in 1976. About half of all grain shipments are made in ships weighing less than 40,000 dwt.

Most of the world's grain production is consumed where it is produced. In 1975, 137 million metric tons, out of a total of 1,024 million metric tons produced, were transported by ship. Grain accounts for half of this amount, corn one-fourth and then barley, oats, rye, sorghum and soybeans. The leading export centers are the U.S., Canada and Argentina, and the major importing zones are once again Japan and Western Europe with 21.6 million metric tons and 44.9 million metric tons respectively in 1975. The USSR has recently assumed an important place among importers because of its bad harvests, which have forced the Soviets to buy grain from the United States.

Bauxite and Aluminum

Production and Use

Bauxite, an impure mixture of earthy hydrous aluminum oxides and hydroxides, is the principal source of aluminum. In preparing aluminum, bauxite is treated by electrolysis in a bath of cryolite at 1,200°C. The process requires a considerable amount of electricity.

Red bauxite is true aluminum ore, the richest of the nonferrous ores, with grades ranging from 20% to 28%. There are two types of bauxite mines. The first type, situated in countries of temperate climate, is usually old, very deep and often quite difficult to mine and has only limited reserves. The second type, located in tropical countries, is generally new, shallow and easy to mine and has extensive reserves, especially since bauxite is still forming in many cases.

According to the statistics of the League of Nations, in 1935 the total bauxite tonnage mined in the world came to 1.8 million metric tons. France was by far the largest producer, with 512,000 metric tons, followed by the United States with 237,000 metric tons. By 1975 world tonnage had risen to 81 million metric tons, but the large producers were no longer those in the northern hemisphere. Australia, whose production rose from 30,000 metric tons in 1962 to 22 million metric tons in 1971, emerged as the world's leading producer, followed by Jamaica with 13.4 million metric tons.

According to the U.N., aluminum production increased from 260,000 metric tons in 1935 to 13 million metric tons in 1975. The table below compares production tonnage in bauxite and aluminum and underlines their astonishingly rapid growth. It also shows the concentration of bauxite in two locations, Australia and the Caribbean area (Jamaica, Surinam and Guyana), which account for more than one-half of world production.

BAUXITE AND ALUMINUM PRODUCTION, 1935-1975

	Bauxite-thousands of metric tons			Aluminum-thousands of metric tons	
	1935	1975		1935	1975
Australia	0	22,000	United States	54	4,109
Jamaica	0	13,400	USSR	26	1,950
Guinea	0	7,600	Japan	4.5	1,102
Surinam	113	7,000	Canada	21	930
USSR	132	6,000	Norway	15	620
Guyana	140	3,000	West Germany	71	533
Greece	130	3,000	France	22	359
France	512	2,900	United Kingdom	15	252
Hungary	211	2,900	Australia	—	207
Yugoslavia	216	2,300	Italy	14	192
United States	237	2,000	Others	17.5	2,510
Other	109	9,400	World	260	12,765
World	1,800	81,500			

Australian bauxite production is confined to two extremely rich sites in the extreme northeast of the country: Weipa in Queensland, with two billion metric tons of reserves, is the world's leading source of bauxite exports; Gove in the Northern Territory, is entirely a desert. All production, however, is in the hands of three American firms, a Canadian firm (Alcan) and a French firm (Pechiney-Ugine). The Caribbean suppliers have a distinct advantage over the others because they can supply the United States directly with aluminum, already treated at low cost due to the group's cheap electricity.

Aluminum is used industrially in a limited number of countries: the United States uses 40% of the world production; the USSR 12%; Japan 11% and Canada 9%—a total of more than two-thirds of the world's supply. Aluminum production is rapidly expanding because of demand from aerospace (without an alloy of aluminum and titanium, no jet would be able to take off), shipbuilding, auto manufacturing and other heavy industry. And the demand for both aluminum and its numerous alloys shows no sign of slowing.

Shipment (See Maps 14 and 15)

It is estimated that roughly 60% of the bauxite and aluminum is transported by ship. World trade in the two products amounted to 41.2 million metric tons in 1975, down from 42.4 million in 1974 but up from 38.1 million in 1973. The commercial networks are relatively well integrated, and the aluminum producers can choose, depending on the situation, between treating the ore themselves with oxidization and sending the aluminum thus produced to electrolysis factories or to ship the untreated bauxite and transform it at the electrolysis units.

Exports of bauxite and aluminum were 41.2 million metric tons in 1975, including 11.8 million from Australia and 8.5 million from Jamaica, and were oriented toward ultimate buyers in proportion to their respective economic power: North America, which bought 18.5 million metric tons; Europe, which bought 15.1 million; Japan, which bought 5.2 million, and so forth. Inter-American trade is also very important.

The aluminum production cycle is more integrated than that of the coal or steel industry, but none of the three approach the level of integration of the oil industry. Therefore, it is not possible to obtain an overview of market prices for their production and shipment.

Phosphates

Production

Although three kinds of fertilizers are currently produced—phosphates (70 million metric tons), nitrogen (25 million metric tons) and potassium (20 million metric tons)—only phosphates are transported by ship. Phosphate production can be broken down as follows:

PHOSPHATE PRODUCTION

	1935	1975
	(in thousands of metric tons)	
United States	3,210	26,000
USSR	2,375	17,800
Morocco	1,150	12,500
Nauru, Pacific islands	1,000	4,650
Tunisia	1,500	2,300
China	—	2,250
Togo	—	1,800
Other countries	1,465	4,800
World	10,700	70,300

As we see in this chart, phosphate production in 1935 totaled 10.7 million metric tons. Its output doubled in 1945 and has now advanced to more than 70 million metric tons, of which 82% is accounted for by the three leading producers, the U.S., the Soviet Union and Morocco. The United States and the USSR have dominated phosphate production for more than 40 years.

Morocco, the number three producer, has also played a dominant role with its famous mine at Khouribga, 84 miles from Casablanca. The discovery of phosphates in the Spanish Sahara was a boon because of the size and quality of the reserves. This mine is now under Moroccan control, in the wake of the famous "green march," with Spain retaining only a 35% interest in the phosphate company.

The miracle of Nauru is an old one. As far back as 1934 the island was producing 500,000 metric tons of the richest phosphates in the world, with a grade of 85% to 88%. Achieving independence in 1968, Nauru, with its eight square miles and about 7,000 inhabitants, has a per capita GNP of $34,800 (the highest in the world), thanks to its phosphates. The phosphates are mined by 2,000 foreign workers. Together with other islands and atolls—Christmas, Ocean, Gilbert and Ellice—production currently stands at 4.6 million metric tons.

Shipment (See Maps 6, 14 and 15)

The two largest phosphate exporters are Morocco and the United States (the former having surpassed the latter) with respective exports of 12.6 million and 10 million metric tons. Heavy demand made it possible for Morocco to quadruple its prices in 1973, only to cut them in half several years later. In addition to the fertilizer industry, which accounts for 80% of all phosphates consumed, detergents and cattle feed also use the material.

In 1975 the shipment of 1,492 million metric tons of oil and 635 million metric tons of the five major categories of dry bulk goods—a total of 2,127 million metric tons—accounted for about 76% of the world maritime shipments, an estimated 3.043 million metric tons, and the combined metric tons/mile figure of 12,848 billion was 84% of the world total, an estimated 15,363 billion for all products. The value of bulk cargoes, which are shipped over longer distances, is less at the point of embarkation than that of other goods which use maritime transport. However the impact of shipping costs add to their value at the port of delivery. Therefore efforts have been made to improve the productivity of the world bulk cargo fleet, most notably by increasing ship size, modernizing the fleet and standardizing cargoes.

Liquefied Natural Gas

Production and Use (See Map 3)

Several years ago, natural gas could only be used close to the point of extraction, but everything changed quickly with the advent of long-distance pipelines, followed by the introduction of large liquefied natural gas (LNG) carriers. Here again the marriage of energy and transportation has been a beneficial one. The following table gives a global breakdown of the production of natural gas and of corresponding reserves.

NATURAL GAS PRODUCTION AND RESERVES

rank	country	Gas production in billions of cubic feet (cubic meters)				Reserves in billions of cubic feet (cubic meters)		rank
	North America	22,575	(645)					
1	United States			19,460	(556)	217,000	(6,200)	3
4	Canada			3,115	(89)	52,500	(1,500)	6
	Latin America	2,135	(61)					
	Mexico			770	(22)	11,900	(340)	
	Venezuela			420	(12)	41,650	(1,190)	
	Argentina			280	(8)	70,000	(200)	
	Chile			245	(7)	2,275	(65)	
	Middle East	1,085	(31)					
	Iran			770	(22)	322,000	(9,200)	2
	Asia-Oceania	2,380	(68)					
5	China			1,400	(40)	24,745	(707)	
	Indonesia			245	(7)	15,050	(430)	
	Australia			210	(6)	32,200	(920)	
2	USSR	11,200	(320)	11,200	(320)	910,000	(26,000)	1
	Rumania	840	(24)	840	(24)			
	Western Europe	6,160	(176)					
3	Netherlands			3,500	(100)	70,000	(2,000)	5
6	United Kingdom			1,190	(34)	49,000	(1,400)	
	West Germany			560	(16)	8,155	(233)	
	Italy			560	(16)	9,905	(283)	
	France			245	(7)	5,250	(150)	
	Africa	840	(24)					
	Libya			420	(12)	26,250	(750)	
	Algeria			245	(7)	124,950	(3,570)	4
	Other	735	(21)					
	World	47,950	(1,370)					

Source: *Oil and Gas Journal,* February 1977.

(For a detailed analysis of natural gas resources, which are found in generally the same areas as oil, see the discussion of oil production by country.)

The heating power of natural gas, measured in kilocalories (kC), varies according to where the gas is produced.[14] The countries in Europe whose gas has the least heating value are East Germany with 5.7 kC and Bulgaria, Hungary, Belgium, Italy and the Netherlands, which range from 8.4 to 8.8 kC. The heating value of gas in Argentina, Brazil, Mexico, Taiwan and Iran ranges from 8 to 8.8 kC. France, Poland, Australia, Britain, Canada, the USSR and Algeria possess gas resources with a heat-

14. N.B.: One metric ton of oil has the equivalent caloric value of 38,500 cubic feet (1,100 cubic meters) of natural gas and 1.5 metric tons of coal, and one ton of petroleum products has the equivalent caloric value of 52,500-56,000 cubic feet (1,000-1,600 cubic meters).

ing value ranging from 9 to 9.65 kC. The highest gas heating value is found in Venezuela, Colombia, Brunei (9.5) and Tunisia (11).

As we have seen, the production of natural gas is half that of oil and is concentrated among a handful of major producers including the United States, Canada and the Soviet Union. However, production of natural gas is growing faster proportionally than that of any other source of energy. In contrast to oil, natural gas is ready for use without major processing and, like oil, can be moved through pipelines. But although land transport is easy, it is not feasible to transport gas in its natural state by ship because of the space required. Therefore, the gas is liquefied and loaded onto specially equipped ships known as liquefied natural gas (LNG) carriers. Through a process of compression and cooling at -160°C, the volume of the gas is reduced, yet it retains its energy potential and is easily transportable. While liquefaction is an expensive process, the cost is not excessive in view of the power available when the gas is returned to its natural state. Regasification is a simple operation in view of the physical difference between the low temperature of LNG and that of the surrounding atmosphere. Moreover, byproducts recovered from the process are used by the chemical industry in the manufacture of several products.

In summary, natural gas is a vital component of the world's energy picture. Its important uses include space heating, refrigeration and industrial production, and it may have potential as a fuel for motor vehicles. Two byproducts of natural gas are butane and propane, both of which are used as fuels. Propane is also used in petrochemical production.

Shipment (See Maps 5 and 15)

The major importers of LNG, as noted earlier, are Europe, Japan and the United States. The major exporters are, in the order of their experience in the industry, countries in North Africa, the U.S. (Alaska) and Brunei and in 1977-78 various nations in the Middle East and Indonesia. Shipments of liquefied gases in 1976 totaled roughly 525 billion cubic feet (15 billion cubic meters) out of a total capacity of 563.5 billion cubic feet (16.1 billion cubic meters). This figure is expected to increase threefold over the next two years and the United States is expected to consume half of that amount. The table shows the existing networks and those which are being established.

PRESENT AND PLANNED LNG CAPACITY
(in billions of cubic feet)

Exporter	Algeria		Libya		Middle East		Brunei, Indonesia		U.S. (Alaska)		Total	
Importer	Present	Planned for 1977-78	Present	Planned for 1977-78	Present	Planned for 1977-78	Present	Planned for 1977-78	Present	Planned for 1977-78	Present	Planned for 1977-78
Japan	–	–	–	–	–	140	245	368	53	–	298	508
Europe	123	123	130	–	–	–	–	–	–	–	252	123
U.S.	14	490	–	–	–	–	–	–	–	–	14	490
Total	137	613	130	–	–	140	245	368	53	–	564	1121

By 1983 the United States may be consuming as much as 2,800 billion cubic feet. On a world scale, the greatest uncertainty centers on the price of gas to be established between various continents in relation to other energy sources and, most importantly, to oil. Abu Dhabi had concluded a 20-year agreement to provide Japan with 105 billion cubic feet annually for $0.86 cif per million Btu. Later Abu Dhabi renegotiated the agreement at more than double the price, or between $2.05 and $2.10 cif per million Btu, which places its gas almost on a parity with oil.

The major obstacle is no longer technological, but financial. The global product of 6,300 billion cubic feet—the equivalent of 150 million metric tons of crude oil—estimated for 1985 will require an investment of $30 billion in 1976 dollars. Because of the financial requirements, attempts are being made to establish organizations comprised of a gas-producing country, a major oil company and a gas-importing country.

Maritime trade in liquefied petroleum gases, which rose from 9.7 million to 10.5 million metric tons from 1973 to 1974, decreased in 1975. Trade in petrochemical gases (ammonia, butadiene, propylene, ethelyne) was on the order of four million metric tons that year.

Containers (See Map 11)

A large portion of the cargoes on the main shipping lines are now containerized. By 1972 an estimated 44% of the loading and unloading of regular-line ships carrying the 10 major types of goods to and from the United States was containerized. This percentage has since risen substantially. Between Europe and the Far East the proportion currently exceeds 50%. An interesting example of integrated transportation is the Transsea system, which links Basel to Tokyo in 35 days. The containers travel by sea to the Soviet ports on the Baltic and the Black Sea. They are then taken by train to Moscow, the major crossroads, which sends them on to the Siberian port of Nahodka (north of Vladivostok). Nahodka has three maritime links to Japan, where the goods are reloaded and sent on to South Korea, Thailand, Formosa, Singapore, Manila and Hong Kong. This mixed formula, which poses a serious competitive threat to purely maritime modes of transport, is also competing with land transportation. Container transport is also moving into the Caribbean and West Africa and in 1977 began to penetrate the links between Europe and New Zealand and Europe and South Africa. The harbor installations of the Persian Gulf are scheduled to be refurbished within three years.

The roll-on/roll-off ships (vessels whose cargo, e.g., vehicles, is rolled on and rolled off) have potential for underdeveloped countries because their loading ramps help to economize on port installations and dockside equipment. They are, in fact, making a considerable impact in these countries, similar to that of pallet-carrying ships, or pallet freighters, which are designed to exploit fully the efficiency and low cost of the pallet. The creation of new roll-on/roll-off services is periodically announced, as for example in the spring of 1976, when a service was opened linking Felixstowe in Great Britain with Rotterdam, Antwerp, Dammam and Jedda.

Barge-carrying ships serve a large number of developing countries in the Mediterranean region, the Red Sea, the Persian Gulf, Latin America, the Indian subcontinent and the Far East. These ships make it possible to avoid the traffic in overcrowded ports, but they cannot always utilize their advantage because, as we saw before, 17 out of 27 of the ships have cellular holds and special frames for carrying containers. They must therefore use the same specialized installations as the container ships.

General Cargo (See Map 11)

The notion of general cargo is difficult to grasp; there is sometimes a tendency to confuse it with the cargoes of the regular lines, in the same way that freight taken on for ballast can be confused with tramp shipping. In fact, regular-line ships often take on cargo for ballast; conversely, tramp ships are beginning to specialize more and more in order to take over some of the traditional business of the regular lines: automobiles, sugars, cements, fertilizers, wood chips, etc.

There is thus a significant "osmosis" among different kinds of world shipping, shifting the brunt of excess capacity that has hit the oil tanker fleet first to the mixed oil-and-ore carriers, then to the pure ore carriers, and finally to freighters and the whole "dry fleet." In 1975 the depression in the market for bulk carriers (partially compensated by the demand for grains) generated delays in the demand for general merchandise carriers, and in 1976 world tonnage increased by 8%. Two continuing problems in this area are the scarcity of small-scale ships (the same thing is happening with oil) and backups in the ports, of which Lagos with its cement ships is the most famous example. Ships are even unloaded on occasion by helicopter.

The United States share of world trade in dry goods, is difficult to assess. The capacity of its fleet is 14.9 million register tons (out of 372 million register tons in the world), divided into two categories: ships on reserve 1.7 million register tons and those in use 13.2 million register tons; and ships used on the Great Lakes 1.6 million register tons (of which 1.5 million are more than 20 years old) and those used on the open sea 13.3 million. To the extent that it is possible to make a correlation between the available fleet and the global trade carried on by nonspecialized ships, this trade has declined as a portion of total shipping to the benefit of oil, bulk cargo and containers, to say nothing of air transport. But it has certainly increased in tonnage over the years as part of a general economic expansion.

Another indicator of the modest development in shipping miscellaneous goods by traditional freighters is the creation of new lines. 1974-75 witnessed a considerable increase of new initiatives in this direction in the eastern Mediterranean and the Persian Gulf, a trend bolstered by the reopening of the Suez Canal. The ports most directly affected are usually the Mediterranean ports, connected by ground transport to northern Europe, and those in Lebanon, Syria and Turkey, which relay goods by rail and truck.

For many reasons, there will be a renewed utilization of ships hauling miscellaneous cargoes. Inflation has had a considerable impact on the costs of those ships that were in heavy demand. According to *Fairplay International Shipping Weekly*, a British publication, from 1967 to 1975 the 20-foot container rose in price from $848 in 1967 to $2,500 in 1975 and the cost of the container ship went from $7.4 million to $48.76 million. At about the same time the classic "tweendeck" ship went from $2.12 million in 1965 to $8.45 million in 1975. Fuel costs for fast ships have increased rapidly, while those for the standard freighters have remained more constant. But the real advantage of freighters is their capacity to take on the widest range of cargoes. Because they have access to all ports, they also make it possible for far-sighted shippers to shift from declining trade sectors to more vigorous ones. The newly independent countries are beginning to use freighters to assert their independence, since they lack the expensive cargoes appropriate for container ships and roll-on/roll-off ships, as well as the necessary harbor equipment. These needs will give new life to shipyards and help renew a fleet in which ships less than five years old make up only 21% of the total, as opposed to a comparable figure of 87% for container ships.

Passengers (See Map 10)

Only British and Soviet ships remain active in long-distance international passenger travel. The increased number of crossings by the *Queen Elizabeth II* and the continued success of the *Mikhail-Lermontov* on the Leningrad-New York line must be weighed against the retirement of the *France* in 1974, the *Michelangelo* and the *Raffaello* in 1975 and the decommissioning of the *Leonardo da Vinci* in 1976.

Tourist activity slowed in 1974 and 1975 after prices began to reflect the cost increases for fuels. Tourism in the countries of the Organization for Economic Cooperation and Development (OECD) fell in 1974 to 17.3 million passengers, only 3.6% of which traveled by ship. 1975 appears to have been better, but domestic tourism is developing faster than international tourism, even when ships particularly well adapted to cruises are in use and, in the Mediterranean region, can take advantage of the reopening of the Suez to visit such regions as the Red Sea, Somalia, the Indian Ocean and Kenya. Despite fluctuations in the business cycle, it is likely that tourism, and especially interest in cruises, will develop at a sustained pace for a long time. Ships compete successfully with airplanes on short runs such as across the English Channel and the Baltic Sea.

Propulsion in Maritime Transport

Propulsion has received more attention since 1973, when OPEC countries increased the price of crude oil, thus tripling the cost of ship fuel. The following figures bear this out:

FUEL COSTS AS % OF OPERATING EXPENSES

	Oil tanker, 200,000 dwt	Bulk carrier, 25,000 dwt	Container ship, Australia-Far East type	Regular-line freighter, 16,000 dwt
1970	14%	10%	17%	8%
1975	37%	29%	40%	22.5%

A second way to understand the importance of propulsion in maritime transport is simply to weigh the engine, along with the entire engine compartment, shafts, propellers and auxiliary equipment and compare the total with the displacement weight of the ship. A third way is to compare the construction costs of the engine compartment with those of the entire ship.

PROPULSION AS A FACTOR IN SHIPPING

		As percentage of:	
		weight	costs
1)	roll-on/roll-off ships, 20,000 dwt, two engines, one shaft (30,000 hp)	7%	35%
2)	LNG carrier, 410,104 cubic feet, one turbine, one shaft (45,000 hp)	6%	22%
3)	oil-ore tanker, 160,000 dwt, one engine (32,000 hp)	7%	25%
4)	freighter, 17,500 dwt, one engine (23,000 hp)	17%	30%
5)	container ship, 48,000 dwt, two engines (54,000 hp)	12%	26%

In the case of the LNG carrier, the ratio of propulsion to costs is low because of the sophistication of the holds and the hull; in the case of the oil-ore tanker, on the other hand, that percentage is low because of the relative simplicity of the holds and the hull. The ratio of propulsion to weight is high on container ships because of the relative compactness of the ship.

The advantages of the steam turbine in propulsion have long been a subject of debate. To remain competitive turbine output has been increased by raising pressures and temperatures and by improving the super-heated phrase. But the rise in energy prices has pushed the cost threshold well above the level at which this turbine is economical, and it is rarely used on newer oil tankers. For this reason many shipyards have closed down their turbine services.

However, the gas turbine continues to be used in such vessels as container ships, where smaller bulk, reduced maintenance and speed make up for the added cost of fuel consumption. Some researchers have also studied the possibility of using "pasty" fuels, made of a mixture of standard fuel, water and coal dust in maritime transport.

Rises in fossil fuel prices have also rekindled interest in nuclear fuel. The number of nuclear-powered vessels, including submarines, now in use is estimated from 200 to 3,000. Civilian nuclear ships include the American multicargo freighter *Savannah*, the German bulk carrier *Otto Hahn*, the Japanese oil tanker *Mutsu* and the Soviet icebreaker *Arktika*.[15] Tikkoo, a shipping company, announced at the beginning of 1977 that it was considering, in collaboration with American shipbuilders, the construction of three nuclear-powered oil tankers weighing 600,000 dwt. These ships would radically alter the terms of competition with other tankers because of greater carrying capacity and a maximum speed 25% higher than that of turbine-propelled ships. At a time when the cost of oil is forcing turbine-propelled ships to reduce their speed, fuel costs for nuclear-powered ships are a very small part of their annual operating expenses. This makes high speeds economically feasible, and improves the productivity of the investment.

Adaptation of the Fleet

Ships are constantly being added to or removed from any given fleet. A newly built ship is called an entry. The launching of the new ship is the result of a forecast, made months and years in advance, of future transportation needs. New ships replace old or outmoded ships and reflect the increase in traffic. Th experience of the past few years, however, has shown the fallibility of expansion forecasts. Roughly 60 million dwt "fell" on the market in 1974, again in 1975 and once again in 1976, including some 40 million dwt in oil tankers each year (which means four or five VLCCs per week). But fluctuations in the world demand for oil

15. The *Arktika* succeeded, in August 1977, in linking the mouth of the Lena in Siberia with the North Pole, opening up the possibility of commercial exchanges between the Soviet Union and Canada via this route.

had created an excess capacity at the end of 1976, a time when 78 million dwt were still under construction or on order.

CARGOES → SHIPS ↓	LIQUID — BULK — LIQUEFIED GASES: natural gas	petroleum (and other gases)	OIL: crude oil	finished products: dirty	clean	other (wine, etc.)	DRY CARGO — GENERAL CARGO: dry bulk	LOADING UNITS: containers	trailers	barges	pallets, vehicles, etc.	heavy items	refrigerated products	fish, whales	wood	oil exploration platform supply	general cargo	PASSENGERS
LNG tanker	x																	
LPG tanker		x																
dirty tanker			x															
clean tanker					x													
dirty tanker with reheaters			x	x														
dirty tanker (for wines, etc.)						x												
bulk carrier							x	x										
oil-ore, combined carrier (oil-bulk-ore)			x				x	x										
bulk carriers (containers)							x	x	x									
container ship								x									x	
multicargo container ship		x					x	x	x		x		x				x	
polythermal ship								x					x				x	
roll-on/roll-off ship								x	x		x							
barge carrier								x		x								
tug carrier, pallet carrier, vehicle transport								x	x		x							
car ferry								x	x								x	x
factory ship														x				
pulp-and-paper ship															x			
supply vessel																x		
general cargo vessel								x		x	x						x	
multicargo vessel								x		x							x	x
freighter, cruiser																	x	x

The ships listed do not necessarily take on every one of the cargoes mentioned in the columns; for example, a multi-cargo container carrier is not equipped to take on gases and dry bulk cargoes and trailers and vehicles, etc.

An interesting example of ship renovation to match cargo is found in ships designed to transport sheep, converted oil tankers that carry sheep to various Arab countries for ritual slaughter. At the end of 1975, the *Tindfonn* shifted from a capacity of 51,412 metric tons of oil to 50,000 sheep.

A normal "exit" from the fleet is the demolition of old or outmoded ships. They are sold off "at weight," or by the displacement ton when the ship is empty. The value of certain salvageable metals and the utility of certain equipment is added to the price of scrap iron. The main demolition yards are in Taiwan and Spain. There are similar yards in Pakistan, China, South Korea, Yugoslavia, Italy and the United Kingdom. The tonnage scrapped and the prices paid by the demolition yards vary according to the supply and demand situation in shipping and according to the level of shipping costs, which is a function of the general situation. Demolition is by definition a radical way of adjusting capacity with overall demand. Two million dwt were demolished in 1974, but this figure increased to 12 million dwt in 1975 (including 300 oil tankers totaling nine million dwt) and to 15 million dwt in 1976 (of which 11 million came from oil tankers). Prices have been oscillating from $60 to $120 per displacement ton when empty.

The following table shows how prices for new, used and demolished ships have been following a similar evolution, with an increase in costs due to inflation and certain feverish movements due to demand, to the extent that prices of used ships actually surpassed prices of new ones in 1973.

SHIP PRICES

	1969	1970	1971	1972	1973	1974	1975	1976
	millions of dollars							
Price of new ships on order at year end (tanker, 210,000 dwt)	19.0	31.0	33.5	31.0	47.0	42.0	38.0	34.0
Price of used tanker, (200,000 dwt, built 1969-70)	—	40.0	30.0	30.0	52.0	23.0	10.0	9.0
Price of scrap metal (Far East; tanker, 210,000 dwt)	1.54	2.10	1.74	1.68	3.85	4.21	2.91	3.03

Source: Fearnley-Egers.

Versatility increases a ship's usefulness. The most common example is the OBO (oil-bulk-ore) carrier, which can move from oil to bulk cargo and back again for an extended period or on each trip, or even between legs of a single trip. This adjustment capacity is important, as the table below shows.

BREAKDOWN OF CARGOES OF OBOs OF MORE THAN 18,000 dwt
(millions of metric tons transported annually)

	Oil		Bulk		Total
	millions of tons	%	millions of tons	%	millions of tons
1969	58.6	71	23.8	29	82.4
1970	61.5	63	35.5	37	97.0
1971	96.7	85	17.5	15	114.2
1972	132.2	85	22.7	15	154.9
1973	166.2	81	39.6	19	205.8
1974	139.9	58	100.9	42	240.8
1975	112.4	51	106.6	49	219.0
1976	117.0	53	103.0	47	220.0

Source: Fearnley-Egers.

However, aside from this case, neither the ships nor the cargoes can be locked into one category.

One dramatic way of adapting transport capacity to needs is the decommissioning of ships, which takes place when operating costs exceed income for an extended period. At the beginning of 1977, oil tankers totaling 33 million dwt were decommissioned. This represented 10% of the current fleet. Figures showed that 5.5 million dwt, or 2.5% of the capacity of the dry fleet, had been decommissioned. Of course, while a ship is out of service, fixed costs, and particularly capital charges, are still paid. The only exceptions are the crew expenses and certain insurance premiums, but these savings are offset by costs for security, maintenance and berthing. The accidental causes of ship exits are shipwrecks, fires and unexplained losses, which, from 1965 to 1975, have amounted to one million register tons.

In the case of excess capacity, orders can be canceled, changed or delayed. Ship prices and indemnification are a reflection of the balance of forces between shippers and shipyards. Indemnities obtained by shipyards on canceled oil tanker orders have gone as high as 50% of the price. This rationalization of the market, which took hold in 1975 (affecting tankers totaling 45 million dwt) and which continued in 1976 (totaling 11 million dtw), has been offset by deliveries (45 million dwt and 40 million dwt in 1975 and 1976 respectively) and its effects are beginning to fade. Moreover an excessive number of conversions may transfer excess capacity from one type of ship—e.g., oil tankers—to others—ore haulers, container ships and so forth.

Some other remedies for overcapacity just transfer problems to another sector. An oil company that does not renew a long-term time charter or that sells its tankers to the shipping company of a producer nation falls into this category. Still other measures, currently the subject of much discussion, are used in oil transport. The reduction of speed, as we have indicated above, reduces the cost of fuel per transported ton. By reducing the number of tons transported annually, a slowdown has the effect of absorbing the total excess capacity.

Ships are also used as floating storage space, and there is now a regulation requiring separate ballast tanks. Under this rule, certain tanks can no longer be filled with oil in one direction and water in the other, but must be used exclusively for ballast. The shippers and the oil companies are fighting this regulation because it considerably increases their costs. It is applicable to ships of more than 70,000 dwt after Jan. 1, 1976, but there are proposals to make it retroactive.

Finally, a series of operating practices are being utilized to adapt capacity to need. To increase capacity, sea speed can be accelerated, layovers and maintenance stops can be shortened and the number of such stops can be reduced. To reduce capacity, the opposite measures are taken. There are current moves to reduce oil tanker speeds from 15-16 knots to 10-11 knots. One final way of adapting capacities to needs, or more precisely of not adapting them, is state intervention in the natural mechanisms of the market, which introduces rigidities and thereby reduces the productivity of maritime transport at the international level.

World Organization of Maritime Transport

Maritime transport is a world in itself. We might even say that it is the world because it links every country touching the sea, almost every commodity and every profession involved in production and distribution.

Free as the open sea itself, a ship is not tied to any specific route, nor to the import and export needs of a specific country. These facts permit smaller nations to become major shipping powers. For example, on July 1, 1977, Liberia's fleet represented 79.9 million gross register tons (grt), Norway's 27.9 million grt, Greece's 29.5 million grt, and Panama's 19.5 million grt, or about 40% (156.8 million grt) of a world total of 393.7 million grt.

The unequal development of certain maritime nations can be traced in history dating back to the Vikings of Norway and to the Greeks of the fifth century B.C. The remarkable growth of fleets of certain Communist countries (the USSR, Poland and East Germany) is a result of strategic and political considerations as well as the desire to accumulate hard currencies. The Soviet Union moved from 11th place in 1960, with 3.4 million grt, to sixth place in 1977 with 21.4 million, overtaking Panama with 19.5 million grt. The notion of equilibrium also has its place on the seas. Handling imports fob and exports caf (cost, assurance and freight) at its own rates, protected by bilateralism, the fleet of the Soviet-bloc nations operates through its widely distributed ports in the Baltic, north of the North Sea, on the Black Sea and on the China Sea, picking up business on the international routes with prices as much as 20% below the going rate. Construction programs in these countries are still underway.

Since World War II the fleets of certain non-Communist countries have also experienced incredible growth because of their ship registration practices. Flags of convenience are granted by the free-registration countries to shippers who seek to escape regulations imposed by most nations, particularly on questions of safety (of the ship as well as of the crew and the environment) but also in the area of wages and insurance. The advantages for the shipper are, on one hand, a reduction in the wages and size of the crew and, on the other hand, extremely low taxation (essentially a renewable registration fee and no taxes on revenues).

Flags of convenience began in 1939 when the United States wanted to supply England and France without undermining its neutrality and used the Panamanian flag to do so. At the end of the war, the U.S. found itself confronted with an excess capacity that was not economically viable because of American operating costs, particularly wages. To avoid decommissioning ships that were practically new, shippers obtained authorization from the U.S. government to operate them under a flag of necessity by fulfilling certain conditions (which are still in effect), namely that the shipper be American and that the ships could be placed under the American flag if their services were required in the interests of national defense.

Since then non-American shippers have taken advantage of the flag of convenience, and there are now seven countries where it can be obtained: Liberia, which has the largest fleet in the world (followed by Japan, the United Kingdom and Norway); Panama; Honduras; Lebanon and three countries whose recent development has been very rapid—Cyprus, Somalia and Singapore. The flags of these seven countries flew over 7,813 of the world's 67,945 ships in July 1977, representing 109.51 million grt out of 393.7 million grt, which is about one ship out of nine and more than one-fourth of total capacity. (The difference between one-ninth and one-fourth indicates the size of these ships, especially the oil tankers registered in Liberia.)

Flags of convenience have also had a negative effect on shipping. Of world tonnage lost at sea from 1950 to 1970, Liberia's share was twice and Panama's three times that of the OECD countries combined. Such accidents have had detrimental effects on the environment. The free-registration countries do not always have the means to inspect the ship hulls and engines nor to check the qualifications of the personnel, including officers.

Two-thirds of the oil shipped in the world is handled not by oil companies but by independent shippers who lease their ships to the oil companies. The term "independent shipping" immediately conjures up Norwegians and Greeks, such as Stavros Niarchos or Aristotle Onassis. But there are also such figures as the Hong Kong-based shipper Yue-Kong Pao, who single-handedly built up a fleet of 150 ships after starting, in 1955, with a 1927 coal-powered freighter.

Before a discussion of chartering, we should note that maritime transport is a "game" of chance in which it is possible to make and to lose a great deal of money. In this game a shipper has two main defenses against loss: to place all or part of his fleet on a long-term basis or to spread out the risks. Thus, from the 21st floor of his office building in Hong Kong, Yue-Kong Pao, in September 1975, was overseeing the operation of 42 oil tankers, 10 multicargo bulk carriers, two LNG tankers and 75 dry ships, with 20 oil tankers, three LNG tankers and two dry ships on order. This fleet makes Yue-Kong Pao the largest independent shipper in the world, with a fleet larger than Exxon or Shell, two companies involved in single-cargo shipping. However, it is the independents that make it possible for the oil companies to play off their transport needs and the capacities of their own fleets.

Maritime transport is subject to fluctuation because it depends on sea conditions and the state of the economy. In the case of oil, seasonal fluctuations, which are foreseeable, are complicated by economic fluctuations. An oil company therefore has an interest in controlling a nucleus of its own ships, complemented by a reserve of chartered ships. The ships chartered on a long-term basis make up the permanent fleets of the oil companies and offer them the advantage of lightening their financing costs. Ships chartered on a short-term basis, for a spot voyage or for several consecutive trips, make it possible to deal with the ups and downs of the market. Some of these fluctuations are seasonal: the heavy winter oil consumption of the northern hemisphere and the same phenomenon during the southern winter balance each other out. Other fluctuations are unforeseeable and are often the result of politics. One example is the closing of the Suez Canal.

The costs of the permanent fleet are known, while those of ships chartered on a spot basis are not. In any event, charters, whether short or long term, essentially deflect the hazards of oil transport away from oil companies. The situation of the independent shippers since 1974 is proof of this: oil companies have stopped using them for spot leases wherever possible, and they are not renewing the long-term leases as they expire.

Supply and demand are another aspect of the game of maritime transport. This game is regulated by charter brokers. They serve as intermediaries between producers seeking a ship to lease and shippers seeking to lease one. They make use of a network of information and communication that makes it possible to put parties in contact with one another and to conclude a contract, finalized by the signature of a "charter party." The clauses of the contract deal with the nature of the cargo; the ports of origin and delivery; the necessary layovers (called "lay-days"); the fees for late delivery (called demurrages) and the charter rate, the arrangements for payment and the currency in which it will be made.

Spot leasings are calculated in terms of the tons transported. Carrying costs in the case of oil are expressed as an index. Worldscale 100 is a base rate for transporting oil over various world routes calculated for a theoretical ship, the T2, which dates back to World War II. Worldscale 100 was, for example, $16.50 per long ton for the Ras Tanura (Saudi Arabia)-Rotterdam route (via the Cape) on Jan. 1, 1977. A lease agreement of W 30 means that a ton of oil carried from Ras Tanura to Rotterdam was calculated at 0.30 x $16.50, or $4.95 per long ton and $4.87 per metric ton. Long-term charters (one, three and five years) give the chartering party the right to use the ship as if he were the owner, accepting the variations in operating costs, including certain kinds of insurance, whereas the fixed costs, and particularly wages, are borne by the shipper.

As a general rule, a time charter is a charge calculated on the basis of a daily or monthly rental rate computed in relation to the ship's dead weight and sometimes supplemented by a fixed fee. For example, a freighter weighing 28,000 dwt was chartered at $4.85 per dwt per month, plus $1,500 per month, thus having a monthly charter fee of $4.85 x 28,000 + $1,500 or $137,300.

One variant of the time charter is the "no frills" agreement, whereby the shipper charters his ship without a crew. This type of charter has its greatest appeal when the charterer's rent includes repayment on capital. It is a form of leasing practiced in particular by British Petroleum's (BP) shipping fleet. BP purchased four ships from Japanese shipyards through a subsidiary, which charters the ship to BP without crew and at a rate that makes it the owner at the end of a 10-year period. This subsidiary naturally includes several banks, whose importance should not be underestimated in maritime transport.

Maritime brokers and charter parties negotiate many, but not all contracts. Some are handled directly. When the deal is an important one, it is handled through the receiving party on one side and shippers and their representatives on the other. The forwarding agents also pick up the business of small customers. Prices are established by the ton or in cubic feet or meters, and price conditions are specified for pickup and delivery. The transaction is formalized by a bill of lading.

Two types of transport available to shippers are regular-line ships and tramp ships. The ship on a regular line is like a bus and the tramp ship is like a taxi. The former serves a certain number of ports on a specific route on specified days. Regularity and frequency are increased if several bus companies come together to form a conference. There are more than 200 such conferences in the world, each of them with an average of six members each. They are often criticized for controlling the market, sharing out cargo along determined routes with quotas enforced by penalties and setting prices at excessive levels. But conferences have indisputable benefits. They regularize schedules and stabilize shipping costs; under these conditions, customers can make precise forecasts of their costs and can adjust their production programs. Conferences also protect shippers against themselves, against the excesses of competition that might prompt them to abandon certain kinds of shipping or to ruin one another. In any case, experience shows that these agreements are neither airtight nor eternal, and that the "outsiders" in turn protect customers from the excesses of oligopoly and state intervention. Moreover, various formulas act to lower rates: preferential rates for important types of cargo, rebates, promotional rates and the like. Conferences restrain competition, but they enable the companies to make profits.

"Tramping" is sometimes used as a term for the tramp ship, a "vagabond" ship which, in the terms of our earlier analogy, is like a taxi. A tramp is an all-purpose ship that goes from one port to the next subject to the work contracted by its owner.

Tramping is in decline. As we saw earlier, a considerable portion of the shipments of dry bulk cargoes are contracted on a per-trip basis, but the tendency among large shippers and large-scale charterers is to seek the security of long-term charter contracts, leaving only a minimum of business to chance, i.e., to tramping. Moreover, the all-purpose ship, as represented by the Liberty ship developed during World War II (11,000 dwt, 11.5 knots, 2,500 hp) is giving way to the specialized ship, whose productivity is greater. The role of the all-purpose ship has nonetheless received a new impetus from standardized ships such as the Japanese *Freedom* and the *S D 14* of Austin and Pickerill (14,900 dwt, 14.9 knots, 7,500 hp), which is still very popular among shippers.

Essentially international, maritime transport has given rise to numerous worldwide organizations. On the governmental level, these include the United Nations Conference on Trade and Development (UNCTAD), with its commission on maritime transport, and the Intergovernmental Maritime Consultative Organization (IMCO), which is also part of the United Nations. UNCTAD is more specialized in economic and commercial questions, while IMCO is more oriented toward technological questions. Created in 1959, it formulated the safety measures and means of combating pollution that are developed in international conferences. As a sign that it has gone beyond its consultative role, the organization is planning to drop the "C" in its initials and will henceforth be known as the IMO. Finally, the OECD has a Committee on Transportation.

Among shippers, existing organizations include the International Chamber of Shipping, which encompasses 31 associations from 26 countries; the International Shipping Federation, which represents shippers in negotiations with governments and trade unions in the maritime commissions of the ILO; the Council of European National Shippers' Associations (CENSA); the Committee of the Shippers' Associations of the European Community; and Intertanko, which is an association of independent tanker owners.

Shipping agents of virtually every country are also organized into national associations. In addition, there are the organizations involved in ship classification: Lloyds, the Bureau Veritas, the American Bureau of Shipping and Norske Veritas. Other groups include the International Chamber of the Merchant Marine, the International Port Association, the International Chamber of Commerce and the International Office of Containers.

The sea has been an important element of freedom since the beginning of time. But it has also allowed the more powerful to exploit the weaker. The underdeveloped countries know this, and now having attained political freedom, they are also demanding freedom in the economic sphere and in maritime transport. These nations realize that a national fleet is the tool and symbol of independence and that shipping costs constitute a substantial part of the value added to their natural resources. However, in asserting their independence, these countries sometimes institute a set of protectionist and discriminatory measures that first create upheaval in the maritime transport market and then reverberate onto shipbuilding.

According to H. P. Drewry, a broker, the oil tanker fleet of OPEC either in service or on order in mid-1976 totaled 11.3 million grt. That figure is comparable to the goal of the Arab Maritime Petroleum Tanker Co. (AMPT), an association that includes many important oil-producing countries: Kuwait, Saudi Arabia, Qatar, Bahrein, Abu Dhabi, Iraq, Libya and Algeria. This fleet will be joined by the fleets being built or planned by the other nations and the fleets being built or planned by individual governments within AMPT such as Kuwait.

All of these newly rich countries are adding to the excess capacity of the world oil tanker fleet when they buy unused ships at bargain basement prices. They are lowering productivity in transportation when they aim at having 40% of their exports carried by their own ships, as opposed to the current 30% figure. (This objective presupposes control over 113 million dwt, or one-third of the current world fleet.) Nigeria, in July 1976, declared its right, effective immediately, to furnish up to 50% of the marine tonnage for the shipment of its oil.

This is undoubtedly an abuse of power and a poor allocation of world resources. The Code of Conduct of maritime conferences invites similar abuses. On June 30, 1975, 32 countries signed a U.N. accord proposing to share world maritime traffic on the regular lines, including bulk carriers, on a 40-40-20 basis between importing countries, exporting countries and third, or shipper, countries. The implications of this have not yet become evident.

Infrastructure

The transport of goods by ship would not be nearly as organized and efficient without the support systems available today. A ship at sea is supported by a much more complicated infrastructure than is usually imagined. A port, which is the first thing that comes to mind, is much more than a place, or a sufficiently deep and sheltered body of water where ships load and unload. There are a multiplicity of activities involved in a port call. Furthermore, ports are intimately linked to communications networks and roads.

Like a plane in flight, a ship is permanently in touch with land to aid navigation or, in the case of the tramp freighter, to know its destination. More recently ships have been linked to space for navigational purposes through receiver-computers that work with data from satellites in polar orbit. Such equipment is used especially in heavily traveled zones such as the English Channel.

The channel (see Map 8) and the Suez Canal are good examples of unavoidable and delicate passages. Others, such as the Strait of Malacca, became a problem only after the draft of oil tankers was deepened. When growth in ship size became a permanent phenomenon, there was talk of building a canal across the Malaysian peninsula to the north, at the Isthmus of Kra.

The importance of such passages was emphasized by the closing of the Suez Canal in 1967. According to a 1972 UNCTAD study, the closing generated extra expenses totaling $4,355 million for maritime shipping in the 1967-71 period ($2,860 million for oil and $1,495 million for dry goods). The $10 billion mark was passed during the 1967-75 period. The reopening of the canal benefited some goods more than oil, and the areas most affected have undoubtedly been southern Europe and the Soviet Union, as well as the countries of the Persian Gulf and the Indian Ocean. The canal is currently open to oil tankers of 110,000 dwt empty and 70,000 dwt fully loaded. Plans to eventually open Suez to fully loaded ships of 300,000 dwt are being considered.

Competing with or (depending on one's viewpoint) complementing oil tankers are pipelines. The Sumed (Suez-Mediterranean) pipeline, which handles 80 million metric tons a year, has been in operation alongside the canal since the beginning of 1977. It was designed to serve ships whose size bars them from the waterway. In fact, these two methods of transport, both of which are controlled by the Egyptian government, do not really compete with one another, but both compete with the Cape of Good Hope route. The cost of passing through the canal was set as a function of the cost of rounding the Cape. The same is true of the pipeline.

The Suez Canal was for a long time the main factor in slowing down the tonnage race in oil tankers, in the same way that the Panama Canal continues to contain the size of bulk cargo carriers (e.g., the Panamax type scarcely exceeds 70,000 dwt).[16] But to overcome this obstacle, it was still necessary for the demands of transportation to justify large ships and for technology to be capable of building them, conditions that ripened just before the Suez Canal closing of 1967.

Another obstacle to the growth of the largest ships (the oil tankers) was the shallowness of ports. Solutions to this problem included development of the single-point mooring buoy (SPMB). SPMB consists of buoys linked to storage tanks on shore by an underwater sealine and a floating conduit to the ship, which is at anchor and can drift to a certain extent around this fixed point. This technique, which is still being developed, can now be applied to ships of 500,000 dwt and is also used in the extraction of crude oil from some sea-based drilling platforms. Other innovations include the direct unloading of a large ship at sea by smaller ships capable of entering the harbor in question. Shell Oil has practiced this method in the English Channel for some time.

New ports have been built to accommodate large ships in such favorable locations as Antifer, France (see Map 8) and Bantry Bay, Ireland. Another technique has been to limit the draft of newer ships, in comparison with the growth in other dimensions, in order to enable them to use as many ports as possible.

In order to evaluate the depths necessary for receiving ships, the following simple and approximate formula can be used:

$$\text{draft} = \frac{\text{dead weight} + 14}{40,000}$$

where the draft is in meters and the dead weight is in tons.

This formula applies exactly to the 270,000 metric tons of the British

16. According to the *Financial Times* of Oct. 29, 1977, the treaty of Sept. 9, 1977, between the United States and Panama provided for a study by these countries of the possible creation of a second canal, without locks, which would facilitate the passage of large tankers carrying Alaskan oil to the East Coast of the United States.

Petroleum ships (see p. 12), which have a draft of 20.7 meters, or 68 feet, and less exactly to Shell's *Batillus*, whose draft is 28.6 meters, or 94 feet. Of course, the improvement of the port begins with ensuring access to the channel, which includes maintenance of the traditional channel markers as well as the water levels necessary to the maneuver and berthing of ships 1,000 feet long.

The ports accessible to an oil tanker weighing 250,000 dwt are indicated in the following list. It should be noted that the United States cannot receive tankers of more than 80,000 dwt on the East Coast or in the Gulf of Mexico. Therefore the delivery is "broken down" in the Netherlands Antilles. The island of Bonaire has recently completed ship-handling facilities with a capacity greater than any port on the American continent. It is accessible to ships of up to 500,000 dwt. Two pipelines of 24 inches in diameter each handle 420,000 cubic feet an hour, allowing ships of any size to respect the traditional 24-hour period allotted for loading and unloading. (An oil tanker generally uses its pumps for loading, and unloading is handled by pumps on shore and sometimes by gravity.)

In recent years normal ship operation has undergone a significant change: a reduction in the length of stopovers. In the past a typical freighter could easily spend two-thirds of its time in port and the other third at sea, and increases in navigational speed would not only have been useless but even costly in fuel consumption. Development of the standardized container at the end of the 1950s stimulated an intensive mechanization and acceleration of the dockside cargo-handling process and a consequent reduction in the length of port calls. After reducing the length of stopovers, it became important to reduce transit time in order to offer a service that approached that of the airplane in its frequency and speed. However, container ships require heavy investments in loading equipment and large storage areas, in effect amounting to the construction of a specialized port.

A similar innovation to the container ship is the roll-on/roll-off ship, designed in such a way that vehicles can be rolled aboard and ashore. But it also involves the use of dockside equipment. Like container ships, roll-on/roll-off ships are built for cargo-handling speed. Lloyd's monthly publication cited the case of a roll-on/roll-off ship capable of taking on 2,000 passengers, 400 cars and 240 truck trailers in a little over five hours.

Barge carriers are able to avoid the traditional port calls, unless they are taking on or delivering containers. With bulk freight, the ship is passive. Loading and unloading are done at special locations, which are usually owned by the industries receiving the goods, where cross-beams with rolling bridges handle the dry bulk goods. For scrap metal a magnet is used. Installations for liquefied gas carriers are outside of the tradi-

MAJOR PORTS OF EMBARKATION AND DEBARKATION: WORLD OIL TANKERS
(See Map 16)

PORTS ACCESSIBLE TO TANKERS OF MORE THAN 150,000 DWT
(as of December 1975)

Port	Maximum ship size (thousands dwt)	Port	Maximum ship size (thousands dwt)	Port	Maximum ship size (thousands dwt)
MIDDLE EAST		**SOUTH AMERICA AND THE CARIBBEAN**		**France:**	
Abu Dhabi:				Fos-sur-Mer	250
Das Island	250 (350)	Bahamas:		Le Havre	250
Dubai:		Freeport	380	Le Verdon	100 (290)
Fateh	300	Brazil:		Sete	275
Iraq:		Sao Sebastio	300	Greece:	
Mina al Bakir	350	Netherlands Antilles:		Agioi Theodoroi	250
Israel:		Aruba	285	Ireland:	
Elath	350	Bonaire	500	Bantry Bay	330
Haifa	110 (250)	Curacao	500	Italy:	
Kuwait:		Bullen Baai	500	Ancona	300
Mina al Ahmadi	400 (500)	Trinidad:		Augusta	280 (300)
Neutral Zone:		Galeota Point	250	Gaeta	250
Ras al Khafji	250 (300)	Pointe a Pierre	265	Gela	500
Oman:		Virgin Islands:		Genoa	500
Mena al Fahal	320 (500)	St. Croix	140 (260)	Milazzo	330
Qatar:				Porto Torres	300
Halul Island	500	**NORTH AMERICA**		Savona	250
Umm Said	300	Canada:		Tarento	210 (300)
Saudi Arabia:		Come-by-Chance	320	Netherlands:	
Ju'Aymah	500	Point Tupper	350	Amsterdam	80 (250)
Ras Tanura	500	St. John	350	Rotterdam	280 (330)
Turkey:				Norway:	
Izmit	250	**ASIA**		Mongstad	300
		Brunei:		Slagen	250 (300)
AFRICA		Seria	250	Stavanger	100 (210)
Algeria:		Japan:		Spain:	
Arzew	150	Atsumi	200	Algeciras	250 (300)
Congo:		Chiba	250	Bilbao	500
Djeno	250	Kawasaki	250	Cartagena	260
Gabon:		Kure	500	Malaga	300
Gamba	80 (250)	Kudamatsu	70 (250)	Sweden:	
Libya:		Nagasaki	110 (300)	Brofjorden	500
Es Sider	210 (280)	Niigata	280	Gothenburg	225
Marsa el Brega	300	Oita	250	Lysekil	350
Ras Lanuf	355	Okinawa	500	United Kingdom:	
Zuetina	250	Shimotsu	250	Coryton	100 (280)
Nigeria:		Tokuyama	250	Finnart	330
Bonny	375	Yokkaichi	300	Immingham	110 (250)
Brass River	250	Yokohama	300	Isle of Grain	60 (230)
Calabar	70 (250)	Taiwan (Formosa):		Liverpool	90 (250)
Escravos	350	Kaohsiung	140 (250)	Milford Haven	250 (300)
Forcados	250			Southampton	100 (250)
Tunisia:		**EUROPE**		Thameshaven	80 (250)
La Skirra	110 (180)	Belgium:		West Germany:	
		Zeebrugge	60 (260)	Brunsbuettel	60 (250)
				Wilhelmshaven	250

Note: Figures in parentheses show size of largest ship that port can receive after partial unloading.
Source: H. P. Drewry, Shippings Consultants Ltd.

tional ports, and the actual loading and unloading operations involve no more than pumping liquid into completely isolated pipelines.

After reaching port, cargo must be transferred from maritime to ground transportation. To facilitate the process a well-equipped port offers an entire network of railroads; wide, navigable waterways; freeways and pipelines. But the transition between ship and land also involves the need for storage space. Storage capacities impose limits on the carrying capacity of ships, and they in turn are controlled by the pace of production in the factories. If we suppose that a port is the transport link for a single refinery, then, according to a theoretical oil industry rule, at any given moment the capacity of the largest oil tanker, expressed in dead weight tons, is twice the capacity of the largest distillation and refining operation, expressed in barrels per day.

In 1967 the largest tanker, the *Idemitsu Maru*, had a capacity of 209,000 tons and the largest refinery had an operating capacity of 100,000 barrels per day. In 1973 the year of the "sea change," the largest ship in service, weighed 400,000 dwt, and its counterpart, the largest existing refinery, had a capacity of 200,000 barrels a day. Since one metric ton, on the average, equals a little more than seven barrels of crude, the ship's cargo represents roughly 2 x 7.5, or 15 operating days for the refinery. Port fees and storage charges wipe out the marginal productivity gains of the ship's size. What is true for tankers is equally true for container ships.

Economies of scale have spurred growth in ship size. But the pace of this growth has been regulated by the pace of technical progress which has had to overcome numerous difficulties: in oil tankers, problems of deformations, torsions, vibrations, etc. and the tossing about of cargo; or in bulk carriers, weakness within the structures of container ships with large hold panels and tapered hulls. Other difficulties are found in the port facilities and during passage through certain canals, channels or shallows that must provide ships with the necessary depth and even room for sideward movement—in the locks of the Suez Canal, for example.

Finally, financial and economic constraints dictate that optimization of the ship's operations is feasible only if it can be coordinated with optimization of the rest of the shipping process. Improvements in the ship have to take account of the cost of harbor infrastructure, where storage plays a large role, and more generally the cost of everything that precedes and follows maritime transport. The questions of whether one carries crude or refined oil, bauxite or aluminum, live cattle or refrigerated meat all depend on the integration of maritime transport into the larger chain of production, upstream and downstream.

Air Transport

Introduction

As the most recent innovation in transportation, aviation brought to existing communication networks both speed and independence from the constraints of roads and other ground transportation. Air transport provided the most direct and rapid routes, thanks to "that navigable ocean at the doorstep of every home," as the sky was described by Sir George Cayley, the 19th century British scientist and pioneer of mechanical flight.

At the beginning of the 20th century, the sky held out the prospect of absolute freedom; the development of a machine capable of navigating it was the dream of aviation's pioneers. Unfortunately, because of World War I, the airplane became a weapon before it could serve as a means of transportation. Dominated by the military from the beginning, aviation developed in successive phases according to the changing national defense requirements of various countries.

In 1919 the first commercial airlines began with planes that were direct descendants of those used in World War I. Similarly it was the Allied military fleet in World War II, and especially the Air Transport Command, that gave new impetus to commercial aviation in the 1945-50 period, raising it to a level of sophistication never before attained.

During World War II the airplane had acquired power, weight and range: from the 12-ton, two-engine airbus of the 1930s, with its limited range, to the 50-ton four-engine plane of the postwar period, with a capability of transoceanic flight carrying more than 60 passengers. The wartime economy also made possible the accelerated research and development of jet propulsion. Twelve years after the end of World War II, this technological breakthrough spawned the first generation of large jet transports. The Korean and Vietnam wars were arenas for the refinement of large air transports, which were part of the Military Air Transport Service, while the nature of the small-scale guerrilla operations in these conflicts spurred development of the helicopter, which until that time had only seen limited use.

After World War I, various governments, realizing the potential of civil aviation, moved quickly to build both military and civilian air power. As a fast, spectacular way of exerting political, cultural and economic influence the airplane proved indispensable, available at a moment's notice and capable of generating further rapid transport capacity. The evolution of Italian aviation in the period between the two world wars and its role in the invasion of Ethiopia were good illustrations of this concept. Since then the principle of free movement in the air, as originally conceived in aviation law and endorsed by the Versailles Treaty and the Chicago Conference of 1944, has remained a pious wish. The international legal structure of air transport has made it anything but "free as the open sky," and instead has hemmed it with the constraints of competing national sovereignties.

Nonetheless, in a little over half a century and despite the obstacles of a restrictive legal framework, airlines have managed to create the links in a network that covers the entire world. Air transport today is a fact of daily life, and its impact is increasingly felt in the world economy. Curiously enough, this evolution could only occur through a combination of the most traditional aspects of commercial relations and the audacious innovations of a transportation mode freed from the constraints of geography.

The very first commercial air service was opened between Paris and London in 1919. This conformed to an economic law which stated that every possible method of communication will be established between two centers capable of generating a sufficient volume of business. Because of their importance as industrial, commercial and financial centers, the capitals of Europe quite logically constituted the essential poles for the first intercity air networks. This initial phase was followed by an era of technical innovation and long-distance flights. New techniques improved the plane, adapting it to the requirements of its new functions. Speed, range, comfort and safety each made the airplane economically more viable. Long-distance flights opened up the skies to continental and intercontinental travel. Extending their exploits over seas and deserts, aviation's pioneers often established regional operations, forerunners of the long-distance routes laid down in the 1930s. In 1932 the French magazine *Illustration* published a map of the world showing 51 of the most important long-distance flights of the 1922-32 period. This map could easily be super-imposed, with little modification, on today's air routes.

During the 1930s commerical airlines were established. In 1931 Great Britain's Imperial Airways began service on the Cape of Good Hope route, making 26 stops in a week as it moved south from Cairo. On the North American continent and in Europe, the links in the air networks grew each year and the service became more frequent and better organized. Several long-distance services were launched in 1935 and since then have become international routes from England to Australia, from the

United States to the Far East and Oceania by way of the Pacific islands, and from Europe to South America, where French and German airlines made essential contributions to the emergence of regional air service. These first lines were, for the most part, tenuous links, more for political interests and prestige than commercial viability. They were, nonetheless, the framework upon which the world air networks of today were built.

In addition to linking major cities, the transport plane quickly proved to be the ideal means of integrating isolated regions into modern life. Air transport opened up deserts to cultivation, linked islands to continents, established ties to inaccessible areas and prompted the development of tourism.

In certain underdeveloped regions, the airplane existed side by side with the most primitive methods of transportation. The airplane and the mule were the two most widely used modes of travel in large parts of Latin America. Inhabitants of certain parts of northern Canada assimilated the airplane into their way of life years ago at a time when they could still be amazed by a bicycle. In New Guinea the gold fields of Wau were opened up after 1928, when a 48-mile air route linked the mines to the coast. The dense jungle, which had previously required 10 days of walking with minimal loads, was crossed by Junker W-34s and G-31s in 20 minutes. In 1936 the Wau-Salamaua route was transporting 500 metric tons a month. The opening up of many of Colombia's mineral resources provides similar examples. Today, thanks to air transport, the most isolated regions of the world, whatever their latitude, have been exposed to development on a scale not always appreciated.

During this pioneering period, many of contemporary aviation's objectives were already being pursued despite flimsy and often inadequate equipment, the length of flights and the risks involved. It was consistent performance that astonished the world in 1924 when Peltier-Doisy and Besin averaged 113 miles an hour between Paris and Shanghai in their Breguet 19. The shortcut provided by the polar routes prompted Lindbergh and his wife, in 1931, to fly from Washington to Tokyo in their Lockheed hydroplane *Sirius*. A desire for well-spaced service moved Air France and Deutsche Lufthansa in 1930 to coordinate the schedules of their weekly flights to Latin America.

The 1930 performance of the Hunter brothers, who refueled in flight and remained aloft for 23 days and one hour, was hailed as a feat of human tenacity. A similar tribute should be paid to the engine that operated continuously for 550 hours. However the huge 7,200-hp Dornier DOX hydroplane in its 1938 flights to North and South America showed that a large-scale plane consumed an excessive amount of fuel and so did not have the advantage of extra cargo capacity on a long flight. Its twelve 600-hp engines consumed 422 gallons per hour and thus absorbed the plane's entire carrying capacity of 22 metric tons on a transatlantic flight.

Recent public attention focused on the Concorde has to some extent evoked the legendary feats of the past. Commentaries abound, some lyrical and some critical, assessing in various ways the costs of a project whose economic benefits are by no means unanimously proclaimed, even if its operational accomplishments are indisputable. To avoid illusions, both the achievements of the past and the potential for the future must be analyzed realistically. Aviation is no panacea; it is a tool for movement through the air, and as such it suffers because of the energy it must consume to overcome the natural laws of gravity. But in return, it produces speed. It is this quality that should guide any attempt to assess rationally air transport's contribution to the economy of the modern world.

Fleets

The construction of any vehicle is always a search for the best possible compromise among all the elements that go into its movement. For anything "heavier than air," motion above ground demands some kind of lift, which in turn requires a sustaining surface that moves at a certain speed and is propelled by mechanical force. Before it shows any economic results an airplane must expend energy, an important part of which is used in movement to stay aloft. However, civil aviation does not proportionately consume great quantities of oil. In 1970 Europe burned 600 million metric tons of crude oil, 23% of which was used for various kinds of transportation, with the airplane accounting for only 2.1%.

The entire growth of air transportation is linked to the evolution of engines, their output, fuel consumption, weight and bulk. All of these qualitative elements have a direct effect on establishing the optimum energy payload for an airplane. Great progress has been made in this area since the first planes. Fuel consumption levels of 10.5 ounces per hp per hour in 1930 were reduced to six ounces per hp per hour with the introduction in 1955 of the compound engine, which reused the residual energy of the exhaust to activate turbines coupled to the propeller. Despite their initial high fuel consumption, jet engines attained progressively greater levels of fuel efficiency. In 1976 American airline companies reduced fuel consumption by 2.4 million metric tons from the level of 1973, while carrying 21 million more passengers. Jet engines also grew increasingly lighter, while their thrust increased, contributing to an overall reduction in weight since their introduction.

The jet airplane nonetheless remains a major consumer of fuel, converting 4.4 pounds of kerosene into propulsive force every second. The long-range four-engine plane of the 1955-57 period consumed 400 gallons of high-octane fuel per flight hour in order to carry nine metric tons at

300 miles an hour. However, in each of these cases, output is not significantly different per kilometric unit; it even increases progressively with high-power jets as shown in the formula below:

	DC-6B	DC-8	DC-10

$$O = \frac{tkm}{kgf} \qquad \frac{4,500\ tkm}{1,200\ kgf} = 3.70 \qquad \frac{24,300\ tkm}{6,000\ kgf} = 4 \qquad \frac{36,000\ tkm}{8,000\ kg} = 4.5$$

O: output per flight hour.
tkm: number of tons x kilometers per hour (payload x hourly speed).
kgf: kilograms of fuel.

In another illustration, the table below clearly shows that the transport plane has only a modest payload compared to its total weight, a problem further complicated by the transportation of its own fuel:

MEANS OF TRANSPORTATION	FREIGHT AS PERCENTAGE OF TOTAL WEIGHT
Railroad	50 - 60%
River barge	80%
Truck	60 - 70%
Ship	60 - 75%
Transport plane	15 - 25%

This is why the aviation industry and the airlines, instead of competing with trains and ships, have gone to considerable lengths to find ways of promoting the real superiority of air transport in terms of speed and space.

The slogan of "farther and faster" inspired aviation research for an extended period. There was a time when these two elements seemed irreconcilable. Speed was the strength of the small planes, which created little resistance but had limited range. Long flights required a lot of fuel and a lot of power to lift this fuel supply off the ground, adding weight and thereby limiting speed.

Research sought to lighten the structures and the engines in order to gain more range and to carry more weight. New designs lowered engine weight per unit of power and thereby reduced fuel consumption at the same time that frames were becoming less encumbered, as double-wing planes gave way to single-wing models with more graceful fuselages. This was the era of streamlined struts, of aerodynamic-coverings and the first retractable landing gear. Airplanes grew more maneuverable, their drag diminished both in equivalent power and consumption, and they flew farther and faster.

The first high-altitude flights made possible the development of large transport planes, followed by jets and jumbo jets, which realized the most economical synthesis of weight, volume, range and speed. With the reduction of air density at higher altitudes, the plane's resistance, or drag, does not increase as a square function of its speed, as would be the case on the ground. To go twice as fast, the airplane does not have to overcome four times as much drag; at sufficiently high altitudes, the low air density compensates for increased drag. The power required to improve performance at subsonic levels can still be utilized at that point and at still higher levels because the propulsive power of the jet actually increases with speed.

Thus patient research in reducing weight and fuel consumption, combined with the increase in available power, resulted in a considerable increase in payload and range as well as speed. Power makes it possible to take off safely with considerable payloads and to take them to altitudes where a minimum of drag and an optimum level of fuel consumption make possible a trip at the most desirable speed.

The following table indicates the most representative types of airplanes during four decades of air transport.

MAJOR PLANES OF THE PAST DECADES

Decades	Types of planes	Total weight in metric tons	Payload*	Engine power**	Cruising speed in miles per hour (kilometers per hour)	
1935	Douglas DC-3	11 t	3 t MR	2× 1,200 hp	156 mph	(260 km/h)
to	Junker 52	12 t	3 t MR	3× 660 hp	120 mph	(200 km/h)
1974	Douglas DC-4	33 t	6 t LR	4× 1,450 hp	234 mph	(390 km/h)
	Lockheed Constellation	48 t	7 t LR	4× 2,500 hp	300 mph	(500 km/h)
1945	Lockheed Super G	54 t	9 t LR	4× 2,700 hp	288 mph	(480 km/h)
to	Douglas DC-6B	52 t	9 t LR	4× 2,500 hp	300 mph	(500 km/h)
1954	Douglas DC-7	60 t	11 t LR	4× 2,750 hp	318 mph	(530 km/h)
	Boeing Stratocruiser	64 t	17 t LR	4× 3,250 hp	312 mph	(520 km/h)
	Lockheed 1949 Super Star	70 t	12 t LR	4× 3,400 hp	336 mph	(560 km/h)
1955	Douglas DC-7C	64 t	12 t LR	4× 3,400 hp	336 mph	(560 km/h)
to	Boeing 707	115 t	20 t LR	4× 4,500 kgt	540 mph	(900 km/h)
1964	Douglas DC-8	120 t	20 t LR	4× 4,500 kgt	540 mph	(900 km/h)
	De Havilland Comet IV	70 t	15 t	4× 4,765 kgt	492 mph	(820 km/h)
	Boeing 707 - 320C	150 t	40 t C	4× 7,000 kgt	540 mph	(900 km/h)
1965	Douglas DC 8-63C	150 t	40 t C	4× 8,000 kgt	540 mph	(900 km/h)
to	Boeing 747C	320 t	90 t C	4×20,000 kgt	564 mph	(940 km/h)
1974	Douglas DC-10	186 t	40 t LR	3×24,000 kgt	576 mph	(960 km/h)
	Lockheed 1011	204 t	40 t LR	3×24,000 kgt	570 mph	(950 km/h)

*Payloads are the maximum weight in metric tons carried by medium-range (MR), long-range (LR) and cargo (C) planes.
**Engine power is expressed in horsepower (hp) for combustion engines and in kilogram thrust (kgt) for turbojets.

There is an obvious parallel between increases in speed and total weight and advances in engine power. This table, which considers the most widely used long-range planes, could be reproduced with comparatively the same results for medium-range planes, which are lighter but have evolved since the mid-1930s toward a similar combination of higher tonnage and speed. The European Airbus, weighing 140 metric tons and carrying 300 passengers, flies at 564 miles (940 km) per hour.

Throughout the evolution of air travel, airlines have made great progress in providing added space and personal services made possible through the development of larger planes. Yet, for sound economic reasons, airlines expanded their operations to reach a mass market and many of the frills of an earlier air travel generation have been dropped. Such cost-cutting measures are justified in view of the enormous investments required for equipment worth at least $120 a pound. The revenue realized by a few additional seats or a few hundred more pounds adds up over the 3,500 hours of annual flying time.

In addition to airplanes, which are the mainstays of world air transport, there has always been an interest in more specialized operations. Thus from time to time, proponents of higher payload capacity attempt to revive the dirigible, which was abandoned after the crash of the *Hindenberg* in 1937. Kept aloft by a mass of lighter-than-air gas—helium or hydrogen—the dirigible theoretically can carry a much larger payload than the airplane, although at much lower speeds. Because of its vertical takeoff and landing capability, it needs only a very simple infrastructure. Necessarily slower than the airplane because of the drag of its volume, the dirigible moves at speeds from 60 to 120 miles per hour with a quiet engine that consumes relatively little fuel. There are already plans to use nuclear propulsion, which with the considerable carrying capacity of the modern dirigible would make it a serious rival of the ship more than of the airplane. But it would have a cost per ton-mile significantly lower than that of the most economical plane.

All the progress in aviation over the past 40 years could be put to use in a revival of the dirigible. The *Graf Zeppelin* crossed the Atlantic more than 150 times, traveled 900,000 miles and carried 50,000 passengers without incident over more than 35 years. This and other pre-World War II models were abandoned as too dangerous because they used hydrogen, a flammable gas, for fuel. This problem has been overcome by the use of helium, an inert, nonflammable gas, but there remain uncertainties about construction costs and the reliability of an apparatus that, because of its volume, would remain quite vulnerable to all sorts of atmospheric fluctuations, particularly at the low altitudes envisioned for its use.

In the same search for aircraft to compete with surface transport, the hydroplane appears to have potential. The requirements of airport infrastructure for very large airplanes become economically prohibitive, but seaplanes need only water to take off and land and thus far less expensive support equipment.

Seaplanes were effectively the first planes to attain large dimensions, after their invention in France in 1910 and further refinement in other countries. During this period, only bodies of water provided sufficiently long and unobstructed surfaces for the acceleration and takeoff of large planes. The absence of landing gear eliminated a substantial amount of weight, making possible a larger payload and a greater range as well as important fuel savings. Yet performance in general was not significantly different from that of regular airplanes of equal tonnage and engine power. For these reasons the Dorniers and the Savoia-Marchettis used by Italian companies were all seaplanes. The same was true of the Shorts that established regular service between Great Britain, India and East Africa. Latecoere seaplanes flew the airmail routes of the North Atlantic. In 1929 the giant 7,200-hp Dornier DOX astounded the world when it took off from Lake Constance in Germany with 169 passengers. The same plane opened the era of transoceanic flights. Shortly before World War II, the Dixie Clippers of Pan American Airways began regular North Atlantic service, via the Azores and Lisbon, making more than 2,000 crossings.

The advances in airplane technology from 1939 to 1945 eclipsed the advantages of the seaplane. Nevertheless, after the war the Martin Co. experimented with large-scale jet-propelled seaplanes in the U.S., and the Compagnie Generale d'Hydroaviation in France is currently attempting to revive this type of plane. In West Germany the Dornier Co., which has years of experience in the field, is working with different types of airships weighing roughly 1,000 metric tons.

The need for little or no airport infrastructure and the numerous bodies of water available for landing and takeoff has obviously renewed enthusiasm for large seaplanes. Furthermore, this type of plane, with its solid but relatively simple structure, has potential as an "airborne freighter" and is well suited to extensive containerization. Its large increase in dimension and weight does not entail a proportional rise in energy use, however, thus allowing more room for freight and shortening delivery time. But it remains to be seen whether the floating docks required for loading and unloading and the transportation links between cities and landing areas will erode the savings on runways and landing equipment.

Except for the albatross, birds require little space for landing and takeoff. The airplane, on the other hand, needs extensive ground space for acceleration and deceleration at the beginning and at the end of its flight. Since the earliest phases of aviation, the inventors have sought to free planes from the runway. The autogiro and the helicopter achieved this objective before World War II. But helicopters did not begin to make serious progress until 1950. Unfortunately, the extremely high cost of the apparatus that moves the helicopter's blades and the corresponding expenditure in energy quickly placed limits on purely commercial uses.

The few airlines that had helicopters were ultimately forced to give them up because of the cost of keeping them in service. Since then, helicopters have generally been limited to such services as short hops between airports and cities, emergencies and transportation to and from otherwise inaccessible locations. As one example, the oil industry uses helicopters extensively to provide support services to offshore drilling operations.

The helicopter undoubtedly has its limits for large-scale transportation. The largest helicopters do not exceed 13 to 15 metric tons, and their payload capacity is no greater than that of an airplane because of the very heavy engines needed to provide stabilization while maintaining stationary positions. (Almost all helicopters weighing more than four metric tons have two engines or, better still, two turbines.) Over short distances the helicopter can use a sling to carry up to 40% of its total weight. But beyond a certain distance, its extra power becomes a handicap resulting in excessive fuel consumption. The helicopter also lacks speed because of an aerodynamic phenomena related to the rotation of the blades and the torque of the engine, which increases dangerously beyond certain levels. Nevertheless, under normal operating conditions and with proper maintenance, the helicopter is a very safe and reliable tool.

Among the high-tonnage helicopter models are the "flying cranes" such as the Sikorsky S 64, which weighs 40 metric tons (including 22 payload tons), and the remarkable Soviet helicopters such as the V-12, which can lift 40 metric tons to an altitude of 7,382 feet.

Thus in its attempts to get away from an ever more costly infrastructure, the air transport industry must come to terms with other obstacles that increase the costs of its operations. Within these limits the industry is attempting to solve the problem of air traffic density over airports during rush hours. One possible solution, the vertical takeoff and landing (VTOL) craft, would combine the speed and fuel advantages of the plane with the flexibility of the helicopter. The VTOL may be either a helicopter that by a mechanical procedure can fly like a plane, held aloft by a short wing, or a plane equipped for either vertical takeoff or landing or to land at such an angle that its runway distance would be greatly reduced.

In a simple but extremely costly VTOL model, a set of vertical jet engines are added to a standard airplane, giving it a total thrust that exceeds the weight of the plane and enabling a vertical takeoff prior to lateral acceleration. However, such a procedure consumes a huge quantity of fuel, even though the takeoff jets can also be used to propel the plane in normal flight. Many experimental versions of this VTOL have been used in ongoing research in Europe and the U.S., but thus far none has proved viable.

A more practicable development is the slow-flying plane whose special wing keeps it aloft at speeds low enough for the plane to take off and land in a very small area. France's Breguet 941, whose performance in this area has yet to be equaled, is a 24-ton turboprop that flies at 450 miles an hour, powered by very large propellers. When their thrust is turned downward and triple flaps extending the length of the wing are deflected down, the plane can take off within 984 feet. Considerable study on ways to integrate such a plane into the network of interurban air routes has been made in the U.S. in cooperation with McDonnell-Douglas and Eastern Airlines.

Canada, primarily because of its climate, and Latin America, because of its terrain, make wide use of this all-purpose air transport. A gigantic airlift using this plane—the only transportation available in a totally deserted region—made possible the construction of a 300-mile (500-km) railway linking the iron mines of Labrador with Sept-Iles on the St. Lawrence in Canada.

Small-scale versions of VTOLs are already widespread. After the Beaver, the Otter and the Twin Otter, De Havilland Aircraft of Canada (DHAC) is producing a DH-7, combining four 1,120-hp turbine engines with wide-diameter rotating blades capable of 1,100 rpm. Weighing 18.5 metric tons, the DH-7 can carry a load of five metric tons over 435 miles. It requires only 1,148 feet for takeoff and 820 feet for landing; its takeoff slope is 18%. Designed to transport either 48 passengers or freight, this plane has a novel advantage: its sound level is the lowest ever. For the moment, the silent and low-cost DH-7 is only a small carrier, but it is an undoubted success within the general framework of VTOLs. Along similar lines there is wide experimentation in the use of fluid flaps to facilitate flight. In this approach a specially prepared wing uses the rigidity of a stream of hot gas from the exhaust.

The interplay of physical laws and the ingenuity of aerospace research has, over a quarter of a century, provided air transport with its most sophisticated equipment. This equipment is characterized by an extraordinary productivity; payloads and speeds have grown steadily and have spurred each other's expansion. As early as 1948, the capacity of a cargo plane such as the Boeing Stratocruiser flying at 300 miles an hour with a load of 19 metric tons, was the equivalent of a train with 40 cars. Today, if an airline attempted to integrate a plane like Lockheed's C-5A Galaxy military transport into its fleet, the problems confronting it would be more akin to those of a shipper than of an airline.

The world fleet of transport planes is quite modest in size. About 5,360 planes account for all air transport. To be exact, at the beginning of 1976 there was a total of 8,290 units each weighing nine metric tons or more. Of this total 1,420 were equipped with alternative engines and 1,510 with turboprops, for a total of 2,930 propeller planes, with an average tonnage and a productivity qualitatively lower than the most widely used jets.[1]

Thus, despite the fanfare a mere 8,000 airplanes are the basis of an industry whose prodigious activities have been trumpeted for 30 years and have reached virtually every country in the world. Many aviation firms ignored this and paid a heavy price after they set up large-scale standardized production lines, without having a clear understanding of the tightness of the market and the speed with which it can be saturated.

In 1918 the French aviation industry showed impressive figures: an output of 3,000 planes a year, with 9,000 frames and 20,000 engines supplied to other countries. France led the world in this field, and French companies competed with German, Canadian, British and Italian producers. But they had yet to come up against Lockheed, Douglas, Boeing and the other American manufacturers.

In 1949, 31 years later, the United States had reproduced, in a five-year span, the same operation that French aviation industry had built between 1914 and 1918, but on a more developed scale and with new materials. The U.S. had an industrial potential capable of moving into standardized production at very high levels of output, which met the airline's need for equipment and at the same time offered both on-the-spot and follow-up services that were difficult to match. Despite the potential of the British aviation industry and its wartime production achievements and the ideas of the French builders, who started from scratch after years of inactivity, Europe found it impossible to overcome a handicap of more than 10 years during which powerful U.S. companies such as Douglas had been able to turn out more than 10,000 DC-3s and C-47s as well as 2,500 DC-4s and four-engine C-54s.

With production in full stride after the restoration of peace, American airplanes took over the world market with models such as Lockheed's Constellation and Super G and the Douglas DC-6s and the DC-7s, of which over 1,000 were produced. In the medium-range class, Europe countered the American Convair with several excellent aircraft, including the four-turbine Viscount (438 models sold) and the Fokker two-turbine F-27 (395 models sold).

1. These figures do not include data for the Soviet Union or the People's Republic of China because information is inadequate. In 1975, 196 planes of Soviet origin were in use in various countries belonging to the OACI (Organisation de l'aviation civile internationale), including 104 turboprops. Aeroflot is known to be involved in all aspects of general aviation, as well as in air transport. For this reason, it has a large fleet of planes, probably exceeding 2,000, including many light ones. Moreover, with more than 80 million passengers and 2.5 million metric tons of freight, the USSR has a fleet of modern transport planes. We should note, however, that the free market laws of standardized production and levels of profitability are not similarly applicable in a planned economy.

U.S. supremacy in jet production was initially threatened by the De Havilland Comet, which was followed by the S.E. Caravelle, of which 278 were produced and sold throughout the world, including the United States. But American builders realized and corrected their shortcomings, and recovered with the introduction of the Boeing 700 series and the Douglas DC-8s, whose many versions and derivations assured them a comfortable market dominance. Sales for the two series totaled 4,200, of which 3,095 were Boeing's.

The following table shows the evolution of the world airplane fleet over the past 15 years:

WORLD AIRPLANE FLEET 1960 - 1975

	1960	1965	1970	1975
airplanes equipped with turbojet engines	388	1,311	3,757	5,096
airplanes equipped with turbo-propeller engines	723	997	1,531	1,562
airplanes equipped with standard propeller-driven engines	3,903	3,332	1,987	1,480
TOTAL	5,014	5,640	7,275	8,138
world air traffic (millions of km-tons)	12,340	23,450	47,810	71,130

From the chart, we see that the growth in air traffic is much more rapid than the increase in the number of planes in service, whose total number shows slow progress, underlining the high productivity of jets. It should also be pointed out that the U.S. proportion of the world air fleet was the same in 1975 as it was in 1960—75%. This preponderance shows the impact of standardized production on a limited market. It not only exacts a price for the qualitative error of a poor plane, but also penalizes the planning error that brings a perfectly good plane into the market too early or too late. Technical quality, foresight, production speed and the spark of genius which produces a plane that spawns several more generations all play a role in this process. If a plane responds to a wide variety of needs and offers a unified concept of utilization and maintenance, there is no room for competitors.

This combination was what enabled Douglas, with its DC-4s, DC-6s and DC-7s, and later Boeing, with its 707s, 720s, 727s and 737s, to hold a preponderant place in the world market over a 35-year period, selling their planes to long-, medium-, and short-range carriers, regular airlines and air transport companies. Boeing has continued this process with its "all-purpose" jets, of which it has built more than 3,000 since 1958. It has also sold 342 of its major passenger model, the 747. McDonnell-Douglas has covered the market less thoroughly, managing to sell only 250 "jumbo" DC-10s in a production line requiring sales of 400 or more for financial equilibrium.

Standardized production and the tightness of the market make specialization unprofitable. This has not prevented the world aviation industry from conceiving and producing cargo planes with remarkable adaptability, as well as slower, less-expensive planes and short-haul carriers made for optimum performance on specified routes. Yet the airplane "made to order" does not carry much weight in the industry because its markets are too small and it is too expensive in the long run.

Engineering modifications must be tied to cost efficiency. A well-made fuselage may add speed and/or lower fuel consumption. But if a few added inches make it possible to accommodate an extra row of seats, is it not sensible to sacrifice a little speed for the millions of extra passenger miles that the plane can offer the buyer? And despite the apparent impracticality of a cylindrical fuselage for transporting people, would it not be economical in heavy-traffic areas to use a "quick change" plane whose interior could be rapidly transformed to carry either passengers or cargo. The plane could then be in constant use, which would lower its annual fixed costs per flight hour.

Although the market for passenger and freight planes is tight, as a result of their productiveness and efficiency, there is one area of aviation with slightly larger outlets. This field is called general aviation and encompasses all activities of civil aviation outside of public transport. Airplanes, helicopters and gliders used for business, private travel or pilot training fall into this category. They serve as agricultural equipment, recreation craft, taxies or small transports. General aviation includes the small, or "third-level," firms using planes with a takeoff weight of less than 7.5 metric tons. Attempts to categorize these air firms often fail. Many small transport companies grow, regroup and in effect are only partially or temporarily involved in general aviation, while large national or international companies that have nothing to do with aviation often buy heavy transport planes for their needs. The general aviation fleet—excluding airlines—totals 237,828 planes, more than double the 108,000 in use 10 years ago. This is a more impressive figure than the 8,000 transport planes in use, but it is still a far cry from the 325 million automobiles on the world's highways. The United States, with its space, industrial wealth and high living standards, is again the leader in this category. It has four-fifths of the world fleet—175,000 planes—including 20,000 with more than one engine and 1,200 jets. France is in second place, with 6,000 planes and 1,200 gliders, followed closely by Canada, and then Australia and Germany, with nearly 4,000 planes. Europe has some 16,000 planes involved in general aviation, or less than one-tenth of the U.S. fleet.

General aviation is an area in which the wide range of uses, the different tonnages and the extent of the market give countries a chance to use their industrial potential, even if they are not competitive in the category of large planes. The U.S. predominates, with well-known companies such as Beechcraft, Piper and Cessna, particularly in the production of propeller engines, where it has an almost total monopoly in the smaller sizes. Europe, and France in particular, also have a wide variety of small standardized aircraft that are popular with foreign buyers.

In contrast to commercial aviation, which must consider economic imperatives that remain relatively constant on all routes and in all spheres of activity, general aviation offers a vast array of activities which a multipurpose plane could never satisfy. The flying school, the shuttle service and the agricultural sector each require very different types of planes and planes that are constantly evolving. Over a 10-year period the planes used by farmers as well as by company directors have been better adapted to their objectives. The expansion of the business airplane has been closely tied to the increasing international orientation of many companies, and in Europe the Common Market has helped to promote this process.

Thus the general fleet seems to be expanding independently and sometimes at the expense of the commercial transport fleets. An important part of the intercity freight previously carried by the regular airlines is now handled by general aviation in order to save time. Not only is this fleet increasingly penetrating the daily activities of the most developed nations, but it is also gaining ground in those countries where the airplane is the only way to reach remote areas. Prospects for expansion in this field focus on the speed, convenience and other advantages afforded by the small airplane. The general aviation market is thus open for continued expansion, but sales are even more critical in this sector than in the commercial transport field.

The multiple effects of the economic crisis of 1974-75 and the continuing price increases for petroleum products have had a constraining effect on world air transport activities. Because until recently many companies overstocked on new equipment, airplane purchases seem to be marking time. These conditions are causing deep concern at the top levels of the aviation industry, particularly in the United States. However in Europe the commercialization of the Concorde and the success of the Airbus are cause for some optimism.

The Concorde and the Airbus possess markedly different qualities: advanced technology and high-priced performance on one hand and consistency and low noise on the other. The development of the Concorde was part of the optimistic perspective that reigned in air transportation before the economic downturn and fuel problems of the mid-1970s. At the time of its entry into commercial use, the Concorde was viewed as the vehicle that would conquer the skies. Few airplanes have aroused as much public passion or given rise to as many political quarrels.

Technically, the Concorde is a success. Its utility, speed and comfort provide a real advantage to people who do a lot of traveling and who have the means to pay for exceptional service. The crucial question, however, is precisely how many such travelers there are. How many are there now, and how many will there be in the short, medium and long term? Such statistics are absolutely essential because they set the parameters for the number of supersonic transport (SST) planes that can be produced. According to certain estimates, 40 SSTs would be sufficient today to meet the world demand for long-distance high-speed travel by first-class passengers, or those who can pay the price of a trip on the Concorde. Although this is only an estimate, it shows that the supersonic plane, limited by its special requirements and by the dimensions of its market, can hardly justify large-scale production. Any thought of amortizing its construction through the production of several hundred units is illusory.[2]

Some criticism of the Concorde has also focused on the operating costs of a plane that consumes, depending on the phase of the flight, from 11 to 17.6 pounds of jet fuel per second, a rate considered prohibitive since the increase in oil prices. However, when the Concorde was conceived, the oil crisis had not been foreseen, and at any rate an exceptional expense would have probably been justified by the exceptional service to be rendered. Ironically, another drawback is the speed of the Concorde. Precisely because it spans longitudes and meridians with such ease, the SST clashes with local time zones and the personal schedules of people who cannot easily adapt to arrivals and departures in the middle of the night. It must therefore wait until the appropriate time for its landing and these waits are expensive.

If the initial years of its commercial use prove satisfactory, the Concorde will undoubtedly win the approval of many of those who today are opposed to it. It may be only the first in a series of new planes that will generate innovation in the future. Thus the plan to have the supersonic jet flown by an American airline during its stopover time in the U.S. foreshadows what might become the routine use of such a plane by several different national airlines. The Concorde is undoubtedly a costly experiment, but it may yet yield profitable results.

Despite all the publicity about the Concorde, it was the Airbus that

2. Development, planning, construction and test flights cost France and England $5,760 million. The first series of 16 planes will cost each country $1,200 million.

posed real problems for European builders. The Airbus was initially conceived by Boeing, McDonnell-Douglas and Lockheed when those companies were seeking a plane to succeed the current generation of jets. But the European Airbus was already in the air and showing signs of a promising career at a time when American builders were just unveiling their plans for the 1980s.[3]

An economical nonpolluting plane is the new goal of the aviation industry. Engine designers are now as preoccupied with putting a quiet, modest jet engine with 10 to 12 metric tons of thrust on the market as with perfecting large jet engines with 20 metric tons of thrust. America, like Europe, is concentrating on planes that are derived from a single idea. Increased fuel costs must be overcome by procedures that reduce energy consumption without compromising the performance level which has proved so profitable for expanding markets. In addition, jet design should seek to be compatible with the world struggle against noise and air pollution, particularly in proximity to inhabited areas. The airplane of the 1980s will have 200 seats, two to three jet engines and a "supercritical" wing. Such a formula will make it possible to lighten the plane significantly, thereby requiring only two jet engines, instead of three, in the 20 metric ton thrust class. It will eliminate much overcapacity (300 to 500 seats), which over the past 10 years has benefited no one except a few charter companies.

A thicker, shorter wing with a smaller slope will provide more aerodynamic maneuverability. It will be fully reinforced, but with a lighter structure than today's wings. Boeing with its B-7X7 and Douglas with its DCX-200 already meet these standards. The Boeing model will use three CFM 56 engines with 10 metric tons of thrust, built jointly by General Electric and SNECMA (Societe nationale d'etude et de construction des moteurs d'avion), and its fuselage will have a diameter of 198 inches, placing it between the 707 and the 747 (236 inches). The considerably shortened fuselage of the McDonnell-Douglas three-engine DC-10 maintains the same breadth, and the two engines will be of the same class as those currently available in the 20 to 25 metric ton thrust range (General Electric CE 6-50, Rolls-Royce RB 211, and Pratt and Whitney JT 9D). Lockheed, on the other hand, is offering a shorter and more economical version of the L-1011, the "500" model. The company foresees no significant modification of the wing or the RB 211 jet engines, which are favored by Britain and its Commonwealth partners.

It should be noted that in Europe, the Airbus is already fulfilling the need for planes that place economy ahead of top performance. Its high

3. In 1975 the Airbus recorded 32 sales and 24 options with French companies and six foreign companies, including South African Airways and India's domestic airway. Today, the interest aroused among new clients, above all with Eastern Airlines in the United States, has created hopes that this series could result in 150 units sold.

level of efficiency is a result of the use of numerous elements of advanced technology in its construction: the aerodynamics of the wing, a high-dilution jet engine equipped with an afterburner, the form of its fuselage and innovations that permit it to use standard airport equipment in the same way as most planes currently in service. Improved control over all technical aspects of operation, which has an indirect impact on maintenance cost, is one of several points that make the European A-300 a rival of the large three-engine jets, the DC-10 and the L-1011, as well as the 727, the most widely used medium-range airplane in the world. The world market for an airplane of this kind is estimated at several hundred.

The current Airbus is built for medium-range, but in its B-11 version, it would undoubtedly become a very long-range plane equipped with four CFM jet engines producing 11 metric tons of thrust and would have all the fundamental elements of today's A-300 B2, including the fuselage length. This Franco-American CFM 56 engine, equipped with an after-burner, is also the basis of projects by the French SNTAS (Societe nouvelle des industries aeronautique et spatiale) to build AS-200s with two, three and four engines for a generation beyond the 1980s. Similarly, the Breguet-Dassault firm has projected, in cooperation with McDonnell-Douglas, the development of a Mercury 200 using the same type of engine. This 160-seat two-engine plane, called the ASMR, would be a candidate to succeed the 727, the DC-9 and the Supercaravelle in the area of medium-range carriers. On another front, Boeing hopes to use this new CFM 56 engine formula to renovate its old 707s, which use too much fuel, with a quiet fuel-efficient jet engine.

Obviously there is an international spirit of cooperation. This spirit is prompted by the realization that if the attempts at intercompany agreements give way to unrestrained competition, then each company must conquer the entire market or be left with nothing. This is a bitter prospect for a European industry threatened with extinction in the market for transport planes, but it is no less foreboding for the "Big Three" American companies, two of which would be eliminated as well.

Since the beginning of 1977, increased competition has become a further cause for worry. The Airbus narrowly missed an opportunity to enter the American market. It fit all the requirements of Western Airlines, but the latter ultimately opted for the Boeing 727. Yet this three-engine plane is more than 12 years old and is less a rival of the Airbus than its predecessor was. It appears that Western's decision was not dictated by technological criteria alone. And Boeing, which has yet to develop a plane for the future, seems to be pushing its most successful line, the 727, to the hilt; 1,641 of these planes have been sold or are on order.[4] It has stepped up sales to the point of saturating the medium-

4. In the same way McDonnell-Douglas succeeded in selling 23 of its DC 9-80s to Swissair and Austrian Airlines. The company will shortly sell its 1,000th DC-9.

range market while there is still time, thus enabling work to continue on its future programs with the protection of a comfortable commercial advantage.

This hardening of attitudes does not augur well for cooperation. At this stage the survival of the air transport industry appears dependent on government, because of the important social ramifications. It remains to be seen whether such a relationship will make possible agreements that economic and commercial factors, by themselves, have not produced. The outlook is uncertain but in aviation nothing is ever completely hopeless. The dynamism of the innovators and the imagination of the airlines have more than once turned around a desperate situation in the past.

Beyond the 1980s research is focused on saving energy or replacing petroleum-based fuel with liquid methane, liquid hydrogen or even nuclear power. Long-term study in these areas has greatly increased in the past three years and its impact is expected to extend beyond aerospace.

The introduction of the supercritical wing will undoubtedly result in a wide extension of its uses. Similarly, all the work connected with movable wing will produce numerous results which, thanks to aerodynamic breakthroughs, will have an impact at the level of operations. Technological advances based on cost efficiency will be the source for improvements in planes of the future. Spectacular gadgetry will give way to the durability, practicality and quality that customers will increasingly demand.

Airlines and Their Customers

Historically, all means of transportation were initially used by men for mobility: only later was technological innovation applied to the movement of goods. Aviation was no exception. The cargo plane appeared only after a quarter-century of air travel during which only postal services took advantage of this new mode of transit.

World air traffic is generally evaluated in simple units: number of passengers, tons of cargo, or passenger-miles and ton-miles, the most representative indexes of output. These figures represent the number of people or tons carried, multiplied by the distance traveled, and are used to determine the profitability of air travel.

Statistics on world air travel and transport (see Map 9) are extremely precise for airlines belonging to the International Air Transport Association (IATA), which has 113 members and handles approximately 87% of world traffic on regular airlines. In addition there is the traffic data of companies that do not belong to the IATA but maintain regular national and international service and the figures of the transport companies that do not operate regular lines—the charters—but whose impact on the international level is significant. These airlines are the components of the global figures published regularly by the OACI (Organisation de l'aviation civile internationale) made up of 135 member countries, including the USSR and the People's Republic of China.

The figures for world air travel in 1975 were as follows:[5]

Regular airlines (IATA)	519.8 billion passenger-km
Regular airlines (non-IATA)	112.2 billion passenger-km
Other airlines	112 billion passenger-km
USSR	133 billion passenger-km
Total	877 billion passenger-km

After the economic contraction of the 1974-75 period, the pace of annual growth in air travel appeared to resume in 1976. The figures were up by 11% from 1975, according to initial estimates. The following discussion is based on the latest figures for 1976 and in some cases 1975.

The following table traces the development of air service over the past 20 years:

THE DEVELOPMENT OF AIR SERVICE

	Passengers (millions)	Passenger-km (billions)	Annual rate of increase (%)	Average kilometers traveled per passenger
1954	52	52		895
1955	68	61	17	905
1956	77	71	16	920
1957	86	82	15	950
1958	88	85	4	970
1959	98	98	15	990
1960	106	109	11	1,030
1961	111	117	7	1,055
1962	121	130	11	1,075
1963	135	147	13	1,085
1964	155	171	16	1,105
1965	177	198	16	1,125
1966	200	229	16	1,145
1967	233	273	19	1,170
1968	262	310	14	1,185
1969	293	351	13	1,195
1970	311 (383)	382 (460)	9	1,220
1971	333 (411)	406 (494)	6 (7)	1,230
1972	368 (450)	465 (560)	14 (13)	1,265
1973	404 (489)	520 (618)	12 (10)	1,280
1974	423 (514)	546 (654)	5 (6)	1,280
1975	438 (536)	569 (691)	3 (3)	1,280
1976*	473 (578)	632 (765)	11 (10)	1,318

Note: Figures in parentheses include USSR beginning in 1970.
*Estimated.

5. The USSR became a member of the OACI in 1970. There is thus a discontinuity in the development of world statistics for previous years, depending on whether or not the Soviet Union is included. The People's Republic of China joined the OACI in 1974, but the statistics are not included.

These figures indicate the regularity with which air travel increased over a 20-year period, except for the contraction of 1974-75, which, although foreseen in 1970, was more severe than expected. They also show the increasing length of the average trip. With the advent of long-range jets and their impact on fares, passengers have shown a tendency to lengthen their travels, and average distance has thus increased by 50% in 20 years.

To give a more detailed picture, international travel must be distinguished from domestic travel, which crosses no borders. The U.S. and the USSR currently account for 240 billion and 127 billion passenger-km respectively. The addition of domestic traffic figures for France, Germany, Japan, Canada and Australia equals 419 billion passenger-km or 48% of the world total. Out of the remaining 450 billion/passenger-km in international travel, only 346 billion are logged by the regular airlines.

The following table shows the breakdown of volume by region as a percentage of total traffic.

AIR TRAVEL VOLUME
by Region

	North America	Europe	N.E. Asia S.E. Asia N. Pacific	South America & Caribbean	Africa	Middle East
1965	59.4%	23.4%	8.2%	5.1%	2.4%	1.5%
1970	59.9%	22.8%	9.3%	4.8%	2.3%	1.8%
	50.0%*	35.0%*	7.8%*	3.8%*	1.9%*	1.5%*
1973	46.3%	36.1%	9.8%	4.0%	2.0%	1.9%
1974	44.5%	36.4%	10.7%	4.2%	2.2%	2.0%
1975	41.9%	37.4%	11.6%	4.7%	2.4%	2.0%
1976	40.9%	36.8%	12.6%	4.7%	2.6%	2.4%

*Includes figures for European region of USSR beginning in 1970.

The addition of statistics in 1970 for the USSR raised questions about the previously stable distribution of air traffic over the earlier years. The Soviet Union's impact was notable in the area of domestic travel but negligible in the international sphere; of the 133 billion passenger-km reported by the USSR in 1976, only 6.8 billion were international. The chart shows American airlines losing ground, largely because of heavy international competition from European and Asian airlines from 1970 to 1976.

The following chart shows the "arterial pressure" on air traffic, or the consistency of traffic flows around the major axes of world travel. Only figures for IATA members and their regular services in 1975 are calculated.

AIR TRAFFIC FLOWS

International Long-Distance Routes and Travel Zones	Billions of passenger - km	Percentage of total
North Atlantic and Mid-Atlantic	60	31.5
International Flights within Western Hemisphere	18	9.5
South Atlantic	7	3.7
Europe - Africa	12	6.3
Europe - Asia	30	15.9
International Flights within Europe	32	16.8
Trans-Pacific (North Mid-)	11	5.8
Trans-Pacific (South)	5	2.7
International Flights, Other Regions	15	7.8

The statistics indicate why the North Atlantic is always cited as the key sector and the test area for everything affecting international air travel.

This brief analysis thus gives an approximate breakdown of the flow of air travel. Domestic travel accounts for half of the total, with the United States alone providing 50% of those figures. The remainder, in the international sphere, is spread over charter flight passengers (23%) and the regular services, whose major routes are centered on the North Atlantic, Europe and the Far East (see Maps 10, 12, 14 and 15). We might add that air travel over the North Atlantic, the most widely used international zone in the world, amounts to a daily average of 324 planes flying in both directions. At any hour of the day or night, an average of 95 planes is crossing the ocean (see Map 14).

Another misleading aspect of the statistics is the confusion they create about the number of passengers, seen as individuals. In the discussion on railroads, it is obvious that the total number of individual passengers using suburban trains should be lowered because on a typical working day, the same people come and go. The same thing is true for air travel. In 1970 the president of Air Inter pointed out that the 2.5 million passengers recorded by his company probably amounted in reality to a mere 350,000 people who travel several times a year.

It must also be kept in mind that the figures which are collected from airlines and which ultimately appear in the world data are based on passengers using a specific line, one designated by a number. If in the course of a single trip a passenger uses several lines with different numbers, he will be counted as a different passenger on each flight. It is thus necessary to keep in mind the different kinds of trips made every year by an individual, the round trips that are counted individually and more complicated trips, with several flight numbers, with or without plane changes. The engineer who flies five times a year between Paris and Lyon, who vacations in Rhodes after getting there by way of Rome and Athens and who, in the course of the same year, makes a business trip to Detroit via New York will appear statistically as 20 passengers. So hundreds of millions of passengers actually represent far less awesome numbers. Users of air transport are often a core clientele of regular passengers, especially on the short- and medium-range flights and in high-density traffic zones.

Travelers are generally grouped into two distinct categories: tourists and businessmen. This fundamental distinction, however, is much too simplistic.

There is nothing mysterious about tourist travel. Aside from the various motives that prompt a businessman to extend his trip or to make a detour for recreational reasons, such travel fills a need or desire for rest, relaxation, novelty or escape. The business trip, on the other hand, can arise for many reasons having little to do with the world of business as such. A wife and children following the head of a household to a new job, people looking for work, sailors flying home after the end of a voyage or families traveling to visit far-away relatives are all on "business trips." Other trips of a nontourist nature may fall outside the sphere of business as such: attendance at conferences or conventions for personal, nonprofessional reasons or treatment of an illness, for example.

People may travel on heavy-traffic short-distance routes, such as commuter lines linking large economic centers for the same reasons that prompt them to use their cars or take suburban trains in order to shop, visit friends or amuse themselves, with no specific tourist intentions.

These motives for travel are external to individuals. What interests the marketing services that study air travel are the deeper motivations and real sources of the decision to travel or to stay at home. Their task is to find new customers and new ways of filling the ever-larger planes that the optimism of the boom years placed on a market which has now shrunk. The oil crisis of 1973-74 undoubtedly contributed to the predicament in which the airlines now find themselves, but signs of an oncoming crisis were already visible almost everywhere by 1970. Commercial airlines were no longer thriving or were doing so only with a much greater effort than was necessary in the 1960s. In other words, airline customers were no longer paying the prices necessary to keep revenues at appropriate levels. Why not? Without going into a long analysis, it is possible to identify certain errors that helped to plunge the airlines into crisis.

In an inflationary situation, which by no means precluded a general rise in living standards, potential passengers emerged in direct proportion to the reduction of air fares. The charter companies, drawing on the general appeal of international tourism, were at the cutting edge of this industry. A bonanza was available to any country that would provide the "three Ss" (sun, sand and sea), in the slightest proximity to natural attractions or local color. Together with hotel owners the charter companies began to promote mass migrations of vacationers and to open up this world of exoticism and novel scenery to the people of the industrialized nations. With unbeatably low prices and capacities verging on 100%, these companies clearly tapped a customer market beyond the reach of the regular airlines.

These airlines, already handicapped by the excess capacity of their jumbo jets, reacted badly to the charter flight offensive. They tried to compete on the downside, offering very low prices to travel agencies and tour organizers. Blinded by a spectacular recovery in their bookings, the regular airlines did not see the short- and medium-term dangers closing in on them. The lowering of fares to win back tourists from the charter flights was creating excessive price discrimination against passengers who, aboard the same plane and traveling under the same conditions, had paid the normal fare for business and other nontourist types of travel. It soon became apparent that buying a tourist package was the economical way to travel on business. The trend caught on quickly and the result was a slide in revenues to such dangerously low levels that operating costs were barely being covered.

The regular airlines should not have been so quick to sacrifice their strong points in order to battle the charter companies on their own ground. Regular airlines and charter services approach the market for air travel in vastly different ways. While the regular line could have used some of the dynamism shown by the charters in winning a new clientele to air travel, it was risky to drop fares so drastically at a time when inflation was cutting into revenues. Such economic vulnerability, after the explosion in oil prices in late 1973, brought the airlines to the brink of a grave crisis.

Many observers feel that now is the time to rethink some fundamental questions about the development of an industry that has fallen victim to a severe and unforeseen crisis. The oil price increase was a surprise. But did it really make sense to expect air travel to expand indefinitely at the rate of 16% a year, or in effect to double every five years? The predictions of the most sophisticated forecasters did not prevent reality and the interplay of sovereign interests from destroying such hopes.

The airlines, confronted with a situation in which they were operating largely in the red, had to take action to increase revenues beginning with fare levels. For many years air travel had been one of the rare items whose price fell steadily amidst general inflation in most sectors of economic activity. Starting in 1973, air fares assumed an upward movement whose slope varied from region to region and with different types of travel. Oil prices were largely responsible for this turnabout. But to the extent that elasticity of demand was not operating on all commercial fronts, passenger traffic naturally declined and in a general way: less business travel, fewer tourists. The industry was stagnant at best.

The revival of air travel in 1976 and 1977 shows that in a recovering economy, the demand for transportation is more elastic. It is true that the price increases did not affect certain fares on heavily traveled flights, which remained relatively low. Between rising costs and fluctuating prices, the room for maneuver capable of producing a profit remains quite small, and despite rigorous management, the rise in bookings cannot turn around the poor financial showings of many companies, some of which stretch over decades.

The oil crisis focused attention on the disconcerting ease with which the smooth-running mechanism of growth could be derailed. That mechanism was thought to be completely immune to breakdown, but such confidence overlooked the countries controlling the world's energy sources. The radical change in prices brought about a shift in directions for the airlines.

The so-called no frills airplanes of the recent past are already being discarded for future models that are simpler and more in line with the economic and social concerns of the contemporary world. Will the airlines go so far, as has been suggested, as to do away with inflight meals and the stewardesses who serve them, retaining only the personnel directly involved with the safety of the plane? Perhaps. But what is most important to the passenger is the type of treatment he receives from the airline. There must be a more critical attitude toward those things that in the past gave air travel an aura of luxury, which has slowly disappeared but which still survives, more by reflex than by conscious belief. Airline luxury is expensive and fools no one. Who cares about red carpets and various gadgetry when suitcases are lost in the shuffle between flights?

The passenger is just a traveler who wants no trouble. He wants the carrier to handle any problems that may arise. Of course, plane travel is a problem in itself. Often the traveler is not completely at ease, and long trips provoke some anxiety, however minimal. The passenger must therefore find, in the airline's treatment of him and general attitude toward him, those reassuring qualities that put people at ease. Such traits as deference, amiability and dedication are always appreciated.

The problem of winning over new passengers to air travel is primarily one of information, one which must be solved with the public at large. Advertising is in some ways part of the problem because its target is not always prepared to get the "message." Advertising is often striking; it is rarely informative. Many people still think of the airplane as a plaything for the idle rich and regard travel abroad as something complicated, expensive and difficult. Professionals in the travel industry, unfortunately, often forget that their clients may know little of the world that for them is a daily routine. And it is hardly unusual for such professionals to present information about their speciality in a particularly tedious way.

The question of prices is a delicate one when an industry sets out to conquer a mass market. Price reductions do not always pay off in periods when costs are rising. Nevertheless, the democratization of air travel is quite advanced. The prices of both charters and regular airlines are oriented toward the lowest possible levels. In fact some of the distinction between charter companies and regular airlines seems to be dissipating. On many routes, charter flights are becoming "regularized," and regular airlines are "chartering" increasing numbers of their flights to win their share of the market by cutting fares. All players must still accept the rules of the game, from those who bear the burdens and obligations of a public service to those who do not and who take advantage of this situation to lower prices. On two occasions in 1977, the OACI held meetings of all its member nations in an attempt to update fundamental notions such as "capacity," "unscheduled flights" and "maintaining fares" based on principles and texts written 33 years ago. This was a difficult task in the context of international economic warfare where for several months deregulation and freedom were the catchwords of the Western world.

However in assessing the future of the airplane, reservations about passenger travel give way to considerable optimism about the expanding prospects of air freight. Some even think that the cargo plane will be the means by which civil aviation achieves major international economic successes. For even if air transport is no longer seen as the exclusive domain of a small, wealthy clientele, many nonspecialists still think of air freight only as a way of shipping certain rare items. It is also true that air freight costs are high and unable to compete with surface transportation, where reduced fuel expenses and higher carrying capacity make possible a much lower price level.

Cargo planes transform the space taken up by seats on passenger planes into considerable freight capacity. But they still do not approach the capacities achieved by trucks, ships, trains or barges. While it does provide rapid delivery, air freight has high energy costs, as reflected in its rates and in the volume of goods handled.

In gross tonnage, world traffic in air freight, not including the Soviet Union, rose from 4.6 million metric tons in 1970 to nearly eight million metric tons in 1976 (see Map 11). In 1939 the total was less than 15,000 metric tons. The networks of America's Air Transport Command (ATC) were the basis for the spread of air freight. As the supply line to the Allied forces on every front and the instrument that made possible urgent deliveries beyond the reach of enemy fire, the ATC operated throughout the world. Its shipments exceeded 500,000 metric tons in 1944 and reached 1,450,000 metric tons in 1945. After World War II, it was not until 1958-59 that shipments in civil aviation reached the latter figure.

WORLD AIR FREIGHT

Years	Ton-km (cargo)	Rate of annual increase	Ton-km (mail)	Ton-km
1950	0.7		0.2	0.9
1955	1.240	11	0.37	1.6
1960	2	12	0.6	2.6
1965	4.8	19	1.1	5.9
1970	10.5	17	2.7	13.2
1971	11.5	10	2.5	14
1972	13.3	15	2.4	15.7
1973	15.6	18	2.5	18.1
1974	17	9	2.5	19.5
1976*	19.5	13	2.5	22

*Estimated

The above table shows world air freight from 1950 to 1976 in billions of ton-km. These figures do not include air freight in the Soviet Union, which since 1970 would add roughly two billion ton-km to those figures. The massive use of air freight in the vast, sparsely inhabited territories of the USSR, which have no other transport links, is the reason for this relatively high figure.

During the vigorous expansion of air freight over a 25-year period beginning in 1950, the mail component of the total remained stagnant. Whereas mail was the principal cargo of the first transport planes, bags of mail are now just another cargo. In addition, the ease of travel and the prodigious development of telecommunications have reduced correspondence by proportions significant enough to account for the plateau in mail shipments since 1970.

The possibilities for the shipment of freight are much larger than any comparable movement of travelers. Every individual benefits, to some extent, from modern transport, even if he personally never goes anywhere. Moreover goods are rarely transported more than once. As a result, the extension and development of transport systems is always having an impact on various types of goods. Some observers conclude that for certain kinds of high-priced goods, and in cases where rapid delivery is an economic imperative, the market for air freight is practically unlimited.

We live in an economic framework where "value added" is a central concept and the pace of business activity is constantly accelerating. Air freight is an answer to both of these imperatives. It also offers special advantages of its own, which make it competitive with surface communications even when its price, in tons to the kilometer, is roughly 10 times as high.

Air transport's primary advantage is obviously speed. This speed is all the more attractive because it multiplies benefits. Time saved is a source of profit in itself, but it also has a direct impact on capital tie-ups, represented by the goods during shipment. The result adds up to considerable amounts of money when transportation time is reduced from several weeks, or even several months, to several days. The problems of storage and care of goods in transit, and the costs they generate, can be reduced to a minimum by rapid air transport and its potential to overcome the strictures of seasonal processes. Air freight is a precious link in the distribution chain connecting producers and consumers whatever the distances separating them. For the industrialist, it is another way of expanding his markets.

The growth of airports in the vicinity of large urban centers makes them more accessible without becoming subordinate to the liaison networks that serve them, as in the case of shipping. The airplane is very direct. Its flexibility can make it an indispensable aid to exports, and to variations in exports, because it can adapt to change with a minimum of difficulty. Air freight also eliminates many of the costly ground links, cargo transfers and shipment breakdowns that complicate and impede movement. A truck at each end of the flight is usually enough to complete a door-to-door delivery.

Air freight's second major advantage is the quality of its delivery. In the holds of an airplane, goods are safe from weather and the risks of theft and damage posed by surface transport during transfers and storage time, which the airplane generally eliminates. The caution that necessarily dominates all ground operations involving an airplane has a positive effect on the quality of service and attention paid to freight during loading and unloading. This in turn has a beneficial effect on insurance rates. Air freight is far cheaper to insure than the same freight shipped by ground transport.

A third advantage, which partially results from the second, is that an airplane accepts light packaging. It has no need of the heavy and often bulky crates used on ships. "Air packaging" is a designation for light, resilient containers that reduce costs. Furthermore, the maintenance of certain types of freight at low temperatures poses fewer difficulties for air transport than for other types of transport. Because of these benefits, air transport is already competitive with its rivals.

Air transport serves three types of business. First there is the transportation of goods between major centers of economic activity. Next are the shipments from industrial centers that supply and equip projects in developing markets. Finally, there are pinpoint operations in remote regions where the airplane is used because no surface transport can overcome the terrain, climate or some other geographical obstacle.

The following table illustrates why in calculating transport costs, it is necessary to include all expenses and not merely the costs of the vehicle in question:

SHIPMENT OF TYPEWRITERS FROM WEST GERMANY TO NEW DELHI
(weight — one metric ton, value $1,000)
(Price in U.S. $)

Expenses	Air freight	Surface freight
Packaging	—	60
Pickup	8.25	25.5
Documents	1	15
Dockside handling	—	2
Insurance	3.46	6.95
Customs fees	8	35
Transportation	203	63.97
Delivery	5	42.50
Immobilized capital costs	4.92	24.60
Total shipping costs	233.63	275.52
Total shipping time	6 days	30 days

Source: OACI.

Air freight services are focused on the major passenger travel routes, particularly the domestic American network and the North Atlantic. Europe, by contrast, shows a far more modest concentration because the airplane is no rival for any of the major means of ground transport. Shipments between Europe and Africa and those that move along the Middle Eastern and Far Eastern routes, have roughly the same volume. In contrast, greater use is made of the transpacific lines. The cargo plane gains ground over extremely long distance, but the competition from ships is still quite stiff.

FREIGHT SHIPMENTS IN MILLIONS OF TON-KM ON THE MAJOR TRADE ROUTES*

	North and South America	Intra - North American	North Atlantic	Intra - European	Europe - Africa	South Atlantic	Europe - Middle and Far East	Transpacific
Freight shipments	770	4,700	3,220	590	1,975	375	2,000	1,400
% of world total	4.5	28	19	3.5	12	2.2	12	8.3

*Not including the USSR and the People's Republic of China.

Air freight has developed essentially by taking rush jobs and high-value cargo away from ships.

The intensity of transatlantic and transpacific sea and air shipments is a good illustration, at very different scales of magnitude, of the relative weight of commerce between the different economic centers of the world. Shipments between Europe and Africa and between Europe and the Middle East and Far East are not yet equal in both directions. Cargo planes fly south, loaded with consumer goods and machinery. But while ships return north to Europe with loads of raw materials, the airplane often comes back with a meager payload. There are few products of any value that can be shipped by plane from developing countries except fruits, exotic goods, handicrafts and other fairly low-value consumer goods. But the airplane can transport them cheaply only by observing certain limits. It has no interest in bringing back a cargo, rather than flying home empty, if the extra energy consumed by the load costs more than the additional revenue gained.

Most studies of this market have been pessimistic. Aside from questions of price and transported tonnage, there is often an absence of organization in various aspects of production and distribution. The resources of numerous tropical countries could easily make use of the differences in seasons between the hemispheres by organizing exports of perishable goods in a way that is coordinated with their imports.

To the extent that regular operations and adequate tonnage are developed, the cost of air freight will drop to levels where consumers are not being penalized for this service. Large-scale shipments and low prices always go together. This means that the future of air freight will be determined by its quantitative development and by price levels that make such development possible.

For a long time air freight and passenger travel complemented each other on most airlines. Many airlines are still reluctant to acquire planes equipped for cargo alone and only carry freight in the holds of their medium and long-range passenger planes. Thus for reasons of capacity, airlines are not yet ready to move into a mass market. Air freight accounts for only 15% of the revenues of regular airlines belonging to the IATA. The only exceptions to this situation are the companies that place air freight and the financing it requires at the center of their operations. Their commercial policies are of necessity oriented toward professionals specialized in freight collection, warehousing, handling, trucking and customs procedures. These are the people who, as auxiliaries to air transport companies, prepare freight for shipment on the ground. To operate successfully, they can only handle cargoes that are large and homogeneous enough to be shipped easily.

The emergence of containers, pallets and refrigerator units in freight shipment meshes well with the needs of air freight, which has everything to gain from standardized cargoes that are easy to handle. Containerization, found in all areas of shipping, provides all the advantages of a method that deals with the problems of cargo transfers far more effectively than was possible with a mass of individual items. The airplane itself can be considered a flying container whose entire contents may very well consist of a single shipment to one destination.

As a result of experiments, experts are encouraging an interest in specialized planes to be used exclusively for freight. The basic question is who will begin or, more precisely, who will take the risk. Such risks will ultimately fall on the airplane manufacturer that builds a plane whose success is dependent on a large-scale expansion of air freight or on the airline that undertakes the promotional effort necessary to win over a larger share of the air freight market.

There is no lack of such projects among the builders. Some of the more ambitious plans call for airplanes that weigh as much as 1,500 metric tons and are capable of carrying 1,000 metric tons of freight, including bulk cargo of relatively low value. One such project is the Boeing RC-1, which is 480 feet long and powered by 10 engines capable of producing speeds of Mach 0.65. It would be used to transport crude oil in large-scale operations where the linkup between oil fields and refineries poses particularly difficult problems.

In certain cases a made-to-order plane may be cheaper and more flexible than the construction of a road or a railway, or even a pipeline. Several bolder innovations are aimed at promoting air freight by lowering costs per ton-mile. They include giant hydroplanes, flying machines supported by an air cushion, hybrid creations like the megalifter (half-airplane, half-dirigible), liquid hydrogen engines with revolutionary methods of propulsion and atomic-powered jet engines.

For the air freight companies, increasing business volume by lowering prices remains a problem, given the current state of operations. One key to progress in air freight is better organization of the professional ground auxiliary services. Freight handlers are familiar both with the demand for shipping and the ways to meet it. They can play the role of regulator both for the price and the amount of tonnage shipped and be assured of the best prices in air freight by guaranteeing a certain regularity and quality of shipments. In making their strong commercial potential known to a wide clientele, the freight handlers would be aiding the development of air freight in general.

Well-established institutions and practices undoubtedly stand in the way of the best promotional intentions. Vast installations and warehouses conceived and built for surface transport cannot be abandoned simply because air freight has rendered them obsolete. Many exporters are compelled to make use of the entire array of existing transport facilities and for this reason alone cannot take full advantage of air freight by itself.

The ground services and the airlines could play an even more decisive role with air freight than the travel agencies have played with tourism. Goods are not as demanding as travelers. They can fly night or day, wait several hours for a better connection or take a more indirect route with numerous stopovers. When shipping time has already been cut by weeks or months, a few extra hours in transit is of little concern. This room for maneuver makes it possible to control the flow of freight with maximum flexibility. Nonetheless the freight handlers must maintain a network of information and representation abroad so that they can play the role of exporters. To maintain an adequate and regular flow of goods, they must also cover a market of sufficient scale, which by definition is international.

Air freight will reach maturity only when it loses the false impression still surrounding it. Despite the relatively small number of people who fly, air travel has become a reality for almost everyone. But air freight and air travel have had different economic evolutions. Freighters, barges, buses, trucks and trains all underwent different kinds of development. The same will undoubtedly be true for air transport. The advantage of speed and handicap of high cost place the airplane in a special category. Aside from cost, most of its drawbacks have been minimized in recent years. The progress of the cargo plane in the past indicates a bright future, but its evolution will require time.

Infrastructure

Air travel infrastructure provides a wide variety of activities that contribute to the safety and smooth operation of the airplane. These activities range from installations where airplanes are maintained to radio and telecommunications systems, including relay satellites in outer space. Infrastructure encompasses the most technical aspects of navigational aids and airport design. The following discussion makes no attempt at an in-depth analysis of such a complex field.

The equipment used to guide planes along existing air routes enables the use of more direct routes and favorable winds at different stages of flight, the reduction of waiting time prior to landings and fewer reroutings, all of which have reduced fuel consumption considerably. But because of the various private and public interests at stake and the dimension of the budgets involved, the efficiency of airports has come under intense scrutiny during the current industry crisis.

An airport is the meeting point between air and surface transportation as well as between the world of air travel and its customers. It is a port like any other, with all that such a facility entails in equipment and installations. Beginning with the airstrip of 50 years ago, the integration of airports into the general economy has yielded benefits beyond the air travel industry. In addition to its role in the international movement of people and goods, airports can unlock a region's potential, open it up to trade and tourism and create jobs in places where resources are almost nonexistent.

Because of these significant economic benefits, governments have become involved in the administration of airports from the first stages of conception to the management of the completed facility. Whether it is the national government, a regional or municipal body or an autonomous public entity, the organization in charge must have at its disposal powers that are beyond the capacities of private companies.

The sums involved are considerable. Twenty years ago a runway for large planes already cost $3,840,000 per mile. Today just the initial phase of the development of Roissy-Charles de Gaulle Airport in France cost $408 million. The development of an airport takes up to 25 years and the investments involved require years of amortization. In the past this process was somewhat hidden by the extremely rapid growth of aviation technology.

The inflationary aspects of airport development are currently causing concern all over the world. The economic crisis and the crisis of air transport have further complicated the problem that was already serious under the best of circumstances. The airports built in the postwar period have had to adapt at great expense to the evolution of the sector as a whole. Prospects of a massive increase in traffic in the 1980s prompted the construction of the appropriate airport "superinfrastructure." Roissy-Charles de Gaulle in France, Mirabel in Canada, Narita in Japan and Dallas-Ft. Worth in the U.S. are massive projects designed for a massive flow of air traffic.

In the developing countries the successful beginnings of international tourism have given rise to new infrastructures built to accommodate air traffic on the appropriate scale. The technical aid of the OACI and international cooperation have greatly facilitated such development in these countries, which are dependent on the industrialized nations for both their technology and their tourists. The relatively low cost of land and labor in the developing lands is an asset in this process.

The authorities who built the latest generation of airport facilities are today being criticized for their excessive and ruinous budgets, after they were initially criticized for the narrowness of their conceptions. The need to "think big" was indeed required during a relatively recent era when the crowding of the skies and runways was becoming excessive, costly and dangerous. The introduction of jumbo jets made it possible to reduce the number of flights while increasing capacity. But such planes could not be handled on runways and with equipment built for the passenger jets of an earlier generation.

Earlier air travel forecasts have proven overoptimistic and civil aviation around the world is contemplating the massive airports now considered premature. The future pace of air traffic, which has been marking time for the past two years, holds the key to the situation.

According to the following table, the OACI at the end of 1976 placed the total number of international airports at slightly more than 1,000, with 768 handling regular traffic, 35 handling the traffic of other companies and 209 handling general aviation (see Map 16).

NUMBER OF AIRPORTS HANDLING INTERNATIONAL TRAFFIC

Region	Regular international air transport	International transfer points (regular)	Other international air transport	International transfer points (other)	International general aviation	Total
Africa, Indian Ocean	139	15	2	1	12	169
Caribbean, South America	118	21	0	0	48	187
Europe	199	23	29	0	129	380
Middle East, Southeast Asia	119	30	3	0	10	162
North Atlantic, North America, Pacific	69	37	0	0	10	114
Total	642	126	34	1	209	1,012

However the total number of international airports is only 4.4% of the roughly 23,000 civilian air installations located in OACI member countries. It is evident that domestic air traffic uses far more airports than international traffic. The international installations are concentrated in North America, Europe and the USSR. But all 1,012 of these airports are used by the 240 million international passengers who account for 458 billion passenger-km.

The figures from the following table show annual changes on the major air routes over the past few years.

TRAFFIC OF WORLD'S MAJOR AIRPORTS

Airports	Number of passengers per year (millions)		Tons of freight handled per year (thousands)		Flights
EUROPE					
Paris*	20.0	(5.8)	400	(103)	320,000
London*	29.2	(10.6)	516	(165)	331,000
Frankfurt	13.1	(4)	494	(82)	198,000
Copenhagen	8.0		142		153,000
Zurich	6.4	(2.1)	119	(30)	103,000

Airports	Number of passengers per year (millions)		Tons of freight handled per year (thousands)		Flights
Amsterdam	7.9	(2)	234	(62)	129,000
Madrid	8.4	(1.9)	103	(15)	113,000
NORTH AMERICA					
New York*	41.8	(18.3)	1,189	(178)	766,000
Chicago*	41.9	(13.9)	692	(177)	624,000
Los Angeles	25.9	(8.6)	771	(100)	343,000
Montreal*	6.7	(3.8)	110		135,000
Dallas*	13.2	(4.1)	65	(43)	312,000
SOUTH AMERICA					
Rio de Janeiro*	4.5	(2.2)	73	(18)	63,700
Buenos Aires	4.3		65		68,718
Caracas	2.7		68		62,000
ASIA & THE PACIFIC					
Tokyo	17.7	(4.1)	200	(50)	171,000
Sydney	6.5		105		109,000
Hong Kong	4.4		80		—
Singapore	3.6		58		52,000
Bangkok	2.5		45		49,000
AFRICA					
Dakar	0.4		11		12,000
Johannesburg	3.2		68		62,000
Nairobi	0.9		29		22,000

Note: The figures represent the best estimates for 1974, 1975 and 1976 except for those in parentheses, which are from 1964.

*Cities with several airports, whose traffic flows have been combined in these figures.

This data points up the importance of the American and European airports in contrast to those in other regions of the world with the exception of Japan. The position of Frankfurt, which leads Europe's airports in freight handled, underscores the exporting talents of West Germany.[6] The airports of London and Paris show a volume of traffic consistent with their strategic positions and importance as European capitals. The obvious divergence in the statistics of total volume among countries involved at various levels of modern economic life express an imbalance in trade, accentuated by differing resources and levels of industrial development. Libreville in Gabon handled only slightly more than 200,000 pas-

6. The figure for London is higher, but it represents the three London airports. Frankfurt, with a single airport, handles more than Heathrow: 494,000 tons, as compared to 415,000, in 1976.

sengers in 1974, but this nation has one of the highest concentrations of airports in the world. Thus when viewed in the context of its global points of convergence, air transport again reveals its diversity and the different pressures it exerts on communications systems.

When current statistics on air traffic and airports are compared with those of 10 years ago, the obvious progression emphasizes the problems posed by inadequate infrastructure and the absolute necessity of planning for its expansion. In 1968 and 1969 New York's three airports (Kennedy International, Newark and La Guardia) were swamped and on the verge of breaking all records for late arrivals, with a total air traffic exceeding 500,000 flights a year. With tieups costing from $4,800 to $7,200 per flight hour, the rapidly increasing number of half-hour delays was costing the airlines huge sums of lost revenue. Through considerable expansion and rationalization efforts, New York recorded 766,000 arrivals and departures in 1975. But the 2,260 acres of Kennedy and La Guardia cannot be expanded. Newark, which has yet to reach full utilization, represents the only safety valve for the short range. After that, a new installation located (as in similar situations) 48 to 60 miles from downtown New York will be necessary.

Airport officials are divided on how to handle today's problems. One group calls for investing only in existing facilities with no significant surface extension, rationalizing and automating everything possible with the most advanced techniques available. This position is prevalent in Britain, where officials have abandoned plans for an airport in Maplin, located 53 miles from London, which would have required an initial investment of $1,696 million. London's four airports (Heathrow, Gatwick, Luton and Stansed) will remain as they are until 1990, when 100 million passengers are expected.

The other group began pushing several years ago for innovation and a change of scale to prepare for air transport needs in the year 2000. It has encouraged the construction of airports like the one in Dallas, Tex., which covers 6,800 acres. When it is completed in the 1980s, this airport will be able to handle 1,400 flights a day and receive 55 million passengers in its 13 terminals. Equipped with 39 miles of track and automated transport systems to facilitate access to planes, it will require 10 years to build at a cost of $600 million.

Singapore is planning to spend roughly $480 million on its new airport in Changi, which will handle 10 million passengers by 1982. The initial installation at Rio de Janeiro's new international airport, located about 10 miles from the city, will cost $240 million and will barely handle a million passengers per year. When completed in 1990, however, this airport will be able to receive 10 million passengers a year. The saturation of Haneda Airport in Tokyo has been relieved by the new facility at Narita, about 40 miles outside the city. Covering 1,065 acres and extremely sophisticated, the airport at Narita will initially handle 5.4 million passengers and 410,000 metric tons of freight, expanding to 16 million passengers and 1.4 million metric tons of freight in 1986. The investment is evaluated at $1.2 billion. The future of the Mirabel airport in Canada is planned through the year 2025, when 50 million passengers and 650,000 flights will be handled in a 35,000-acre airport zone, which is larger than the island of Malta.

Other examples could be cited, but they would only highlight the realities of airport economics, i.e., that normally high costs are even greater when runway size directly reflects the importance of the cities being served. Airport construction projects push up the cost of the land susceptible to development and thereby limit expansion. Because their construction naturally involves large-scale projects, these airports are quickly judged incompatible with the population densities near large cities. Locating them far away from cities is a possible solution, but one that often encounters environmental objections.

As contact points for air routes circling the globe, airports conduct their activities in proximity to the cities that built them, but they also act as poles of attraction for the regions and even the countries they serve. In contrast to the traditional railroad station, the diversity of services offered to the public by an airport is surprising. With services ranging from the familiar newspaper and souvenir stands to multifaith chapels, hairdressers, restaurants, hotels, movie theaters, swimming pools, banks and art galleries, one could live in an airport. These facilities are increasingly becoming vast islands, isolated from the adjacent urban areas. As a result, they must generally rely on their own resources, in contrast to seaports, which are usually situated in the heart of a city. Airports receive millions of travelers every year, but several thousand people also go there every day to work—morning, noon and night.

An airport is an economic complex and should be seen as an aspect of development. Its specific contribution must be carefully defined in order to integrate it into the larger networks that it is intended to serve. This service is sometimes lost in the protests of people living close to airports, who are the victims of noise pollution and other nuisances. As a result many see the airport complex not as a source of economic development, jobs and prosperity, but rather as a source of the bothersome byproducts of technology and progress, similar to automobile traffic and real estate speculation.

It is undeniable that people who have jets landing and taking off just above their homes are greatly inconvenienced. Changes in minimum altitude after takeoff and other measures adopted sporadically to minimize the side effects of noise hardly alter the problem. The real solution is a large "no man's land" surrounding the entire airport such as the one at Canada's Mirabel airport. The same thing was done at Lyon-Satolas in

France. Unfortunately, these cases are rare because cities and suburbs generally exist long before an airport is built. As the city and the airport grow, there is often conflict. Roissy airport in Paris has stirred considerable opposition from many of its neighbors in the Parisian suburbs. In Japan the building of Narita, 39 miles from Tokyo, aroused violent opposition from nearby residents of an area where land was already scarce. From the initial phase of land purchases onward, each step in the building of Narita was the occasion for such intense conflict that the newly built airport remained closed for two years.

Ten or 15 years ago, airplanes flew at night almost everywhere in the world; today many airports shut down between 9:00 and 6:00. Such a reduction in operating hours will inevitably have negative effects on all types of service. Slowed by airport closings, the rotation of equipment will decrease, which can only increase overall costs. Travelers will also be inconvenienced by the very early hours at which the first morning flights are scheduled, particularly as airports get farther away from cities.

The rapidity and convenience of links between airports and cities are crucial for short flights, and almost as important for longer ones. In 1976 a hurried traveler spent more time getting from the center of Paris to Trafalgar Square in London than he would have spent making the same trip in 1935. Between time consumed on ground transportation and 30 minutes for the flight itself, the trip lasted roughly two hours. In 1935 the flight took an hour and 20 minutes, but roads into and out of London were quicker because they were far less crowded.

Uncertain traffic conditions force travelers to set aside safety margins that lengthen the overall time spent in transit. The competition from railroads on intercity routes presents a threat to the development of domestic airlines in countries like France or Japan. It is fairly well known that railroads have helped to bail out traffic-clogged airports all over the world. At Orly or Roissy or in Dallas, Tokyo or Montreal, the underground train assures the traveler that he will catch his plane because it avoids the principal sources of delay.

One alternative is the helicopter, but this service is infrequent and expensive for the traveler. One day VTOL airports, handling short-range, quiet and easily serviced airplanes, may solve the problems that airports pose for cities. Nonetheless, the growth of airports today represents a costly and intractable problem, one increasingly thought of as a nuisance, which is giving air transport an image quite contrary to its vocation of bringing people closer together.

The development of civil aviation is complex. Because of the increasing volume of passenger traffic and the growth in size and sophistication of airplanes, it is imperative to build huge airports, virtual cities, with the inevitable conflicts they create among neighboring populations. This whole process costs enormous amounts of money, particularly since refinement of airport facilities does not shield them in any way from the disastrous effects of an economic crisis nor even diminish those effects. One is almost tempted to see the whole thing as a monstrous fraud.

It should be remembered that air transport, a byproduct of military aviation and the logistic innovations of the two world wars, is only part of the overall air power of a nation. Nations may use air power as a lever, and commercial competition among airlines may actually reflect national struggles for influence. Heavy government investments in airport installations are a way of waging this international competition among airlines and exerting influence on other countries. The country or city seeking to attract shipping, tourism or goods in transit can, with government backing, capture a large share of international trade even if its airport installations are losing money. It is the overall balance sheet for the country or the region that counts.

The essential problem, however, is to determine who is going to pay the often considerable costs for this deployment of resources. There are two basic views on the subject. One holds that the various agencies responsible for public services, and ultimately the state, should bear the expenses of air transport infrastructure as they do for maritime transport, harbors and roads. Civil aviation is an essential part of the economic life of a country. It creates access to new resources and generates profits. Therefore, society as a whole should bear the costs of sustaining it. According to the second view, however, the costs of infrastructure involve installations that directly concern only a limited number of companies and people: airlines, owners of airplanes and those who use them. The financial burdens of every aspect of civil aviation should therefore be the exclusive responsibility of its operators and clients.

These opposing views raise delicate questions, which are all the more difficult to resolve because the real situations are rarely as clear-cut as the different viewpoints depict them. The first position is attractive and perhaps even unassailable, from a legal point of view. The second perspective is too narrow and may ultimately penalize groups having little immediate relation to air transport. Yet it is true that government budgets financed by taxation include many expenditures whose utility, logic and significance are a mystery to the most civic-minded individual.

Once again aviation's image is being distorted because of the misconceptions that surround it and the costs involved. It is possible that airport authorities, influenced by the latest marketing and management techniques, are attempting to achieve a direct profitability, which would be difficult under the best of circumstances. Whether this should be the decisive criterion is questionable, especially when the positive benefits of a high-quality international service are bolstering other items in the overall foreign trade balance.

Airports must make themselves attractive to the people who use them, right down to the individual who is seeing someone off. He will no doubt have any number of reactions to the high cost of parking and a farewell drink at the bar.

The revenues of an airport, from rents to landing and parking fees, allow some flexibility in handling operating costs. But the operation as a whole is a means of increasing (or diminishing) the volume of foreign customers, companies, travelers, tourists and businessmen. To this extent, an airport is part of the overall structure of a national economy and can have a very positive effect on the balance of trade. A vast informational campaign is needed to dispel the myth of the huge financial resources at the disposal of civil aviation. The industry has no need to explain why its safety and quality standards are more expensive than in other sectors. It has only to point out that as a means of transportation, it contributes to economic development, the real creator of wealth.

A Brief Survey of Inland Transport

Since a mere eight countries consume 70% of the world's energy, we expect to find corresponding tonnages passing through their ports. This flow is true for oil and gas as well as for other types of goods.

When the cargoes of the big transport ships—oil tankers, LNG tankers, container ships and bulk freighters—arrive at their destinations, they must be transferred to other types of transportation. The latter make up the indispensable counterpart of maritime and air transport systems. But in contrast to their free movement over oceans or through the skies, cargoes are rigidly locked into the inland routes that service harbors and airports, They move over rivers, railways, and roads or, in the case of oil and gas, through pipelines.

Pipelines (See Map 17)

As of Jan. 1, 1975, the world's pipelines could be broken down into the following categories:

WORLD PIPELINES
(in miles)

Countries or regions	Crude Oil	Finished Products	Natural Gas*	TOTAL
Free World	1,182,000	88,200	319,200	525,600
United States	(73,200)	(73,800)	(240,000)	(387,000)
Canada	(12,000)	(3,000)	(19,800)	(34,800)
Western Europe	(6,600)	(5,400)	(45,000)	(57,000)
USSR	22,800	5,200	51,600	82,200
Total	1,204,800	93,400	370,800	607,800

*These figures are for transport pipelines only and do not include other types of networks or the pipelines of NATO.

Source: *Omnium technique de transport par pipeline (OTP).*

The United States is well ahead of the rest of the world in total pipeline length, but its pipelines are the oldest, and the tonnage they move is lower than that of Western Europe. As early as 1865, five years after the discovery of oil in the United States, the first oil pipeline (five miles long and made of cast iron) was in use.

Two pipelines, the Plantation Pipeline, beginning in Baton Rouge, La., and the Colonial Pipeline, beginning in Houston, Tex., currently link refineries to the industrial centers of the East Coast. Totaling more than 3,600 miles in length including their auxiliary lines, they rival both the river transport system on the Mississippi and coastal shipping. The Trans-Alaska pipeline (789 miles long), which went into operation in 1977, links the drilling operations of Prudhoe Bay with the ice-free port of Valdez. The Alaskan pipeline was preferred to the development of an ice breaker oil tanker, tried experimentally in 1969.

There are several other major pipelines in existence. For example, once the 200 million metric tons of oil that flow annually through the Alaskan pipeline arrive at their destination, they are either refined or shipped on to inland refineries through existing pipelines, or they are routed through the Panama Canal.

In September 1977 Canada and the United States agreed to build a natural gas pipeline with a capacity of 1,190 billion cubic feet (34 billion cubic meters) from Prudhoe Bay to the lower 48 states. The 4,000-mile pipeline, which may cost as much as $13 billion to $14 billion, will place the vast Alaskan gas resources at the disposal of Canada and the United States. Canada also has its own interprovincial pipeline, running 2,460 miles from Edmonton to Toronto, with an additional 501-mile extension to Montreal.

The Tapline, which is 30-31 inches in diameter and 1,032 miles long, funnels the output of wells around the Persian Gulf to an outlet on the Mediterranean. This pipeline and the one built by the Iraq Petroleum Company (nationalized in 1972), which also pumps oil to the Mediterranean instead of the Persian Gulf, save oil tankers the long journey around the Arabian peninsula by way of Suez. In principle these pipelines are cheaper than using tankers, but if freight rates fall, they will lose their competitive advantage. Iraq opened a new series of pipelines that allows it to direct its shipments toward either the Mediterranean or the Gulf depending on shifts in the economy or in politics.

The Middle East offers another example of the complex relationships between waterways and ground transport. The Suez Canal, built in the 19th century, has shown its limitations as a modern transportation link on several occasions, and enormous investments have been required to make it viable for larger, more economical ships. Even before the Suez Canal was closed in 1967, large tankers generally took the Cape of Good Hope route, and the smaller ships, which were more expensive to operate, used the canal.

Pipelines are undercutting both the Suez Canal and Cape routes. Since 1970, Israel has been transferring its former canal shipments through the Eilat-Ashkelon pipeline, which is 42 inches in diameter, and has a capacity of 40 million metric tons a year. The 42-inch Sumed line (Suez-Mediterranean) links Suez to Alexandria. The initial project was conceived after the closing of the canal in 1967. After interminable negotiations involving French, Italian and American companies, the Arabs finally took charge of the operation. Fifty percent of the $500 million financing was provided by Egypt; Saudi Arabia, Kuwait and Abu Dhabi each contributed 15%, and Qatar 5%. The current trip from the Persian Gulf to Fos, on France's Mediterranean coast, by way of the Cape, is 21,800 miles and takes 59 days round trip at sustained speeds (which are no longer the most economical due to higher fuel prices); Sumed has reduced this to 9,400 miles and 30 days.

The pipeline works in the following fashion. The Red Sea terminal is at Ain Sukhna, 32 miles south of Suez. The Mediterranean terminal is at Sidi Kerir 16 miles east of Alexandria. Each terminal has 12 reservoirs of 3.5 million cubic feet (100,000 cubic meters). Sidi Kerir has facilities for five tankers and their deliveries and Ain Sukhna can handle three ships simultaneously. Four of the facilities can accommodate the largest 250,000 metric ton ships. The pipe itself has two parallel lines with a current capacity of 40 million metric tons, but this level is expected to rise to 100 million after Egypt constructs an extension to serve Cairo.

There are two types of pipelines in Europe: those which move maritime deliveries inland and those in the North Sea which supply gas and oil to the coasts. The latter pipelines compete directly with ships, which are used in the early stages of drilling or when production is not large enough to justify a pipeline. But the fluctuations of the weather make ship operation difficult and have given rise to an extensive underwater pipeline network.

The longer established lines, such as those from France to Switzerland and southern Germany, serve two functions. They transport crude oil to inland refineries or ship the refined petroleum products, except heavy fuels, from coastal facilities. The latter process is inland.

The pipeline system in Europe is extremely diversified. For example, the upper Rhine region of Germany gets its crude oil through three different pipelines: from the Societe du Pipeline sud-European (SPLSE) on the Mediterranean, from the Nord West Oelleitung beginning in Wilhelmshaven and from the Rhein-Rotterdam-Pipeline originating in Rotterdam. A single refinery in the Ingolstadt region is supplied alternately by the Rhein-Donau-Oelleitung, the Trans-Alpine Line, which comes through the Alps from Trieste, and the Central European Line, which crosses the Alps from Genoa.

In the Soviet Union, a network of pipelines from Siberia, the Urals, the Caucasus and the Ukraine supplies central Russia. Through Mozyr, in the west, a pipeline built by the Comecon completes a 3,000-mile link to the countries of Eastern Europe. China now has a rapidly expanding pipeline network of 1,440 miles.

Gas pipelines and LNG tankers can complement each other, but they can also compete with each other. For example, Algeria is now planning two trans-Mediterranean gas pipelines to replace the use of LNG tankers. One line, with a capacity of 1,400 billion cubic feet (40 billion cubic meters) per year, joins Algeria with southern Spain. The other, carrying 420 million cubic feet (12 million cubic meters) per year, extends from Algeria to Sicily and on to Bologna.

Pipelines also complement and compete with inland shipping and railroads. In France, for example, the construction of two pipelines transporting finished petroleum products inland—the Trapil, linking the Basse-Seine with the Parisian region and the Societe du pipe Mediterranee-Rhone, extending from the Berre area to Lyon and Switzerland—had to overcome the opposition of the inland shippers of both the Seine and the Rhone and even opposition from the French national railways.

These cases illustrate several economic realities. First, the only possible competition for the oil tanker over long distances is the pipeline, and then only in certain cases. Both of these methods are highly capital intensive; capital costs play a much greater role than proportional costs (stemming primarily from energy consumed in shipment). The phenomenal increase in energy costs does not change the fact that a pipeline consumes far more steel than an oil tanker in order to carry the same tonnage over the same distance on an annual basis. For this reason the pipeline has the advantage over ships only in short distances. The Tapline, which crosses Saudi Arabia, and thus avoids the trip around the Cape, or the SPLSE pipeline in the Rhone valley, which eliminates the trip through Gilbraltar and on to the Rhine, illustrate this reality. Several factors are considered in choosing a pipeline's diameter. For the same tonnage over an extended period, a large-diameter pipe requires a higher initial investment and results in more unused capacity, but it loses pressure less readily and thus requires less energy for its operation than the small-diameter pipe. The latter, which is initially less expensive, ultimately requires a large number of pumping stations to counter losses in pressure, until a more sophisticated technology can be developed.

A pipeline is also safer and more reliable than ground transportation, which is subject to climatic and sometimes political contingencies. NATO, for example, has chosen a pipeline to move essential fuels to armies in central Europe.

Inland Shipping (See Map 17)

Rivers

Like the pipeline, traditional river transportation makes it possible to supply inland areas and link them to coasts. But while certain rivers furnish excellent inland links, they do not offer routes to the sea because of rapids or dams. The Nile, the Zaire, the Yellow River, the Zambeze, the Indus and the Ganges are examples of this.

Europe has only two heavily traveled rivers: the Rhine and the Danube. When they are linked, in approximately 1985, by the Rhine-Main-Danube canal, international shipping will be able to make use of a 2,170-mile waterway from Rotterdam to Sulina on the Black Sea. The Rhine could also be extended beyond Basel by an improved canal linking the Saone and the Rhone, thus creating another major axis between the North Sea and the Mediterranean.

China's major river routes include the Yangtze, the earth's most powerful river, which is 3,000 miles long and navigable over 2,400 miles before ending at Shanghai. China also makes use of the Amur, part of which forms the border between the USSR and China.

The Soviet Union has two separate river networks. West of the Urals, the Volga and the canals that connect to it link the Caspian and the Black Seas to Leningrad and also to Belomorsk on the White Sea.

East of the Urals, there is the great network of Siberian rivers: the Ob and its important tributary, the Irtysh, the Yenisey and the Lena. All of them are navigable from June to October, and all of them end at a seaport: the Ob at Novy Port, the Yenisey at Port Dickson on the Kara Sea and the Lena at Tiksi on the Laptev Sea. The Yenisey is a link to Krasnoyarsk, an industrial city on the Trans-Siberian railroad. The Ob provides Novosibirsk, another industrial center, with a link to the sea. The Siberian river network is remarkably well equipped for navigation, and although the severe winter brings shipping to a complete halt, it turns the rivers into solid freeways.

Running perpendicular to these great rivers, the Trans-Siberian railroad is an important transport system. It links up all the developing industrial zones and emerging urban centers: Omsk on the Irtysh, Novosibirsk on the Ob, Krasnoyarsk on the Yenisey, and both Irkutsk and Lake Baikal on the Angara. This infrastructure has made it possible to exploit Siberian oil.

The North American continent has three major river networks. In the United States, the Mississippi and the Missouri, with a combined length of 3,860 miles, link the Great Lakes and the Gulf of Mexico. The St. Lawrence Seaway permits the shipment of large amounts of oil, grains and various bulk items from the interior. In northern Canada, the MacKenzie, which is open to navigation in the summer, is the linkup for all current oil prospecting and production in the area. Thus the Canadian Arctic, like its Soviet counterpart, benefits by its great rivers, on one hand, and by the proximity of major industrial complexes to the south, on the other.

In Brazil, the Amazon and its extension the Maranon are 4,000 miles long. The Amazon has other navigable tributaries, such as the Purus, the Madeira and the Rio Negro. In Argentina the river networks include the Rio de la Plata, the Uruguay, the 1,827 mile long Parana and its tributary the Paraguay. An ambitious project linking the Sao Francisco in Brazil with the Rio de la Plata is under consideration. This region has a remarkable river complex that could not be matched by a road system. Finally, in Venezuela the Orinoco, 1,280 miles long, facilitates the shipment of iron ore and, in the near future, will be handling oil as well.

Africa has no major navigable river linked to the sea with the exception, for short periods, of the lower Zambeze, the Niger and its tributary the Benue.

In summary, river transport is important in the movement of bulk items (coal, ores, grains, fertilizers, paper, pulp, cement and petroleum products), once the adequate infrastructure is in place, because of its capacity to reach areas not open to railways or roads.

Railways and Roads (See Map 17)

Railroads have several important limitations as transport systems. There is very little uniformity because of the multiplicity of national standard regulations and practices. The width of tracks, the gauge, axle capacity and wheelbases vary from one country to the next, to say nothing of the documentation, insurance, and bureaucratic red tape at each border. Railways and roads are also encumbered by the costs of expensive installations and upkeep and by the diversity of rolling stock and vehicles that use them. Another problem for roads, and to a lesser extent railroads, is the increased number of small countries and hence border crossings following the wave of independence in regions like Africa.

The main—and obvious—drawback of railroads and highways is their rigidity. But the railroad remains irreplaceable for heavy transport and for daily service in large metropolitan areas as well as high-speed links between urban centers. Japan's Tokado, for example, takes two hours less than the airplane (including travel to and from the airport) between Tokyo and Osaka.

On a map of world transportation networks, the concentration of railroads and highways, which are often parallel to each other, is surprisingly small: Europe west of the Urals; eastern China, Japan, the Koreas, India (primarily in the north), and the Australian southeast; the coastal region of Africa and Morocco, Algeria, Tunisia, and the southeastern part of South Africa; and the southern edge of Canada from the St.

Lawrence to Vancouver, the United States, Mexico, southern Brazil and northern Argentina.

Invented 150 years ago, the railroad reached its heyday in the years prior to World War I, when it was the only means of transportation widely available. No international body regulated the system and so, it grew in diverse ways. For example, in addition to the "normal" track width used first by England and then adopted by Europe (except for Spain), the United States, Canada, China, Japan and North Africa, there are no less than 15 different track widths in use.

Wide track is used in the USSR, five feet, and in Spain, 5.5 feet. Track reaches widths as large as seven feet in Australia, which also has normal track. India employs three different track sizes. Different types of narrow track as small as 3.3 feet are found in all of Africa, except North Africa including Egypt.

The total personnel employed by railroads is huge: 205,000 workers in Britain; 220,000 in France; 544,500 in the United States; 1,373,320 in India and between three and four million in the Soviet Union.

The most famous railroads have been the transcontinental runs, such as the Trans-Siberian; the frequently renovated (and recently terminated) ancestor of them all, the Oriental Express; the Trans-Australian from Sydney to Freemantle; the Trans-Andean from Buenos Aires to Valparaiso; the Trans-Anatolian from Scutari on the Bosporus (with a northern connection to Iran and a southern connection to the mouth of the Tigris on the Persian Gulf) and the four major transcontinental routes in the U.S. China has the Peking-Canton axis, whose traffic has more than doubled since the construction of an enormous bridge over the Yangtze. In Africa the "Tanzam" railroad connects Lusaka, the capital of Zambia, to the Tanzanian port of Dar es Salaam, making it possible to move more than 20% of the world's copper production from Zambia and Zaire to the Indian Ocean.

During the last 30 years, the length of railway networks has steadily declined in developed nations except in the heavily industrial zones. The decline has been on the order of 30% in the United States, in France outside the corridor between Paris and the southeast and in Britain, and reaches levels of 50% in Germany. In Japan, on the other hand, total track length has remained stable. The Japanese railways are currently building a remarkable underwater railroad tunnel 33 miles long linking the major island, Honshu, to Hokkaido. The mid-point of the tunnel is 149 miles below sea level.

In the USSR, track length has increased by 40%, primarily to meet the needs of Siberian infrastructure. Total track length has increased from 47,740 miles in 1928 to 85,560 in 1975, as opposed to 37,200 in India and 21,700 in France. The USSR is still building new lines, at the rate of 1,850-2,170 miles per five-year plan. Most of these new lines are in

Siberia, such as the new BAM (Baikal, Amur, Maguistral) line, which is 1,950 miles long and runs over seven mountain ranges.

In the 9th five-year plan, builders turned out 2,000 electric locomotives, 3,140 diesels, 370,000 train cars averaging 60 payload tons each and 15,000 coaches. And, unlike most systems, Soviet railroads run at a profit.

While total track length has decreased, freight traffic has been growing over the past 15 years: rising by 50% in France, Germany and Japan; doubling in Canada; tripling in India; and increasing by three and one-half times in the USSR.

Recently high-speed interurban train service has become important. Such services, which have been very successful in Japan and France, have just been introduced in the United States, using French turbotrains. The first lines are already in service between Chicago, Milwaukee and Detroit and between New York, Montreal and Buffalo.

The most recent innovation in surface transport is the specialization of roads in the wealthy countries with ever expanding suburban zones. A world monitoring system under the auspices of the International Road Federation was created in Geneva for all roads open to trucks weighing 30 metric tons. The most successful of these routes is the Pan-American Highway, which runs from Alaska to Chile. The basic idea is an appealing one: each country crossed—and there are 16 in all—contributes to financing on a pro rata basis calculated by the total freeway length across its territory. Thus, for example, Mexico is responsible for 6,386 miles, Brazil for 3,861, but Nicaragua only 235.

Nothing comparable to the Pan-American Highway exists in either Africa or in Asia, but several projects are under construction. The most advanced of these is the Trans-Saharan Road, which will reach as far as Tamanrasset, while extending to the west coast of Africa and to the Indian Ocean, with a long North-South complement in the Trans-East African highway between Cairo and Johannesburg.

The large-scale highway transport envisaged by the IRF is destined to play a complementary role to railroads, which, in every part of the world including Europe, are being overtaken by competition from trucks. In some countries, trucking is displacing both railroads and coastal shipping. In these countries, freight was being delivered to poorly equipped ports, from which it was relayed by inadequate railroads. Western European shipments to Saudi Arabia and Iran are now carried by trucks that cross the Bosporus. The trucks make the trip in four days, crossing eight borders.

Trucking in Afghanistan and Pakistan, on the other hand, as well as the roads through India by way of Delhi and Calcutta and on to Singapore is problematic and will remain that way until the highways envisioned by the IRF are built. It appears that the highway networks con ceived by the Geneva body will initially be built in Africa, which has minimal railway systems.

Motor Vehicles

Motor vehicles are the final link in the extension of world transport systems. The breakdown published by the Society of Motor Manufacturers and Traders distinguished between two types.

The first is made up of 65 million vehicles, comprising one-third of the total world fleet. It handles numerous transport activities involving both people and goods: public works and major construction projects, agricultural equipment, long-distance trucking, and so forth. The second type is used exclusively for the transport of people. It is taking on more and more importance as incomes rise and as tourism expands. The Greyhound Bus company, for example, skillfully built up tourist networks whose success has been copied around the world.

TYPE I VEHICLES

Continent	(in millions)	Country	(in millions)	Percentage of total
North and South America	30.5	United States, Canada	25.5	85%
Asia	14.2	Japan	11.0	80%
Europe	12.0	Britain, France, Germany, Italy	7.0	60%
USSR	4.5			
Africa	2.0	South Africa	0.8	40%
Oceania	1.5	Australia	1.0	70%

TYPE II VEHICLES

Continent	(in millions)	Country	(in millions)	Percentage of total
North and South America	118.0	United States	100.0	85%
Europe	88.0	Britain, France, Germany and Italy	61.0	70%
Asia	14.0	Japan	11.0	80%
Oceania	6.0	Australia and New Zealand	5.7	95%
Africa	4.0	South Africa	2.0	50%
USSR	1.5			

Cars are concentrated in the richest countries of each continent and particularly the largest cities.

Highway transport presents no difficulties in North America, in Europe, in Japan or in other developed countries, because there is an adequate highway infrastructure. The same cannot be said for Africa, where 45 countries combined have barely 600,000 miles of bad highways for a small fleet of four million vehicles.

Transmission of Electricity

In the early development of electricity, it was discovered that the electricity produced by a steam engine or a hydraulic machine was a particularly flexible form of energy with a very high productivity in its mechanical applications. As a result, generators were built in the proximity of coal mining operations, and industries requiring high temperatures or electrolysis procedures relocated to hydraulic power sites. No one really knew how to "transport" electricity economically, so that the factory was tied to the energy source. However, very early technicians explored the possibility of transporting excess capacity to supply energy consumers away from the site. It was therefore at the beginning of the 20th century, after the development of ways to transmit and distribute electricity through insulated power lines and through transformers, that industrial production of electricity grew.

The installations are expensive for two reasons. First of all, transmission and distribution costs make up an important item in the expenditures of electrical companies—more than a third of investment and operating expenses. The organization of a transmission and distribution network, in some situations, can have as much impact on the ultimate cost of energy as production itself. Secondly, the transmission of electricity results in energy losses along the system. The relative importance of such losses varies in direct proportion to the distances involved and in inverse proportion to the tension at which transmission occurs. It is, in other words, a function of geographical realities (the specific locales of production and consumption) and of technical realities (specifics of the long-distance transmission networks).

These factors explain the considerable differences in electrical costs. It is estimated that line losses for the world as a whole average 8.5% of net production; some countries show losses below this average. These include Holland (5.3%), Japan (5.8%) and Germany (6.2%). Other countries are closer to the average, such as the United States (8.1%) or the USSR (8.3%). Sweden (10.6%) or Spain (13.6%) have higher than average losses.

For an alternating current transmission line, fixed capital costs per kilowatt-hour decrease when capacity utilization increases. Operating costs, on the other hand, are proportional to the line's capacity utilization. On a graph of kilowatt-hour costs and capital costs, the real minimum unit costs are found at the point where fixed costs and operating costs are equal. Line losses, on the other hand, diminish noticeably as tension increases (6% per 60 miles at 60 kV, 1% at 400 kV).

Capacity also varies with tension. When the tension level doubles, the transmission capacity quadruples. Generally, a new transmission level is adopted every 20 years to keep up with the developments in installations. This technical threshold has moved on the largest linkages from 116 kV in 1919 to 400 kV in 1960, and a tension of 765 kV appears to be economically viable around 1980. A further level, somewhere between 1,000 and 1,500 kV, will probably be reached by the year 2000. For distances greater than 600 miles, the transmission of electricity on a direct current line is less costly than on an alternating current line. The savings grow out of the need for only two conductors per circuit instead of three, which more than makes up for the additional costs of the most complex terminal equipment. Although energy transmissions over a distance of more than 600 miles are rare, the Soviet Union is considering transmission levels of 3,000-5,000 megawatts over distances approaching 2,500 miles from Siberia to the western region of the country.

At the moment direct-current linkups are used primarily for underground cables, especially between France and England, to carry magnitudes of 160 megawatts. Also under consideration is a linkup that will transmit 600 megawatts from the southern island of New Zealand to the more industrialized northern island.

There are two major trends in the transmission of electrical power. One is based on long-term contracts, which generally assume the creation of special lines.

Long-term contracts take three forms.

—*Barter operations* are those by which electrical energy is exchanged for deliveries of other types of goods. For example, Rumania and Czechoslovakia have a 20-year agreement whereby Rumania supplies two billion kilowatt hours a year to Czechoslovakia at a power of 3,000 megawatts. Similar agreements may be developed between other Eastern European countries.

—*Joint generator construction* contracts cover hydroelectric stations built on a river between two countries. There is also a trend toward joint construction of nuclear power plants. Spain and France, for example, jointly operate the Vandellos plant near Tarragona.

—*Sales of excess energy capacity to other countries* are the third form. In Europe most industrialized countries have more or less developed their existing capacity. Norway, Turkey and the USSR, however, still have important undeveloped resources. Norway nonetheless prefers not to export its resources to give its industry the benefits of relatively low prices. Turkey's facilities, located in the eastern part of the country along the Tigris and the Euphrates, are far from potential markets. The Soviet Union has abundant resources in Siberia.

Short-term agreements take advantage of the differences in daily energy utilization from one country to the next. They are based on daily exchanges and make possible the utilization of complementary hydraulic and thermal resources in adjoining regions. They also permit the coordination of maintenance periods for generators and power stations, with one area's idle capacity being compensated by production from another locale.

These agreements have resulted in increased energy exchanges between European countries. In Europe there are three interconnected networks that correspond to three groups of countries. Studies have been made of the possibility of linking these networks even more tightly together and of facilitating exchanges between the Soviet Union and Western Europe. These studies show that joint utilization of energy reserves would produce an increase of 5,000 megawatts by 1980, the equivalent of 10% of the total current output of the individual grids. When the USSR has completed an interconnected network over its entire territory from Siberia to the Ukraine, the benefits of interlock will be considerably increased, because a larger number of local schedules will be integrated and extra power will be made available to the Asian regions of the country.

Oceans and seas are generally an obstacle to the direct transmission of electricity. But it is possible to transport electricity indirectly in the form of finished goods such as aluminum, whose production requires a large quantity of electricity. Production of such goods can be decentralized in areas such as Africa, which has a fourth of the world's hydroelectric resources, most of which are virtually untapped.

The development of the Inga operation in Zaire was conceived with this problem in mind. The first stage of the operation called for the construction of a hydroelectric power plant and an aluminum factory consuming 70% of the energy produced. Since then, the initial plans have evolved and discussion is now focused on the construction of a gaseous diffusion factory for the production of enriched uranium.

Some scientists are even discussing the utilization of Greenland's hydroelectric resources and the production of hydrogen and ammonia for agricultural fertilizers. These projects would be capable of producing half of the world's ammonia needs by the end of the century.

Such a solution, of course, poses political and economic problems. Transport and handling costs must be low enough to make such an operation economically viable. The treatment of semifinished products could render a region dependent on industrial activity outside its own territory in periods of international tension. But this is not true of the treatment of raw materials, which Europe has to import under any circumstances. The onsite treatment of African bauxite, for example, and its transformation into base metal prior to its export to Europe would create no more difficulties for the latter than the current arrangements in which untreated bauxite is exported for treatment abroad.

Various solutions are offered for the exploitation of hydroelectric resources. One possibility is high-tension transmission over distances of approximately 600 miles. Canada's Hydroquebec has made an attempt along these lines, building facilities for 16,000 megawatts that will be transmitted throughout Quebec and to the northern United States by 735 kV facilities. A second solution is to combine the energy-consuming industrial complex with the production site. An example of this is found in the large Siberian industrial zones where electro-metallurgy, steel production and paper-pulp works have been established to overcome the long-distance transmission costs of electrical power. Finally, onsite production of aluminum or hydrogen solves many problems. Surplus power generated by the electrical treatment can then be used for energy storage or shipment.

In the future the production of electricity will tend to become independent of the immediate energy source, primarily through the use of nuclear power. The transportation of nuclear fuels thus constitutes another way of shipping electrical energy, essentially by placing relatively mobile nuclear power plants at the disposal of consumers.

The transportation of nuclear fuels involves three phases: the movement of uranium ore to the factory where combustible elements are produced; the movement of the fuel to the reactor and the movement of depleted fuels back to the factory for reconversion. The first phase poses no serious risks of radioactive contamination and is essentially handled as little more than a normal bulk shipment. The two other phases, however, pose real safety problems and require special containers. Even though comparison between transport costs for different kinds of energy is a complicated task, the shipment of nuclear fuels is, in the last instance, by far the cheapest. It is thus with nuclear power, whose impact is already felt in the production of electricity, that we will achieve a world in which space will appear isotropic in energy.

Conclusion

There has been an unbelievable expansion in the use of oil and gas. Who, half a century ago, could have imagined that oil production would not merely double, as in the case of coal, but would be 15 times higher than 1930 levels?

A second phenomenon, just as unforeseeable half a century ago, is the concentration of this enormous wealth (whether domestic or imported) in the hands of the richest countries.

Oil and gas have become, through the technologies they have engendered, the key to the world's productive activity. This, moreover, has been accomplished by an "aristocracy" of the eight major powers. But this aristocracy has one vulnerable point: its current oil reserves. These reserves are almost depleted in the United States and Canada, and are not much larger in Latin America; their decline, however, is being offset by imports from the reserves of the Middle East, Africa, Indonesia and Australia (see Graph 4).

We seem to be overwhelmed by oil's impact on our existence, especially after the beginning of actual shortages made it clear that everything would come to a halt without this resource. But this is no reason to give up hope. Various types of energy have evolved throughout history, and nuclear power, still in its early stages, will be a stable part of tomorrow's production. When this occurs, we will be able to begin thinking not about the disappearance of oil but about its selective uses, including fuel for the diesel engines of ships, the key to world transportation, and for power utilities. Oil products are indispensable for petrochemicals, for the fertilizers on which a large part of tomorrow's crops will depend, for proteins to complement meat-deficient diets and many other purposes. At the same time, we can foresee wider use for the raw materials, such as wool and cotton, of developing countries.

Coal's potential rests in its enormous reserves. It will continue to be an irreplaceable counterpart to iron ore in steel production, 78% of which is currently controlled by the eight major powers. The old sources of iron ore are being abandoned, and from now on, it will be imported by large ore carriers from Brazil, Canada and Australia.

Currently dependent for its production on gas, oil and coal, electrical energy, together with nascent nuclear power, remains the most promising energy source for tomorrow. And once again, this energy is in the hands of the "Big Eight." Surely a modus vivendi can be established between nuclear power, electricity production, and the multiple uses of oil by the end of the century. This modus vivendi, of course, is formally dependent on maritime transport (see Graphs 19 and 20).

Air transport is becoming increasingly important in today's world, as reflected in the growth of air routes as well as of mass tourism. The airplane is moving to center stage in the underdeveloped countries, where other forms of transportation remain mediocre at best. Now that the passenger steamer has effectively been eliminated, the merchant marine can devote its energies to the movement of cargo. The airplane has taken over the monopoly of passenger travel, but the day will come when it will also handle as much freight as passenger traffic.

The similarities between the shipping and the airlines industries are striking. Both are resolutely international activities, governed by rigid regulations that are virtually a thousand years old for ships but barely a century old for airplanes. Their movement takes them through two unbounded expanses, the sky and the sea, and they are manned by young men with the same basic training, speaking the same international language—English—and using a single international currency, the dollar. They rely on the same weather reports, the same satellites and the same measurements (feet, miles, etc.).

As we have seen in the course of this work, navigation in the broad sense is the domain of both ships and airplanes. Their parallel increases in tonnage have had identical consequences. The use of oil and LNG tankers is accelerated and is complemented by the great networks that move their cargoes inland, as well as by container ships, which are particularly suited to expanding traffic. Airplane rotation is similarly sped up in the transportation of both passengers and freight.

We have frequently mentioned the importance of the world's eight major powers, the masters of oil and of transportation. But we might also ask whether the power of such an economic entity can endure, for history shows many examples of "great empires" whose power had a beginning and an end. We might well wonder what the reactions of the world's "have not" nations would be to such a shift in the balance of power. It seems impossible that the world can continue to be divided between a complete success for some countries and an immobile despair for others, populated by human masses far removed from everything taken for granted in the developed nations.

By the beginning of the 21st century, we can foresee a slowing of consumption in the wealthy countries and the end of its concentration in those regions. Industries will increasingly be obliged to move to the sources of raw material and energy found in underdeveloped countries. Such a movement might well reverse the transport flows of our own era.

This industrial decentralization seems to us both possible and beneficial. Our children do not understand why an older generation has not made this dream a reality. The links established with such ease by modern transportation acquaint us with new partners whose names are gaining prominence more quickly than we can imagine: China, obviously, but also Brazil, the coastal nations of Africa, Australia and the countries in Southeast Asia. Such cooperation is the real source of hope.

A Brief History of Hydrocarbon Fuels

Oil was created millions of years ago. It developed out of the decomposition of marine flora and fauna, buried under thick layers of sediments. These layers, in turn, formed the rocks that trapped the oil. In some exceptional cases the oil seeped to the surface, forming the asphalt ponds that men have used for thousands of years. Long ago this tar was put to use in China and Persia for foundations and for reinforcing roads. It was also used in Byzantium for "Greek fire." In the 10th century B.C., the Queen of Sheba visited King Solomon to exchange gold for the tar she needed to caulk her ships.

More recently crude oil was highly esteemed for its medicinal value. In 1860 a resident of Titusville, Pa., following the example of the Indians, collected the oil floating on the water of his wells. He put it in little vials and sold it to pharmacists in New York under the name of "Samuel Kier's Balm," strongly recommended against "gout, coughs, rhumatism and toothaches."

A New York banker, who happened to own land in Titusville, decided to go into competition with Kier. He called on the services of an ingenious man named "Colonel" Drake, who rationalized that "if oil rose to the surface in large amounts, there must be a great deal more underground." He hired a blacksmith to drill a hole and, on Aug. 28, 1859, discovered oil. A primitive hand pump went into action. Every available container in the area was requisitioned. One of them was an old barrel that held 41 gallons. This "barrel" became the standard unit of measurement in the oil industry.

From that moment on, the medical applications of oil were forgotten. Drake had hit a well that produced more than a metric ton and a half of oil a day. His success touched off a rush comparable to the earlier gold rush; once a productive well was discovered, forests of oil derricks suddenly appeared. They moved rapidly into the bordering states, and then into Louisiana and Texas.

The discovery was timely because the whale oil then used for lighting was becoming scarce. This shortage led to the development of the "kerosene lamp." Kerosene was so plentiful that some people estimated that "all the lamps in the world would not use it up." As a result of over-production prices fell, and the world had its first oil crisis.

Shortly thereafter an enterprising young man, sensing oil's future and noting how Titusville's successes had been the result of chance, came up with a plan to control this untapped wealth. His name was John D. Rockefeller, and he was not yet 30 years old. Rockefeller's plan was based on two premises:

1) the success of an industry based on crude oil depended on its refinement and ability to be transported, and

2) a new oil industry, including the transportation of oil, would quickly acquire global dimensions.

In collaboration with the railroads, Rockefeller worked out a set of secret agreements that not only allowed him to transport oil more cheaply than his competitors, but also to exploit the wide strips of land conceded to the railroads. He thus placed 90% of all oil shipments under his control, along with the first refineries. When he created the Standard Oil Company in 1882, it was first and foremost a "pool of refiners." During this period, world production consisted of four million metric tons in the United States and one million in Russia, where production had begun 10 years earlier.

By the end of the century, two new rival companies had been created: the Royal Dutch Company of the Netherlands founded in 1890 and the British-owned Shell Transport and Trading Limited founded in 1897. The latter had been created to transport pearl-oyster shells (therefore the name "Shell"), but its focus rapidly turned to the sale and transportation of oil. These two companies fused in 1907 under the name Royal Dutch Shell with Dutch oilman Sir Henry Deterding as chairman.

Standard Oil focused on developing a mass clientele. In an effort to expand the market, a company engineer stationed in China proposed— apparently on the suggestion of his houseboy—providing the population with free makeshift oil lamps and a free initial supply of oil. A market was created and by the 1920s Standard Oil's ships could be seen plying the Yangtze to deliver American oil. The junks took on the task of spreading this unknown source of comfort as far inland as Chungking, 2,400 miles up the Yangtze from Shanghai.

The financial successes of the Anglo-Saxon and Dutch oil companies were not lost on the Germans, who in 1903 gained a concession for the Baghdad railroad, which eventually linked the Bosporus to the oil-rich Persian Gulf. Not to be outdone, the British admiralty, in conjunction with a widely experienced Burma group, created the Anglo-Persian Company in 1909, before any oil had been found in Iran. Twelve years later, Winston Churchill, who once said that "the war was won on a flood tide of oil," negotiated the replacement of Turkish Petroleum with an enormous multinational corporation, the Iraq Petroleum Company (IPC), made up of the British government, the French government (both of which would cede their shares to British and French nationals), Royal Dutch Shell (under Deterding) and Standard Oil. Each of the participants held 23.75% of the capital. Calouste Gulbukian, in his capacity as "negotiating party on his own behalf," was given a share that made him famous as "Mister 5%." All the elements had thus been brought together for developing the oil of the Persian Gulf and for a collaboration of the eight "majors," which, with their subsidiaries, would in effect control virtually all the oil and gas in the world.

The United States, Canada and the USSR, whose first drillings were roughly simultaneous, each have over 100 years in the industry. Indonesian production also dates back to the last century. Venezuela began producing in 1917 and rapidly surpassed Mexico. Iran's industry got underway on the eve of World War I and the other Gulf producers quickly followed suit. China's oil production started in 1933 and Australia began to produce in 1939. Of the African group, Algeria entered the world market in 1956 and was quickly joined by Nigeria in 1958 and by Libya in 1961.

Like oil, natural gas took a long time to win its place in world energy production. In 1910, 91% of that production still consisted of coal gas. This was thought to be irreplaceable for domestic uses and public lighting. Natural gas output did not exceed 525 billion cubic feet, a tiny volume compared to that of the coal gas it was shortly to replace. (These 525 billion cubic feet were the energy equivalent of 19 million metric tons of coal.)

In 1929 the League of Nations published the first official statistics for natural gas production, then at 2,030 billion cubic feet—the equivalent of 58 million metric tons of oil or 4% of the world's energy. The United States accounted for almost all of this production, 1,750 billion cubic feet. Concentrated in Texas and Louisiana, it was far from the large industrial regions in the North, where the gas was shipped through a network of pipelines.

Gradually the advantages of natural gas and its superiority to coal gas became obvious: it had twice the heating power, was cheap, and was even easier to use because it could be pumped through the existing urban pipelines for coal gas.

The United States was the first country to begin shifting to natural gas. The systematic transition continued throughout World War II. When the German blockade threatened to cut off oil shipments from Venezuela and even from Mexico, this transition was proved eminently sensible. During the 1950s Italy became the first European country to commercially exploit natural gas and France followed. Production approached 490 billion cubic feet and between 1957 and 1959 natural gas virtually displaced the older municipal gasworks while using their pipelines. In 1956 scientists drilling for oil in Algeria hit an enormous lake of natural gas. In the USSR the transformation occurred later—in roughly 1963—but it was carried out very quickly.

Natural gas consumption grew rapidly because it proved an ideal energy source for industry, the production of electricity and domestic use. Natural gas, moreover, is a clean, nonpolluting form of energy, well suited to highly populated areas. Its price is linked to the price of oil because it is produced by the same multinational companies.

The first oil wells in the United States and in Russia were discovered almost accidentally. But with the growth of the science of petroleum geology, the search has focused on sedimentary rocks. These rocks cover roughly a fourth of the earth's land surface, or 16,000,000 square miles. The 12,000,000 square miles of submerged lands belonging to the continental shelf are the source of offshore oil. There is very little chance that areas outside the sedimentary zones have what specialists call "traps" of oil or gas (see Maps 3 and 13).

Oilmen first developed those areas where drilling was easiest. But prospectors eventually moved into more and more difficult terrain, where climate and accessibility posed greater problems. The enormous exploration and operating costs, both for extracting and shipping from these areas, prompted increased exploration on the continental shelf. The imminent depletion of certain onshore oil and gas reserves (within 10 years for some areas in the United States), the relatively low cost of shallow offshore drilling and the ease with which oil can be shipped to consumers from offshore platforms contributed to the move. But the most important reason for concentrating on offshore oil has been the desire to diversify petroleum resources outside the control of OPEC and to achieve energy independence.

The 12 million square miles of the continental shelf, equivalent in area to Africa, are potential sites for offshore drilling. Although exploration of this area is still relatively recent, it already accounts for 25% of oil and gas production and will account for 40% within 10 years.

The expansion of offshore oil and gas exploration naturally raised international legal problems. The limits of territorial waters have long been set at three nautical miles, or at six and 12 miles in rare cases. The notion of the continental shelf is just as old, but primarily was applied to fishing and later underwater cables. It therefore did not deal with distances below the seabed. The first offshore drillings were attempted at depths of 17 to 33 feet in the Caspian Sea or, from 1936 onward, at 13 feet in Louisiana. Thereafter drilling depth increased to 99 feet, then to 396 feet on some drilling platforms. The drill now goes as deep as 23,100 feet below sea level.

The agreement signed in Geneva on April 28, 1958 settled the juridical status of the continental shelf, which was officially defined as "the seabed and subsoil of underwater regions adjacent to coasts and islands, outside of territorial waters, up to a depth of 660 feet or, beyond that limit, to a point where water depth permits the development of natural resources."

A distinction is made between "territorial waters" and the "continental shelf." The first term refers to a horizontal distance between the coast and offshore waters. The second term refers to a depth, which can be as little as 33 feet in the Gulf of Mexico or as much as the 660 feet set by the Geneva agreement. Past a depth of 660 feet, a special law permits the extension of any drilling, whether for oil, gas or any other mineral.

Modern geophysicists have several methods to help them locate oil. Using the gravimetric method, oil-bearing rocks, which are fairly dense and deep, can be detected at ground level by slight variations in gravitation. These variations can be measured with extremely sensitive instruments that make it possible to gather information on the form and nature of the rocks at various depths. The seismic method, developed more recently, uses "miniature earthquakes" to find oil. Geophysicists explode underground or underwater charges and then measure the time required for the shockwaves to return to the surface after bouncing off subterranean structures. Once the speed of the waves is known, it is easy to calculate the depths of the formations. By spreading receivers over the terrain under exploration and comparing the rebound times for different waves, they can tell if the rock layers are horizontal or else calculate their slope. Further explosions are set off to develop a map of the underground formations and their profiles.

Finally, logging is a rather expensive but remarkably efficient method. It involves measuring the physical properties of the geological layers targeted for drilling. This procedure, recently invented by the French scientist Conrad Schlumberger, has been used by Schlumberger Limited and several American companies. As drilling becomes more difficult, the services of the logging companies grow more expensive. But these services save drillers much precious time, an important consideration given the fact that some platforms cost $50,000 a day to operate.

The search for hydrocarbon fuels has become a vital activity. Since no government is capable of mounting explorations by itself, they are almost always entrusted to one of the large oil companies or one of their numerous subsidiaries, which are able to transcend most political boundaries. Using similar techniques and employing international management personnel who speak the same technical language, the eight large oil companies, the so-called majors, continue the search for oil around the world.

Extracting oil and gas must be done as expeditiously as possible because of increased drilling and operating costs. Development must occur on a large scale to cover production costs and to obtain the lowest price for transporting oil by tanker. Finally, production must be carried out over a long period because the average operating time for a well has now reached 20 consecutive years.

Onshore drilling often involves installations that last a long time and therefore require very elaborate logistics. It goes without saying that airstrips and helicopter landings are a priority. After these facilities have been established, a road or railway infrastructure is built to handle the movement of heavy equipment—derricks, drilling pipes and water supplies to make drilling mud. A radio and weather station are required. Finally, a repair shop is indispensable. The company must also establish a residential area of trailers and trucks capable of housing a team of 50 to 60 men.

In short, everything must be adapted to the isolation of the field and often to the harsh climate of freezing or torrid terrains. These difficult conditions make it necessary to organize personnel rotations, which in extreme cases, such as the operations in Spitsbergen in the Arctic Ocean, take place every two months. The problems of maintaining the quality of life in harsh climates was first studied and resolved in the Sahara. Visitors to Hassi Messaoud, where the first African oil was found, remember the bushes that were specially flown in or the sign that read "Don't Walk on the Grass" next to the pool.

For a long period drilling operations followed a specific pattern. A series of rods, fastened together, the first of which contained a diamond drill capable of cutting through the hardest soils, was lowered from a derrick. This technique was vastly improved by a method called turbo-drilling, in which the motor turning the rods was no longer on the derrick but on the drill, which was capable of reaching depths of 13,200 feet. This procedure was, in turn, refined by the introduction of a drill on which the rods were replaced by a single, flexible steel tube. Techniques improve on almost a yearly basis. A "bouquet" of drilling heads, such as the one at Frig in the North Sea, can operate 24 drills simultaneously. This innovation has aroused considerable interest and can be used both on and off shore.

Although onshore drilling dates back more than a century, oil companies drilling along seacoasts made no attempt to exploit the shallow depths immediately offshore until after World War I. In 1922 the Russians successfully extended their Baku drillings into the Caspian Sea. After drilling had reached the Gulf of Mexico, U.S. oil companies attempted to use the methods that had proven successful in the Caspian. The initial attempts were disappointing, even though the bayous, coastal rivers and beaches were ideal settings within territorial waters. The first successful drillings in the Western Hemisphere were made in Venezuela in Lake Maracaibo in 1925 at a depth of 17 feet and then in Mexico in 1938 at 33 feet. Only in 1947 was oil struck off the Louisiana coast.

The early fixed platforms slowly gave way to moving platforms, first used in 1949, and then to self-raising platforms, developed in 1956. After that, it became quite normal to move offshore platforms after the depletion of a field. In 1968 there were 250 such platforms in operation, two-thirds of which were in the United States and the rest in the Middle East, Southeast Asia, central Africa and the North Sea.

The usual method of offshore drilling in shallow waters entails laying solid foundations for a permanent platform supporting the derrick, the equipment that separates oil and gas and the storage installations. These platforms, used for the first time in Alaska, can handle 30 to 40 wells simultaneously. Divers can easily work on the wellheads, inspect the pilings and perform other maintenance operations.

For deep-water drilling, platforms have the advantage of being both relatively inexpensive and easy to build, but they have two major drawbacks. The main problems are the limitation on the length of their "legs" and the rigidity of the installations, which makes them useless when the well is depleted. This problem led to the idea of equipping a vessel with a standard derrick that it would carry to a drilling site. The ship would permit a drilling team to move with its equipment from one country, or even continent, to another.

A practical application of this concept was the *Pelican*, a modern French ship transporting all necessary drilling equipment and a reserve of piping. Several propellers fore and aft enabled the ship to maneuver in heavy winds and remain stable in swells. In very bad weather the watch officer could automatically remove the drilling pipe at the wellhead. Later the ship could maneuver to reattach the drill to the wellhead, after locating it by satellites. This technique worked admirably for drilling operations but could not be used once production was underway.

Semisubmersible heavy-tonnage platforms currently operate at depths between 132 and 660 feet. Maintained in position by anchors, the installations float with 66 to 99 feet of equipment submerged. Much has been said of their comforts and accessibility to land by helicopter. Less has been said about the extraordinary performance of these platforms, which stand up to 66-foot swells and winds of up to 120 knots, or 138 miles per hour. Considering the fierce weather conditions of places like the northern Shetlands in midwinter, the construction and durability of such equipment is a tribute to naval engineering. So far only one of these installations has been damaged by rough weather. The major constraint in using the platforms is their enormous operating costs. Gulf Publishing in Houston gives the following estimate for the annual costs of offshore operations around the world:

COSTS OF OFFSHORE OIL OPERATIONS
(in millions of dollars)

Exploration and Drilling	3,400
Production	2,800
Pipelines	445
Transport and Storage	150
	6,795

The refining process always begins with distillation and breakdown, which results in an array of products. First and foremost are the petroleum gases, which are liquefied to produce butane and propane. At 110 °C ordinary gasoline is produced. This product is then reformed, a relatively recent technique used to raise gasoline's octane content. The next product is naphtha, which is the basis of petrochemicals. At 180 °C kerosene and its two variants—jet fuel and all-purpose heating oil—are produced. The next products are the gasoils at 250 °C and the fuel oils at 300 °C. Finally, at 340 °C the bitumens are extracted from heavy fuels with a second, vacuum distillation. The distillation process employs two procedures, cracking and reforming. Cracking involves the use of a catalyst (later recovered) or high temperatures to break down heavy hydrocarbon molecules in petroleum into lighter molecules, which are then isomerized. This is a well-established process, first used in Louisiana in 1940. The second procedure, reforming, is a high-temperature treatment of lower-quality gasoline, also using a recoverable catalyzer.

Petroleum Products

The U.S. Bureau of Mines classifies petroleum products in ascending order of density—gasoline, kerosene, gasoil and fuel oil—and sets the average equivalent of a metric ton at 7.9 barrels.

PETROLEUM PRODUCTS

	(millions of metric tons)	% of total
Fuel Oil	580	27%
Gasoline	530	25%
Gasoil	470	22%
Kerosene	150	7%
Others	320	15%
Refining and Losses	85	4%
World Total	2,135	100%

Fuel oil comprises the largest portion of petroleum products. It is most widely used in the industrialized countries, which alone consume

440 million metric tons (Europe 210 million metric tons; the U.S. and Canada 130 million and Japan 100 million). Forty-five other nations consume an average of only three million metric tons each. Fuel oil is a major energy source for the large industrial countries, which use it to power utilities, heat large buildings and fuel industry. Its utilization has increased almost exactly in proportion to the phaseout of coal in various areas.

However, fuel oil reserves are diminishing, particularly in those heavily industrial areas like North America, Western Europe and Japan, which are most dependent on it. As a result these nations have become interested in nuclear energy, which may eventually account for a significant portion of electricity production, currently 6,000 tetrawatt hours.

Gasoline was initially a secondary product of petroleum refining. The early automobiles ran on oil. However by 1930 gasoline was the dominant fuel used. It is currently the second most important petroleum product in the world and the tonnage produced is roughly equivalent to that of fuel oil. The concentration of consumption is much greater for this fuel. The U.S. and Canada use 310 million metric tons, while Europe accounts for 95 million and Japan 23 million. The rest of the world must make do with 100 million metric tons, or less than two million metric tons per country.

The American gasoline market has continued to grow from year to year. At first production rates were increased, then higher-octane levels were achieved and finally cracking and reforming techniques were improved. But these high-quality fuels are available only to a few rich countries, where 245 million vehicles consume 450 million metric tons of gasoline, or 85% of world production. The rest of the world, with three billion people, uses just 80 million metric tons.

For a long time gasoil held first place among petroleum products, a position it later ceded to the fuel oils increasingly in demand for industrial production and electrical generation. World production of gasoil is currently 470 million metric tons (not including the USSR, Comecon and China). Despite its relative decline, gasoil continues to be the petroleum product with the greatest variety of uses and the one most widely distributed throughout the world. It is the easiest petroleum product to refine and by far the cheapest.

Total kerosene production is approximately 150 million metric tons (not including the USSR). It has two main uses: as a component of airplane fuel and as all-purpose fuel oil for countries without electricity. There are only three large consumers of the kerosene used for airplane fuel (excluding the USSR and China): the United States with 62 million metric tons, Japan with 20 million and Europe with 15 million. Fifty million metric tons of all-purpose kerosene fuel are consumed in regions having no electricity.

New refining techniques make it possible to use olefins such as ethylene, propylene and butadiene and aromatics such as benzene and toluene in the production of petrochemicals. Products include plastic materials, synthetic fibers, detergents, pesticides, explosives and foods such as protein used in cattle feed and even synthetic "meat." Among the most important products of the petrochemical industry are fertilizers for agriculture.

The Oil Crisis and the Future of Electricity

Over the years efficient technologies for the production of electricity have emerged and succeeded each other. Coal, oil, hydraulic power and nuclear energy have each played a role in the production of electrical power. Throughout its development electricity has become progressively more independent of its immediate power source. High-tension wires now transmit electric energy produced by oil-, coal- or nuclear-powered generators to the principal centers of consumption; interconnected networks in the major industrialized countries, particularly in Europe, coordinate the output of the various regional production centers.

The Arab oil embargo of 1973-74 and the radical surge in fuel prices since that time have forced the industrialized countries to reorient their energy policies. Current pricing conditions favor the use of electricity over competing power sources and an exponential growth in the consumption of electrical energy. Utilities that previously relied on one fuel, particularly oil, are diversifying their equipment to burn other sources less vulnerable to price rises and supply cutoffs.

Many utilities have begun shifting to nuclear power, which is relatively easy to transport and not subject to the same economic and political uncertainties as oil. However, recent incidents involving the accidental release of radiation into the atmosphere from nuclear power plants have raised grave concern about the location of these facilities near major centers of population and doubts about the future of nuclear power in general. If the safety questions surrounding the use of nuclear energy can be resolved, the development of breeder reactors, which produce more fuel than they consume, and fusion power may one day provide a vast and almost inexhaustible supply of power.

Energy Growth

The European Development Fund (EDF) attempted to determine the long-term development programs needed to meet energy growth over the next 200 years. With an average per capita consumption equal to about five coal tons (cte) per year, the Europeans and the Japanese currently consume two and a half times less energy than the people of North America (12 cte per capita per year) and 10 times more than the inhabitants of the Third World (0.5 cte per capita per year). Certain studies, especially the second report of the Club of Rome, have predicted that all countries will reach a level of per capita energy consumption double the present rate of the United States, perhaps 20 cte per capita for 20 billion people. Such an increase would raise the total world consumption rate from the current eight billion cte to 400-500 billion cte.

However, the assumptions underlying these calculations are highly questionable. First of all the average level of per capita consumption for the United States seems too high; other studies predict a more realistic rate of about 10 cte per capita. Furthermore, because of the increased acceptance of various birth control methods, the growth of the world population should eventually stabilize at about 10 billion. Based on these estimates, total world energy consumption should reach about 100 billion cte, or 10 cte per capita for 10 billion people, an upper and possibly definitive limit.

Given this forecast of anticipated energy requirements, are there resources to meet these needs? The possible exhaustion of natural energy sources is not really the major problem facing the world. There are vast reserves of oil and coal as well as hydroelectric potential located in underdeveloped regions such as in Asia and Africa. Furthermore, the substitution of nuclear fission energy for the fossil fuels—oil and coal—now used to produce electricity could free these resources for other uses and provide the necessary lead time for the development of fusion and solar power. Therefore the energy dilemma is not so much a scarcity of resources as a need for the proper technology to develop and utilize properly those available.

The major obstacle to energy growth is climate and space, or the lack of it. If the per capita consumption energy rates of the other industrialized nations reach that of the United States, profound climatic changes could result from the interaction of the sun's rays with carbon dioxide pollution produced by the increased burning of fossil fuels. In addition these countries are running out of space. Rather than to continue importing the raw materials, energy supplies and manpower of the Third World in order to produce and export goods in the other direction, they must accept a certain dependency on areas that have much more space and natural resources.

At the same time a progressive deceleration of material growth should have a modifying effect on the energy requirements of the industrial nations. In the Third World, where energy consumption is low, the growth in per capita consumption should rise substantially; similarly, the overall increase in demand for energy should be highest in these countries, which currently contain two-thirds of the world's population.

This scenario, however, extends beyond the 20th century and would probably involve massive changes in civilization as a whole. Until the year 2000, energy requirements will undoubtedly continue to grow in both the developed and developing countries. The former nations must free themselves from energy imports, thereby making oil available for the development of the Third World and allowing time to solve the energy dilemma before it becomes too late.

The Future of Electricity in the Industrial Countries

In Europe, electrical power presently accounts for one-fourth of total secondary energy needs and has the potential for rapid expansion to satisfy the other three-fourths, either as a replacement for the traditional fuels or through new technologies that utilize all its physical properties. The first priorities are the development of "all-electrical" housing and the conversion to electric power for various industrial energy needs.

Over the next five years the massive nuclear reactor programs now underway will satisfy 70 to 80% of Europe's heating needs; if necessary hydraulic energy equipment can be used in tandem. By 1985 electrical power should be able to assume an important share of the industrial energy market and to increase its portion of the residential and tertiary markets. At that point it should represent more than one-third of all energy consumed, compared to the current 25%. After 1985, the growth of electrical power should accelerate. Cogeneration of heat by electrical generators should also undergo significant development. Under this scenario electricity will account for one-half to three-fourths of all energy consumed by the end of the 20th or the beginning of the 21st century, with fossil fuels and alternative energy sources comprising the rest. However, by then the traditional combustible fuels will play only a marginal role in the production of electricity. The energy mix which makes up that gap between one-half and three-fourths will depend largely on the evolution of the costs and technologies involved in transporting heat over moderate distances compared with the costs of transmitting electricity. It will also be affected by the possibilities of using hydrogen directly as a fuel.

The potential market for electricity in the industrial countries has expanded considerably because of the enormous increases in the costs of competing power sources. Only the use of nuclear energy for mass production of electrical power will meet the needs of this expanded market and achieve the necessary diversification of energy sources, which have been dominated since the beginning of the 1960s by imported hydro-carbon fuels. The essential task facing the European nations is to expedite the development of current nuclear power programs for the production of electricity. The use of nuclear energy must not only be accepted politically but also affirmed by the countries that have this capability.

The Future of Electricity in the Third World

The mere presence of energy resources is not enough to ensure a country's economic development. The existence of enormous oil and gas reserves in the Middle East or hydroelectric resources in the Congo has so far not resulted in industrial revolutions similar to those experienced by the developed nations centuries ago. Economic growth depends on many factors: commerce, transportation, industrial production, demography, financial networks and, above all, the attitudes of the population. Development of Third World energy resources is therefore not enough. To guarantee economic growth in the developing countries will require a redistribution of industrial activities on a global level. As noted earlier, the overburdened industrialized nations should accept a decentralization of most energy production and a certain dependency on nations that have more space and a wealth of energy resources.

But the Third World countries must also develop their own industries. To accomplish this, they will need a mobile and versatile source of energy. Electricity appears to have unique advantages for meeting the energy needs of these nations. It can be produced from a wide variety of energy sources: oil, coal, natural gas, nuclear power, tides, winds, garbage, solar power, hydraulic energy and geothermal energy. At the consumption end, it can satisfy several needs by converting one form of energy into another, e.g., providing the power for motors, refrigeration and such processes as electrolysis.

India provides an example of how a developing country can supply its own electrical power through a nuclear reactor program and thereby begin to free itself from the heavy financial burdens of imported oil. Ever since the creation of Indian Atomic Energy in 1948 and the Department of Atomic Energy in 1954, India has aimed for almost total independence in the nuclear sector. To accomplish this, it has established large national laboratories to develop the necessary materials and industrial procedures. The major research center has been the BARC (Bhabha Atomic Research Center) near Bombay, which employs more than 2,000 researchers. A second center has been opened near Madras.

In the initial phase of the program, India decided to order its first reactors from the United States, two of which were provided by General

Electric. An experimental power plant at Tarapur in the Bombay region went into operation in April 1969, and its ability to compete with traditional energy sources was effectively proved. The first enriched uranium fuel was also provided by the United States, but India now buys enriched uranium and transforms it into a fuel locally.

At the beginning of the 1970s, the use of so-called noncommercial energy (wood, grasses, cow dung) had increased slightly as a portion of India's total energy consumption, but demand was also rising for the commerical fuels—coal, oil, hydroelectric power. In order to protect the balance of payments, the government decided to place maximum emphasis on developing coal, hydroelectric power and nuclear energy.

One problem confronting India was that its coal reserves, located in the central and northeastern parts of the country, were so far from certain centers of consumption that transportation costs doubled the price of a ton of coal. Economic analysis showed that nuclear energy would be competitive with coal in areas more than 480 miles from the mining regions. The government then began its nuclear program with 200 megawatt reactors because it did not possess the necessary support systems to accommodate anything larger.

India's nuclear strategy envisaged 12,000 megawatts being provided by nuclear reactors in 1990 and 43,000 megawatts by the year 2000. An initial power plant was ordered from Canada for the site at Rana Pratap Sagar, with two Candu reactors producing 200 megawatts each. Atomic Energy of Canada Ltd. provided the nuclear engineering expertise and Canadian industry provided most of the equipment. Indians contributed less than 20% of the work on the first reactor, but this percentage has increased to nearly 80% of the input on the reactor now under construction in Wapalkamm, near Madras, including all nuclear engineering work.

We should note that while India hopes to achieve energy independence in the future, it is not attempting to reach this goal without help; quite the contrary, it is using carefully selected foreign technologies for the early phases of its program. India is gradually establishing a mining industry, its own production of nuclear fuels and heavy water, and the capacity to process spent radioactive fuels. An industrial complex for nuclear fuels has been built in Hyderabad, and several factories producing heavy water have been built in Baroda and Kota. Since it also has the world's largest thorium reserves, India has been investigating different types of reactors that could use this fuel.

The use of nuclear power will enable India to undertake vast agro-industrial projects that utilize cheap energy, abundant irrigation and readily available fertilizers. Such a complex would employ a total of 1.5 million people and would feed 30 million. Through its existing capacity, India hopes to play an important role in the development of nuclear power in Southeast Asia.

In summary, electric power generated from nuclear sources seems well-suited to the needs of countries undergoing rapid development. Often the relative isolation of coal and hydroelectric resources makes nuclear power economically feasible for major centers of energy consumption. Technology and industry can be mastered by the local populations with the help of techniques developed in the industrial countries. The difficulty is not a technical one; it is political and involves the choice of the people in the developing countries themselves.

New Energy Sources

The idea of using hot springs, geysers and naturally produced steam for energy is an old one. In Greenland, one finds geothermal heating systems in the ruins of the 10th and 11th century Viking homes. In our own time, Iceland makes use of natural hot springs for heating Reykjavik. Less well known is the fact that since 1966 Larderello, Italy, has had 13 geothermal generators with a power of 350,000 kilowatts, capable of producing three billion kilowatt hours. Even certain trains in Italy are run on geothermal power.

At the moment the most important electrical heating stations are in Italy, but the largest to date (Ten Geyser, 908 kW) is scheduled to go into operation in California in 1980. Similar installations are widespread in Japan. There are also geothermal heating systems in Kenya, New Zealand, Mexico, and the USSR, in particular a major project in Kamchatka that is expected to produce electricity more cheaply than is possible with the most efficient hydraulic generators. Similar research is taking place in Djibouti and Java.

The electric power of the world's geothermal generators doubled from 1963 to 1975. It could triple from 1975 to 1980, an indication of the interest in this very cheap energy source.

The world's total geothermal output was 6.5 million kilowatt hours during 1973, primarily in Italy (2.4), the United States (1.4) and New Zealand (1.1), with smaller production levels in Japan, Mexico and Iceland. Yet all these operations combined do not add up to the equivalent of one-half of the electricity output in Greece.

GEOTHERMAL OUTPUT*

	1964	1973
	(in millions of kilowatt hours)	
Italy	2,527	2,480
United States	204	1,453

| | 1964 | 1973 |
	(in millions of kilowatt hours)	
New Zealand	1,194	1,162
Japan	—	248
Mexico	—	183
Iceland	—	24
	3,925	5,550

*Geothermal Resources (U.N., 1975).

Solar energy has its fervent partisans. As a heating source it is quite useful. The 500,000 solar heaters now used in Japan operate without difficulty. There is also a solar oven in France that makes it possible to treat rare metals for specialized technical purposes at temperatures as high as 3000°C. Periodically in recent years researchers have gathered to discuss the transition from heating energy to mechanical energy. But the development of new procedures for energy production is not enough; prices must be competitive with those of traditional hydrocarbon fuels. This has not yet been achieved. Solar energy is essential for recharging satellite batteries and other analogous uses, but it does not have much chance of becoming an important part of the eight million coal ton equivalent currently monopolized by more traditional sources.

Winds and tides are two energy sources that are as old as the world itself. Wind power is an energy source that can be harnessed by local pumping projects, such as those found at Adrar in the Sahara. Using small generators the USSR is currently producing 15 to 30 kW and more in regions with strong, regular winds, such as the southern deserts and the seas of Kamchatka.

In Europe, tides were used to operate small grain mills as early as the 11th century. There are currently only two tide-powered factories in the world. One is in France. With 24 new style turboalternators and a power of 240 kW, it produces 600 megawatt hours. This is a rather average output level but it is free and produces no pollution. The second factory is in the USSR. This is the experimental generator at Kislaya on the coast of the White Sea near Murmansk. If the plant is a success, four more-powerful factories will be built in the same place. The concrete installations will be constructed on shore in Murmansk, then towed and put into place with the techniques used by North Sea oil companies.

In other parts of the world, there are approximately 50 sites where similar energy sources could be developed. Current breakthroughs in technology are making such projects a real possibility. In Argentina there is a plan for a sea-powered plant on the Valdez peninsula, 200 miles south of Bahia Blanca. Another project is under study in Canada to harness tidal power in the Bay of Fundy north of Halifax. Other countries, such as

North and South Korea, are considering similar possibilities.

Bituminous shale was once used as an energy source in England, Russia, Manchuria and France. These operations were abandoned because of competition from the key energy sources, oil and gas, which had low-cost extraction and transportation costs. Nevertheless, the fear of eventual energy shortages is prompting the United States to put considerable sums into efforts to produce energy from bituminous shale at reasonably profitable levels.

The United States has half of the known world reserves; Canada has enormous deposits in the Athabasca tar fields. Thus the world's largest consumer of oil, North America, is also the area best endowed with shale and sands. There are also substantial reserves in Brazil (27% of the world total), somewhat less in Estonia (15%) and in China (9%), where an important project has been launched in Maoming in Kuangtong province.

Up to now liquid hydrogen has been used as a refrigerant and, at extraordinary cost, as a fuel for launching rockets and satellites. The fuel is produced through the electrolysis of water. By the beginning of the next century, liquid hydrogen could be developed into an almost unlimited energy source.

Confronted with a potential oil shortage, nations are looking for alternate fuel sources, the most interesting of which is uranium. The earth's crust contains 100 billion metric tons. In practice, of course, it is impossible to process an ore with such a low yield. But there is already talk of treating seawater, which contains a thousand times less uranium than the average source. Ten thousand times scarcer than iron, but a thousand times more plentiful than gold, the availability of uranium is slowly approaching that of tin.

Uranium is found in crystalline rocks and in certain sedimentary formations from all the geological epochs. It is well distributed in the ground and can be found just about everywhere. It is also simple to detect using a Geiger counter. Explorations are generally conducted at ground level, but in underdeveloped countries lacking a highway infrastructure, detection is first made from the air, and then exploration teams are sent to the site.

A variant of radiometry is emanometry, which detects radon, a water soluble gas whose presence indicates uranium. A second investigative method involves the analysis of underground waters, their mineral salts, the deposits they have left or even the plants they have irrigated. Other standard prospecting techniques, such as the seismic method, have been adapted to the search for radioactive minerals.

Because a metric ton of rock must be unearthed to extract two to four pounds of uranium, one can imagine the enormous dimensions of the underground mines or the vast craters worked by powerful crushers. The underground mines also pose a delicate ventilation problem in the removal of radon, a dangerous radioactive gas that emanates from uranium when it is crushed.

To minimize transportation costs concentrating plants are generally built right next to the mines. The concentration procedure involves grinding the ore into a fine pulp and breaking it down with sulfuric acid. The liquid obtained from this operation is then purified in a complex chemical process. After its concentration, the uranium has a commercial form, the famous "yellow cake." Portions of the huge cake are shipped to other factories to be transformed into reactor fuel.

PRODUCTION AND RESERVES OF URANIUM

Country	Production (in metric tons)	Reserves (thousands of metric tons)
United States	16,000	1,085
Canada	7,600	608
South Africa	5,000	250
France	2,300	81
Niger	1,900	78
Gabon	1,000	32
Spain	170	24
India	150	—
Portugal	84	23
Australia	50	534
Argentina	50	32
Algeria	—	36

Source: *Engineering and Mining Journal*, March 1977.

Thorium, the little-known cousin of uranium, is a potentially useful nuclear fuel that is four times more plentiful than uranium. However, at the moment, the technical problems in making it commercially useful have not been solved and research is continuing. In the meantime this metal, currently a useless byproduct, is accumulating at the pit heads of some uranium mines, in the same place where uranium used to pile up in the era when producers were interested only in radium.

Whereas the standard heating station generates heat from a combustion process involving oxygen and a fossil fuel (coal, lignite, fuel oil, gas etc.), the nuclear power plant produces it from the fission of uranium rods in a nuclear reactor. The heat from the reactor is drawn off by a heat-transferring fluid that circulates around the fuel. A nuclear reactor is thus made up of three elements: a fuel, which can be either natural uranium or enriched uranium (U-235); a moderator, which slows down the neutrons allowing the chain reaction to take place or keeping it going (the most widely used moderators are hydrogen, deuterium, beryllium carbonate or none at all in operations with rapid neutrons); and a heat-conducting fluid, which draws off the heat produced. This fluid can be carbon gas in reactors using enriched uranium and ordinary water or sodium in breeder reactors using helium and heavy water.

In recent years reactors using ordinary water, called light water reactors (LWRs), have predominated. The LWR is currently being produced on a large scale by Westinghouse and General Electric. These two companies have developed two versions of the enriched uranium-ordinary water model: the pressurized water reactor (PWR) and the boiling water reactor (BWR). In the long run this ordinary-water reactor will decline in importance, largely for both technological reasons (its mediocre thermodynamic output) and political reasons. LWRs require enriched uranium, which is produced by only two countries and two groups of nations—the U.S. and the USSR and EURODIF (France, Spain, Belgium and Italy) and URENCO (Germany, the Netherlands and Britain). All other countries are dependent on these producers.

There are also the so-called intermediary models: the natural uranium-heavy water model, developed essentially by the Canadians; and the heavy water-slightly enriched uranium model, which Britain has selected for its electrical equipment.

The future, however, belongs to reactors that allow a much higher utilization of uranium: breeder reactors and "high-temperature" models. Breeder reactors can extract 50 to 80 times as much heating power from a single ton of uranium than is possible with other methods. They transform U-238 into plutonium, which is a nuclear fuel and in the process they create more fuel than they use. The only model that has reached the industrial stage is the rapid-neutron one which uses liquid sodium for heat transfer. The "high-temperature" model should also win an important place over time. Producing heat at a temperature of 750°C, this reactor has an output of 40%, which can be augmented, and it can serve as an energy source for industries as diverse as petrochemicals and steel and eventually for hydrogen production as well. Studies are underway to determine if these reactors can function with a fuel cycle based on U-233 and thorium. Since thorium is more abundant than uranium, the use of such a reactor would increase the final output of fissionable materials.

An estimate made on Jan. 1, 1975 shows that nuclear energy has now become competitive with other sources. It compares two power stations that will begin operation in 1980 and function at top power three-fourths of each year over a 20-year period. The first station operates on fuel oil with two 700-megawatt systems. The second plant is powered by a nuclear reactor with two 925-megawatt systems.

PERCENTAGE OF TOTAL OPERATING COSTS PER KILOWATT HOUR
(in 1975)

	Fossil Fuel Plant	Nuclear Plant
Investments	17%	52%
Operations	10%	20%
Fuels	73%	28%

Investments are more substantial in the case of the nuclear plant ($410,000 per megawatt as against $237,600 for the fossil fuel plant). Fuel cost, on the other hand, which represents three-fourths of the kilowatt hour for the fossil fuel plant (showing the influence of oil prices), is less than a third of the cost of the nuclear plant's kilowatt hour. Thus a nuclear power plant will be far less vulnerable to variations in the prices of basic fuels than the traditional power station.

Exploration now underway guarantees that supplies of fissionable material are neither an obstacle to the development of nuclear power plants nor to building them at any point on the globe. The small quantities of uranium involved (in contrast to the coal tonnages required for a traditional power plant) make the question of transportation an easy one to resolve.

Uranium, moreover, is an element found throughout the earth's crust. There is thus no reason to fear that uranium production will not keep up with demand, even in the early part of the next century, because current reserve estimates are generally on the low side.

WORLD PRODUCTION OF NUCLEAR ENERGY
(billions of kilowatt hours)

	1964	1973	1976
World	15.5	181.0	390
United States	3.3	83.0	201
United Kingdom	8.8	28.0	37
Japan	—	—	37
West Germany	0.1	11.7	25
Canada	0.1	14.3	18
France	0.6	14.0	16
Sweden	—	—	16
Belgium	—	—	10
Switzerland	—	—	9

Sources: United Nations; EDF.

Glossary of Harbor-Related Professions

Stevedore: An individual who handles the loading and unloading of goods, using manual labor (longshoremen) and manages port installations (which usually belong to local governments).

Charterer: In the precise sense, an individual who rents a ship. In the broader sense, an individual who turns over a cargo for delivery and thereby rents the corresponding space for its shipment.

Maritime agent: An individual who represents one or more ships, usually in various inland cities where he seeks out clients. The agent, whose activity is fundamentally a commercial one, is paid on a commission basis.

Freight inspector: A company that verifies the quality of deliveries for the sending or receiving party. These companies often specialize, e.g., in grains, ores, wines, or frozen goods. They are also known as inspection companies.

Shipper: The owner of a ship.

Captain: Legally, the individual responsible for a ship, its crew and its cargo. The captain has the title of commander and is to be distinguished from his second-in-command, who is specifically in charge of the cargo.

Classification board: A group that examines the construction of a ship to assign it a rating. It also makes periodic visits to ships in operation in order to update their ratings.

Legal agent: This individual is attached to the shipper's office in a specific port.

Consignee: The representative of the shipper and the captain in a port, he carries out all administrative, legal, social and commercial operations on their behalf.

Maritime charter and sales broker: Broker who brings together shippers and charterers or shippers and buyers.

Shipbroker: Government official who assists the captain with legal or administrative tasks that the latter is expected to fulfill in a port, particularly when he is a foreigner.

Longshoreman: An individual who loads and unloads ships. He has no specific employer, but sells his labor to a stevedore in keeping with the latter's manpower requirements.

Manager: See Stevedore.

Packer: A specialist in the preparation of all types of packages.

Harbor pilot: A worker specialized in the handling of lines during the docking or departure of a ship.

Pilot: Local individual who assists the captain during the ship's entry to port, departure from port, or movement within port or on rivers.

Towing and salvage: Company with tugs designed to aid ships in normal maneuvers or to bring them aid at sea.

Shipchandler: Company that supplies a ship with food and provisions.

Forwarding agent: An individual who, from inside the port, assures the sorting of cargo, particularly that of small sending and receiving parties. He represents such parties with the shipper and the shipper's representatives and also oversees the formalities of customs.

LIST OF ABBREVIATIONS

AFRA	average freight rate assessment
AMPT	Arab Maritime Petroleum Tanker Company
API	American Petroleum Institute
ATC	Air Transport Command
Btu	British thermal unit
caf	cost, assurance and freight
cif	cost, insurance and freight
CPDP	*Comite professionnel du petrole*
cte	coal ton equivalent
dwt	deadweight ton
fob	free on board
GNP	gross national product
grt	gross register ton
hp	horsepower
IATA	International Air Transport Association
IMCO	Intergovernmental Maritime Consultative Organization
IRF	International Road Federation
JMM	*Journal de la marine marchande*
km	kilometer
LNG	liquefied natural gas
LPG	liquefied petroleum gas
MATS	Military Air Transport Service
MHI	Mitsubishi Heavy Industries
nrt	net register ton
OACI	Organisation de l'aviation civile internationale
OECD	Organization for Economic Cooperation and Development
OPEC	Organization of Petroleum Exporting Countries
rpm	revolutions per minute
twh	tetrawatt hour
UNCTAD	United Nations Conference on Trade and Development
Uniped	Union internationale des producteurs d'energie electrique
UTA	Union de transports aeriens
VTOL	vertical takeoff and landing
W 100	Worldscale 100 (international scale for oil transport)

INDEX

Maps and Graphs

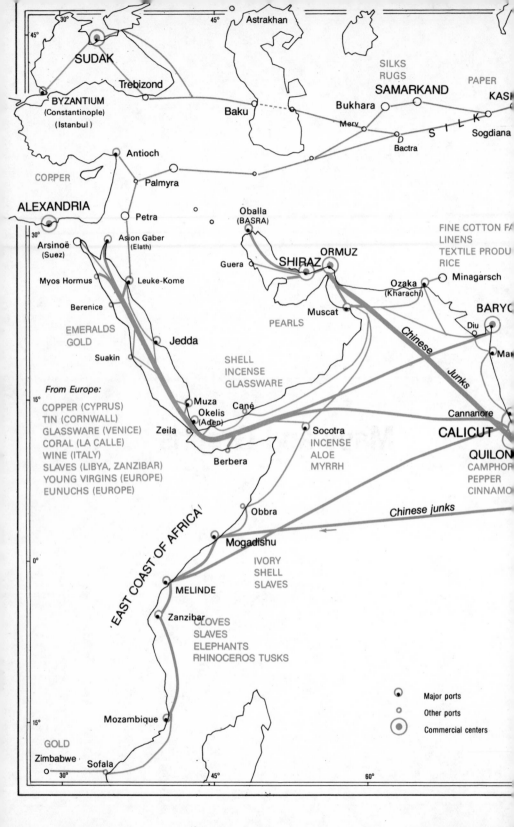

SUDAK

BYZANTIUM
(Constantinople)
(Istanbul)

45°

30°

45°

Astrakhan

Trebizond

Baku

SILKS
RUGS

SAMARKAND

Bukhara

Merv

Bactra

SILK

Sogdiana

PAPER

KASH

Antioch

COPPER

Palmyra

ALEXANDRIA

30°

Petra

Arsinoë
(Suez)

Asion Gaber
(Elath)

Myos Hormus

Leuke-Kome

Berenice

EMERALDS
GOLD

Jedda

Suakin

15°

From Europe:

COPPER (CYPRUS)
TIN (CORNWALL)
GLASSWARE (VENICE)
CORAL (LA CALLE)
WINE (ITALY)
SLAVES (LIBYA, ZANZIBAR)
YOUNG VIRGINS (EUROPE)
EUNUCHS (EUROPE)

Muza
Okelis
(Aden)

Zeila

Berbera

Cané

Oballa
(BASRA)

Guera

SHIRAZ

ORMUZ

FINE COTTON FA
LINENS
TEXTILE PRODU
RICE

Ozaka
(Kharachi)

Minagarsch

Muscat

PEARLS

SHELL
INCENSE
GLASSWARE

BARYC

Diu

Ma

Socotra

INCENSE
ALOE
MYRRH

Chinese

Junks

Cannanore

CALICUT

QUILON

CAMPHOR
PEPPER
CINNAMO

Obbra

Chinese junks

EAST COAST OF AFRICA

Mogadishu

IVORY
SHELL
SLAVES

0°

MELINDE

Zanzibar

CLOVES
SLAVES
ELEPHANTS
RHINOCEROS TUSKS

15°

Mozambique

GOLD

Zimbabwe

Sofala

30°

45°

60°

⊙ Major ports

○ Other ports

◉ Commercial centers

1. WORLD TRAD

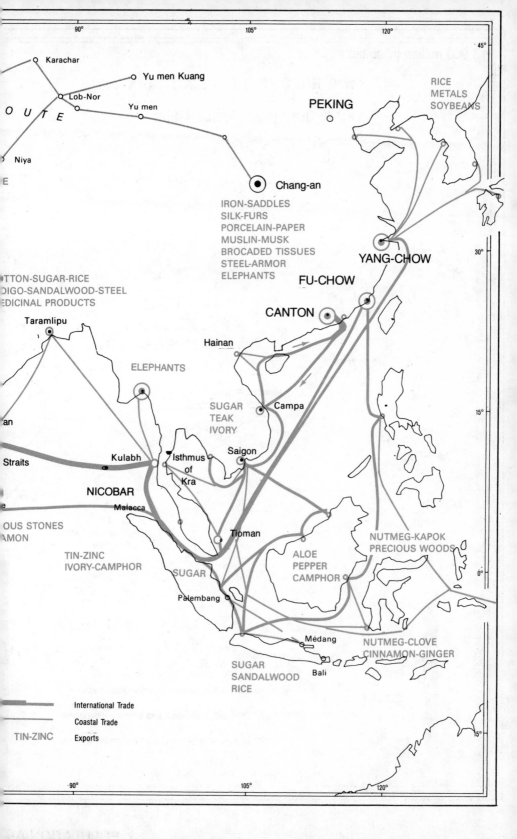

Karachar

Yu men Kuang

Lob-Nor

Yu men

O U T E

Niya

E

PEKING

RICE
METALS
SOYBEANS

● Chang-an

IRON-SADDLES
SILK-FURS
PORCELAIN-PAPER
MUSLIN-MUSK
BROCADED TISSUES
STEEL-ARMOR
ELEPHANTS

OTTON-SUGAR-RICE
DIGO-SANDALWOOD-STEEL
EDICINAL PRODUCTS

Taramlipu

ELEPHANTS

an

Kulabh

Straits

NICOBAR

Malacca

e

OUS STONES
AMON

TIN-ZINC
IVORY-CAMPHOR

SUGAR

Palembang

YANG-CHOW

FU-CHOW

CANTON

Hainan

SUGAR
TEAK
IVORY

Campa

Saigon

Isthmus
of
Kra

Tioman

ALOE
PEPPER
CAMPHOR

NUTMEG-KAPOK
PRECIOUS WOODS

Médang

Bali

NUTMEG-CLOVE
CINNAMON-GINGER

SUGAR
SANDALWOOD
RICE

International Trade

Coastal Trade

TIN-ZINC   Exports

14TH CENTURY

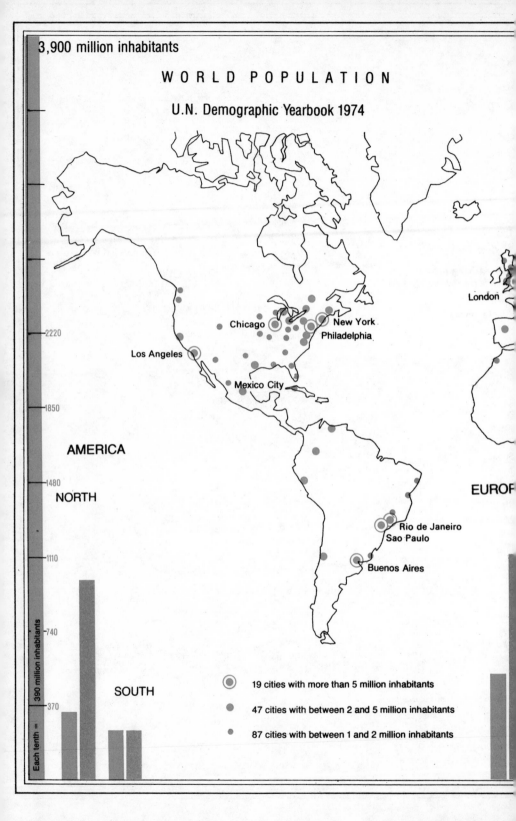

3,900 million inhabitants

WORLD POPULATION

U.N. Demographic Yearbook 1974

London

2220

1850

AMERICA

1480

NORTH

1110

740

390 million inhabitants

SOUTH

Each tenth =

370

EUROP

Chicago

New York

Philadelphia

Los Angeles

Mexico City

Rio de Janeiro
Sao Paulo

Buenos Aires

19 cities with more than 5 million inhabitants

47 cities with between 2 and 5 million inhabitants

87 cities with between 1 and 2 million inhabitants

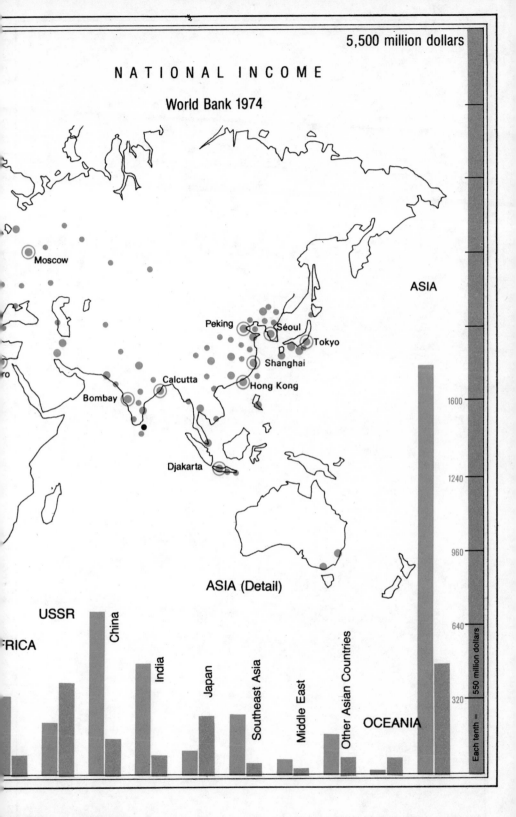

NATIONAL INCOME

World Bank 1974

5,500 million dollars

ASIA

Moscow

Peking
Séoul
Tokyo
Shanghai
Calcutta
Hong Kong
Bombay

Djakarta

ASIA (Detail)

1600

1240

960

USSR

China

India

Japan

Southeast Asia

Middle East

Other Asian Countries

640

Each tenth = 550 million dollars

FRICA

OCEANIA

320

ro

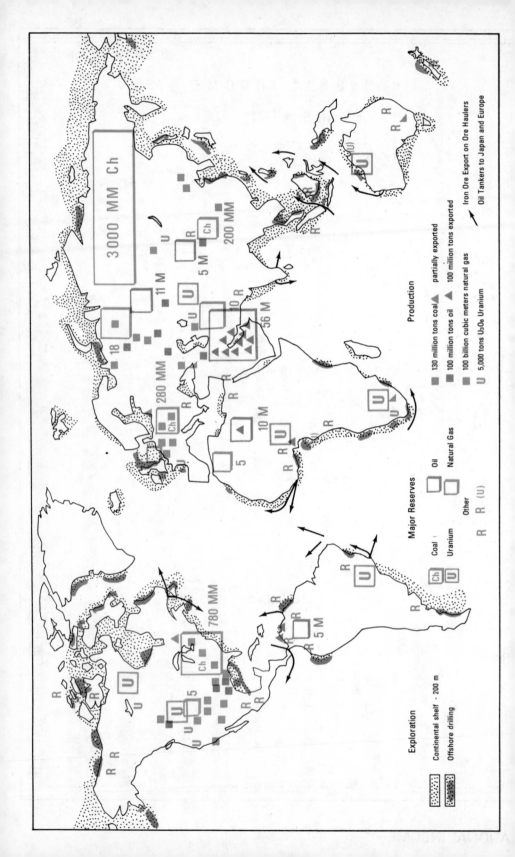

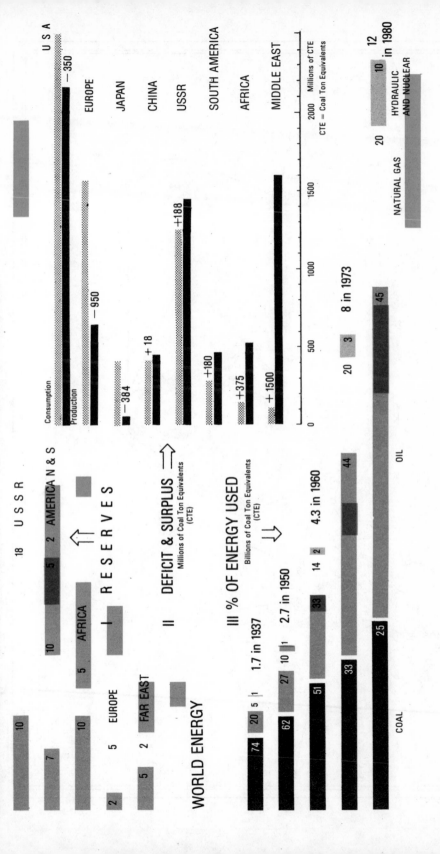

4. WORLD ENERGY

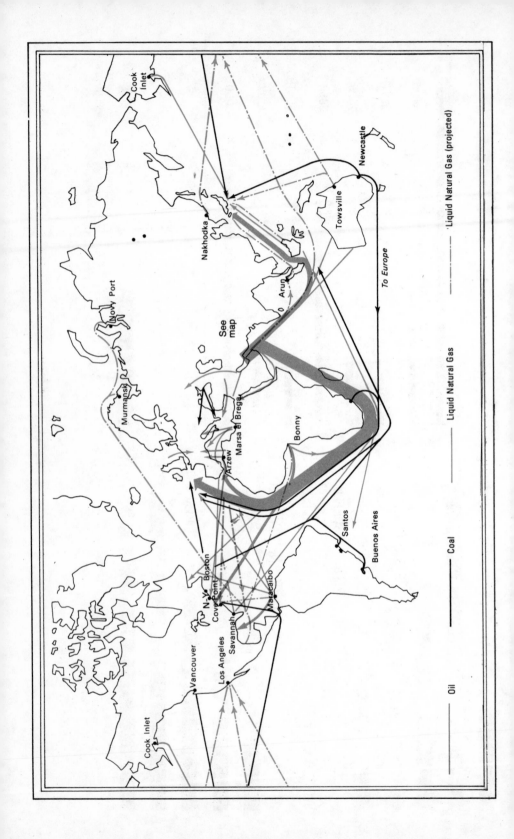

Cook Inlet

Cook Inlet

Vancouver

Los Angeles

Savannah

Maracaibo

Cove Point
N.Y.
Boston

Murmansk

Novy Port

See map

Arzew
Marsa el Brega

Bonny

Santos

Buenos Aires

Nakhodka

Arun

Towsville

Newcastle

To Europe

Oil ——————

Coal ——————

Liquid Natural Gas ——————

Liquid Natural Gas (projected) —·—·—·—

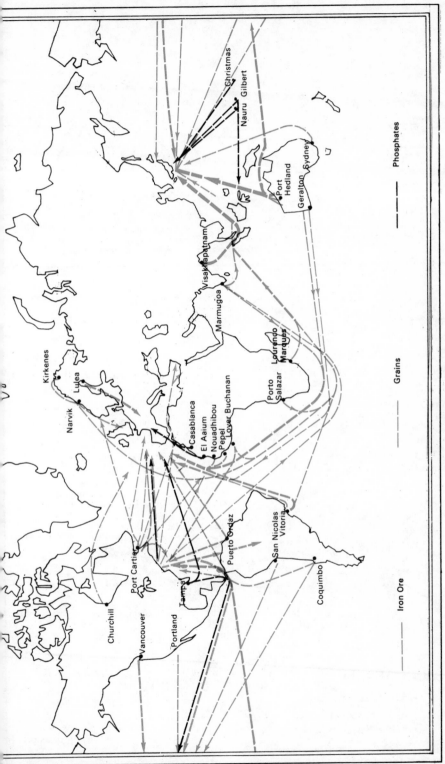

6. MARITIME SHIPPING
(Iron Ore-Grains-Phosphates)

Churchill
Vancouver
Portland
Port Cartier
Tampa
Puerto Ordaz
San Nicolas
Vitoria
Coquimbo

Kirkenes
Narvik
Lulea

Casablanca
El Aaium
Nouadhibou
Pepel
Lower Buchanan

Marmugoa
Visakhapatnam

Porto
Salazar
Lourenço
Marques

Christmas
Nauru
Gilbert

Port
Hedland
Geralton
Sydney

——— Iron Ore

——— Grains

– – – Phosphates

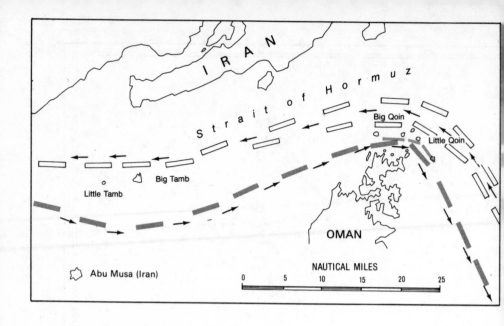

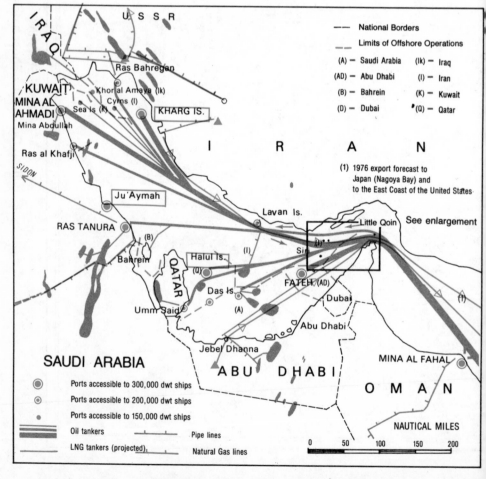

7. TRAFFIC ON THE PERSIAN GULF

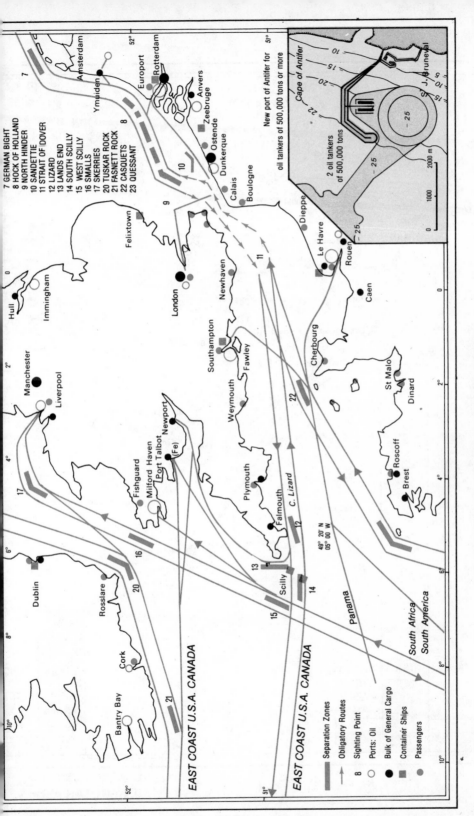

8. TRAFFIC CONTROL IN THE CHANNEL

7 GERMAN BIGHT
8 HOCK OF HOLLAND
9 NORTH HINDER
10 SANDETTIE
11 STRAIT OF DOVER
12 LIZARD
13 LANDS END
14 SOUTH SCILLY
15 WEST SCILLY
16 SMALLS
17 SKERRIES
20 TUSKAR ROCK
21 FASNETT ROCK
22 CASQUETS
23 QUESSANT

New port of Antifer for
oil tankers of 500,000 tons or more

2 oil tankers
of 500,000 tons

Cape of Antifer

J. Bruneval

EAST COAST U.S.A. CANADA

EAST COAST U.S.A. CANADA

Panama

South Africa
South America

49° 20' N
05° 00' W

Amsterdam
Ymuiden
Europort
Rotterdam
Anvers
Zeebruge
Ostende
Dunkerque
Calais
Boulogne
Dieppe
Le Havre
Rouen
Caen
Cherbourg
St Malo
Dinard
Roscoff
Brest

Hull
Immingham
Manchester
Liverpool
Fishguard
Milford Haven
Port Talbot
Newport (Fel)
Dublin
Rosslare
Cork
Bantry Bay

London
Felixtown
Newhaven
Southampton
Fawley
Weymouth
Plymouth
Falmouth
C. Lizard
Scilly

Separation Zones
Obligatory Routes
Sighting Point
Ports: Oil
Bulk of General Cargo
Container Ships
Passengers

2000 m
1000
0

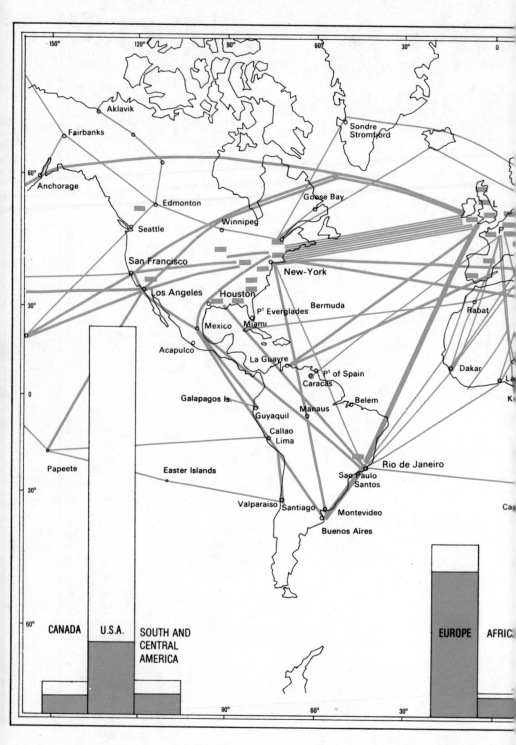

9. REGULAR AIR

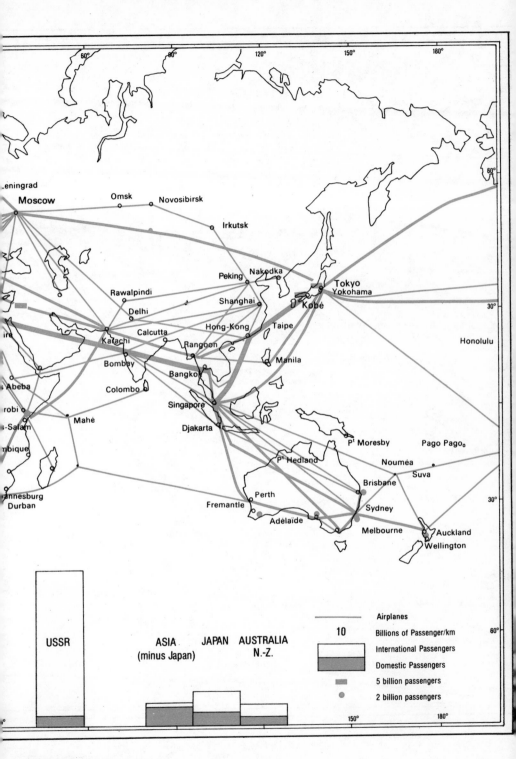

ROUTES (Passengers)

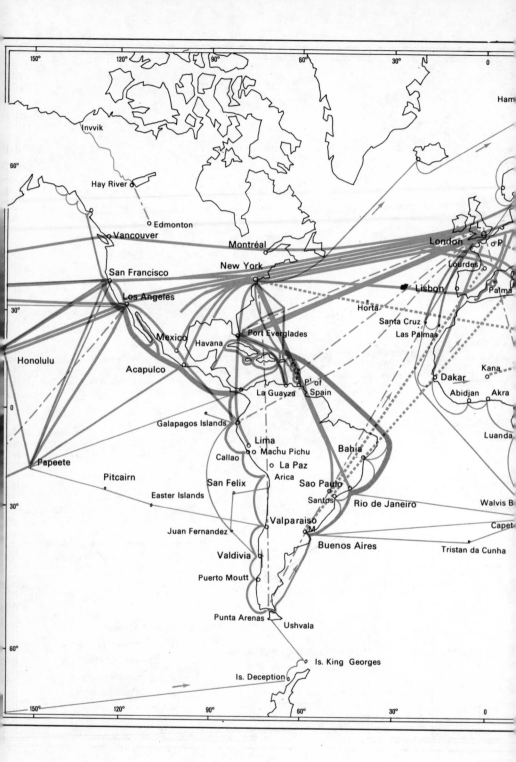

10. CHARTER

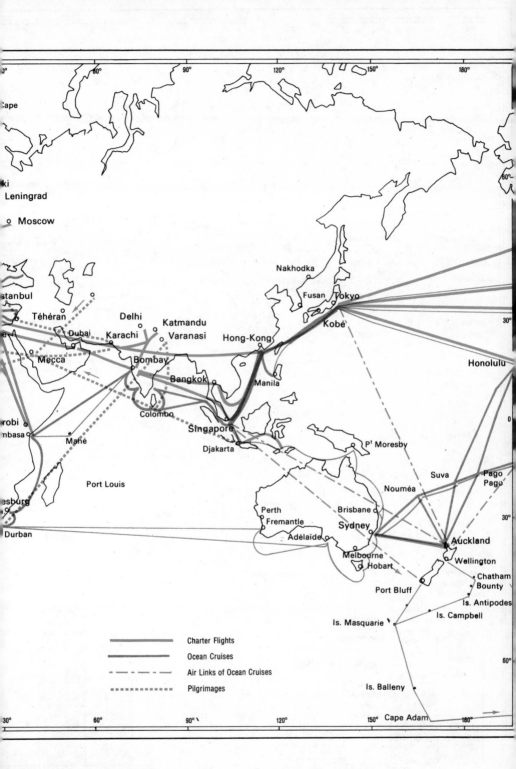

FLIGHTS AND CRUISES

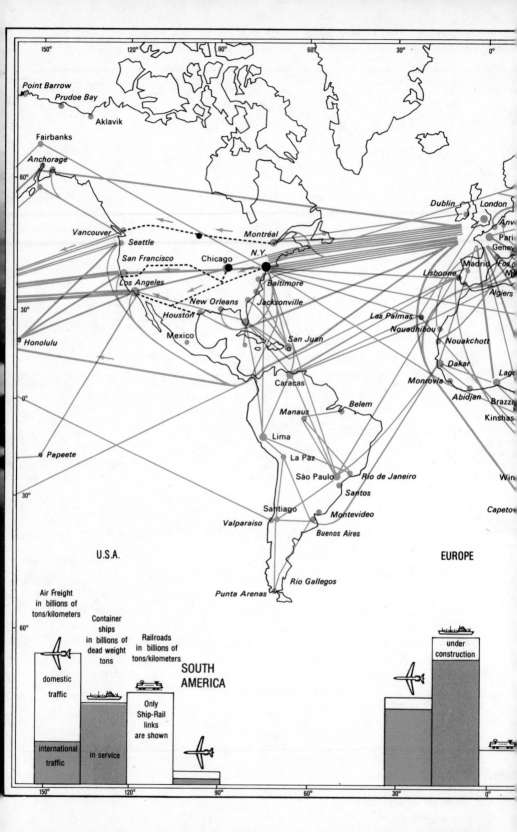

Point Barrow
Prudoe Bay
Aklavik
Fairbanks
Anchorage
60°

Vancouver
Seattle
San Francisco
Los Angeles
Chicago
Montréal
N.Y.
Baltimore
New Orleans
Jacksonville
Houston
Mexico
30°

Honolulu
0°

Papeete
30°

San Juan

Dublin   London
Ànv
Pari
Genev
Lisbonne   Madrid   Fos
N
Algiers

Las Palmas
Nouadhibou
Nouakchott
Dakar   Lago
Monrovia   Abidjan   Brazza
Kinshas

Caracas
Belem
Manaus
Lima
La Paz
Sào Paulo   Rio de Janeiro
Santos
Santiago   Montevideo
Valparaiso   Buenos Aires

Rio Gallegos
Punta Arenas

Win
Capetow

U.S.A.

EUROPE

Air Freight
in billions of
tons/kilometers
60°

Container
ships
in billions of
dead weight
tons

Railroads
in billions of
tons/kilometers

SOUTH
AMERICA

domestic
traffic

Only
Ship-Rail
links
are shown

under
construction

international
traffic

in service

150°   120°   90°   60°   30°   0°

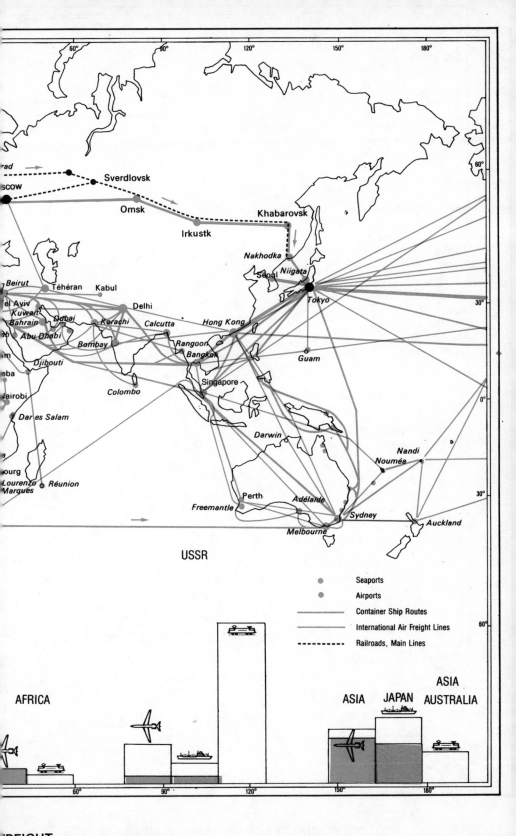

Sverdlovsk

scow

Omsk

Irkustk

Khabarovsk

Nakhodka

Niigata

Seoul

Tokyo

Beirut Téhéran Kabul

el Aviv

Kuwait

Bahrain Dubai

Abu Dhabi Karachi Calcutta Delhi Hong Kong

Bombay

Rangoon

Djibouti Bangkok

Guam

eba

airobi

Colombo Singapore

Dar es Salam

Darwin

Nandi

ourg Nouméa

Lourenzo Réunion

Marques

Perth Adélaïde

Freemantle

Sydney Auckland

Melbourne

USSR

	Seaports
	Airports
	Container Ship Routes
	International Air Freight Lines
	Railroads, Main Lines

ASIA

ASIA JAPAN AUSTRALIA

AFRICA

FREIGHT

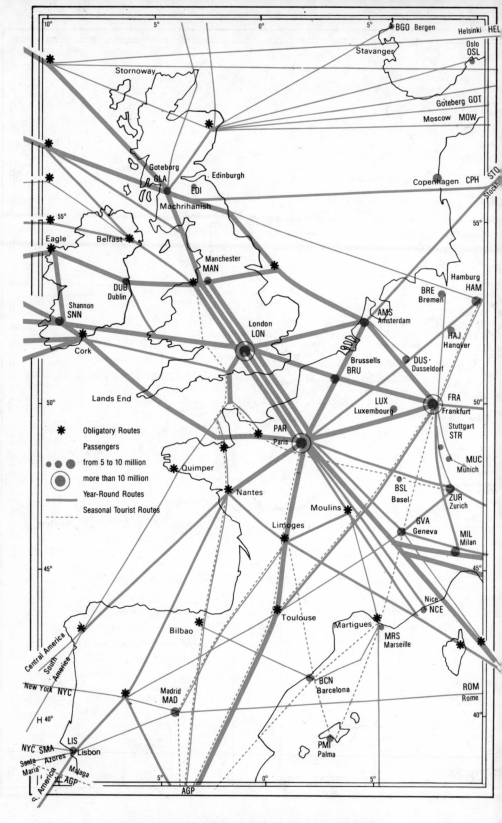

12. COORDINATION OF WESTERN EUROPE AIR TRAFFIC

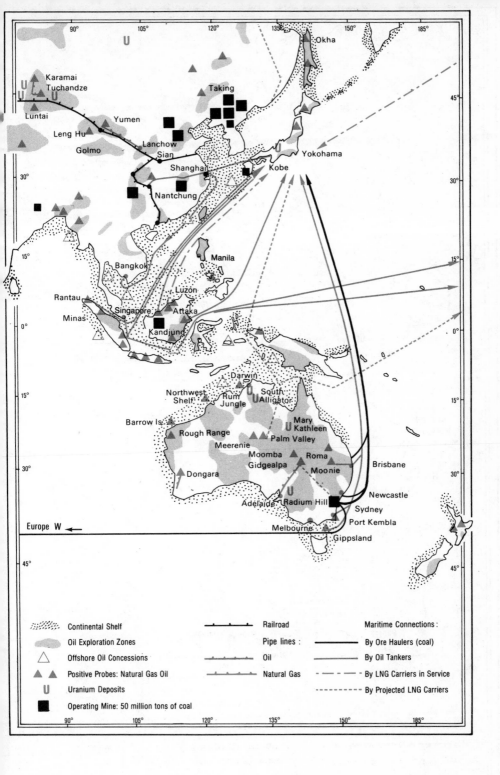

13. ENERGY SOURCES IN EASTERN ASIA

Legend:

- ⠿ Continental Shelf
- Oil Exploration Zones
- △ Offshore Oil Concessions
- ▲ ▲ Positive Probes: Natural Gas Oil
- U Uranium Deposits
- ■ Operating Mine: 50 million tons of coal

Railroad

Pipe lines:
- Oil
- Natural Gas

Maritime Connections:
- By Ore Haulers (coal)
- By Oil Tankers
- By LNG Carriers in Service
- By Projected LNG Carriers

Place names:
Karamai, Tuchandze, Luntai, Yumen, Leng Hu, Golmo, Lanchow, Sian, Taking, Shanghai, Nantchung, Kobe, Yokohama, Okha, Bangkok, Manila, Luzon, Rantau, Minas, Singapore, Attaka, Kandjung, Darwin, Northwest Shelf, Rum Jungle, South Alligator, Mary Kathleen, Barrow Is., Rough Range, Palm Valley, Meerenie, Moomba, Gidgealpa, Roma, Dongara, Moonie, Brisbane, Adelaide, Radium Hill, Newcastle, Sydney, Port Kembla, Melbourne, Gippsland

Europe W ←

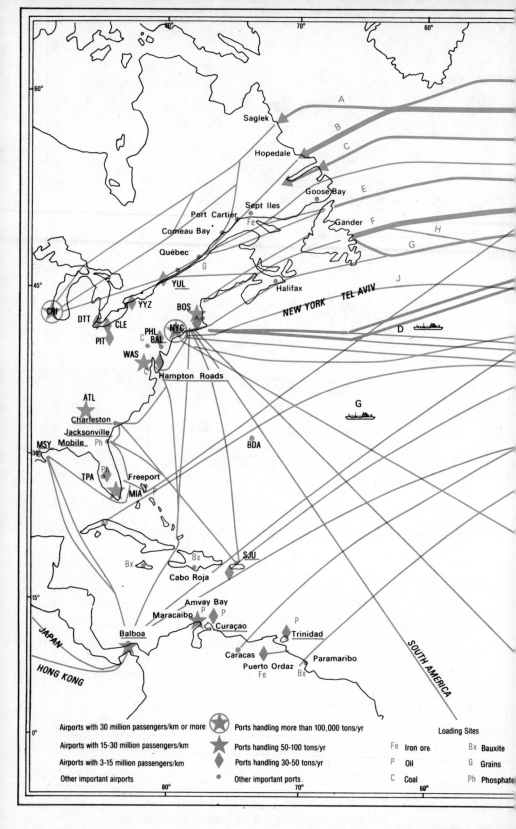

Saglek

Hopedale

Goose Bay

Port Cartier
Sept Iles
Comeau Bay
Québec
G
YUL
Halifax

Gander

NEW YORK   TEL AVIV

A
B
C
E
F
H
G
J
D

YYZ   BOS
DTT   CLE
CRI
PIT
PHL   NYC
BAL
C
WAS
C
Hampton Roads

ATL

Charleston
Jacksonville
MSY   Mobile   Ph
TPA   Ph
Freeport
MIA   P

BDA

G

SJU

Cabo Roja
Bx
Bx

Amvay Bay
Maracaibo   P   P
Curaçao   P   Trinidad
Balboa
Caracas
Puerto Ordaz   Paramaribo
Fe   Bx

JAPAN

HONG KONG

SOUTH AMERICA

⊛ Airports with 30 million passengers/km or more	⬟ Ports handling more than 100,000 tons/yr
★ Airports with 15-30 million passengers/km	★ Ports handling 50-100 tons/yr
◆ Airports with 3-15 million passengers/km	◆ Ports handling 30-50 tons/yr
● Other important airports	● Other important ports

Loading Sites

Fe Iron ore   Bx Bauxite
P   Oil   G   Grains
C   Coal   Ph Phosphate

60°   70°   60°

80°   70°   60°

14. NORTH ATLAN

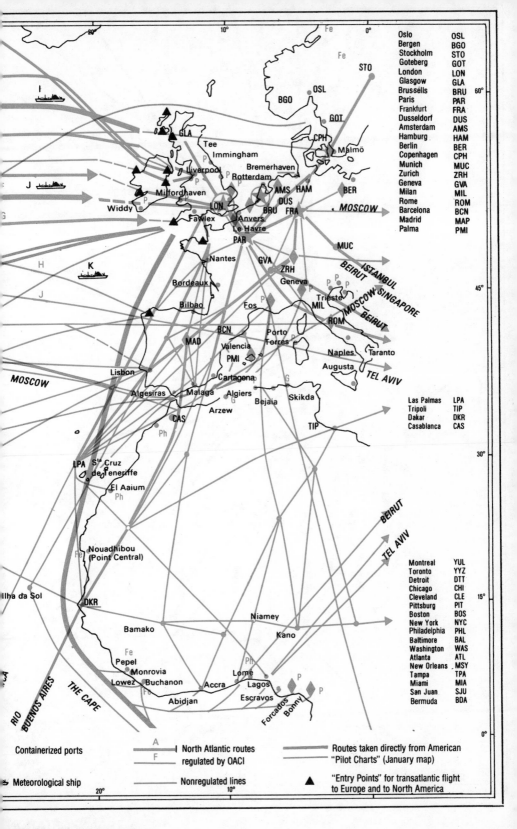

AIR AND SHIP ROUTES

Map labels:

Oslo	OSL
Bergen	BGO
Stockholm	STO
Goteberg	GOT
London	LON
Glasgow	GLA
Brussells	BRU
Paris	PAR
Frankfurt	FRA
Dusseldorf	DUS
Amsterdam	AMS
Hamburg	HAM
Berlin	BER
Copenhagen	CPH
Munich	MUC
Zurich	ZRH
Geneva	GVA
Milan	MIL
Rome	ROM
Barcelona	BCN
Madrid	MAP
Palma	PMI

Las Palmas	LPA
Tripoli	TIP
Dakar	DKR
Casablanca	CAS

Montreal	YUL
Toronto	YYZ
Detroit	DTT
Chicago	CHI
Cleveland	CLE
Pittsburg	PIT
Boston	BOS
New York	NYC
Philadelphia	PHL
Baltimore	BAL
Washington	WAS
Atlanta	ATL
New Orleans	MSY
Tampa	TPA
Miami	MIA
San Juan	SJU
Bermuda	BDA

Legend:

Containerized ports

Meteorological ship

North Atlantic routes regulated by OACI

Nonregulated lines

Routes taken directly from American "Pilot Charts" (January map)

"Entry Points" for transatlantic flight to Europe and to North America

Place names on map:
Oslo, Bergen, Stockholm, Goteberg, London, Glasgow, Brussels, Paris, Frankfurt, Dusseldorf, Amsterdam, Hamburg, Berlin, Copenhagen, Munich, Zurich, Geneva, Milan, Rome, Barcelona, Madrid, Palma, Malmö, Tee, Immingham, Bremerhaven, Rotterdam, Liverpool, Milfordhaven, Widdy, Fawlex, Anvers, Le Havre, Nantes, Bordeaux, Bilbao, Fos, Geneva, Trieste, Nantes, Porto Torres, Valencia, Naples, Taranto, Augusta, Lisbon, Algesiras, Malaga, Algiers, Bejaia, Skikda, Arzew, Cartagena, Cas, MOSCOW, ISTANBUL, BEIRUT, SINGAPORE, TEL AVIV, St Cruz de Tenerife, El Aaium, Nouadhibou (Point Central), Ilha da Sol, Dakar, Niamey, Bamako, Kano, Pepel, Monrovia, Lowez, Buchanon, Accra, Lome, Lagos, Escravos, Abidjan, Forcados, Bonny, RIO, BUENOS AIRES, THE CAPE

Fairbanks
Anchorage
45°
Cook Inlet (Alaska)
Vancouver
Seattle
San Francisco
Los Angeles
30°
Los Angeles
Panama
15°
Honolulu
Panama
Peru
Chile

150°
135°
120°
105°
90°

Guam

Tokyo
Yokohama
Niigata

Harbin
Kirin
Vladivostok
Nakhodka
Wosan
Fushun
Shenyand
Seoul
Daegu
Pusan
Inchon
Hsinkang
Peking
Lien Yun Chang
Nanking
Shanghai
Changchow
Ningspo
Wuhan
Foochow
Changsha
Kaoshiung
Swatow
Hong-Kong
Chungking
Chengtu
Haiphong
Da Nang
Cam Ranh
Hanoi
Saigon
Bangkok
Rangoon
Middle East

Naha
Keelung

Fe
B
Ph
Cu
Manila
Cebu

Brunei
Miri
Fe
Cu
Mn

Port
Klang
Fe

15. TRANSPORTATION

IN EASTERN ASIA

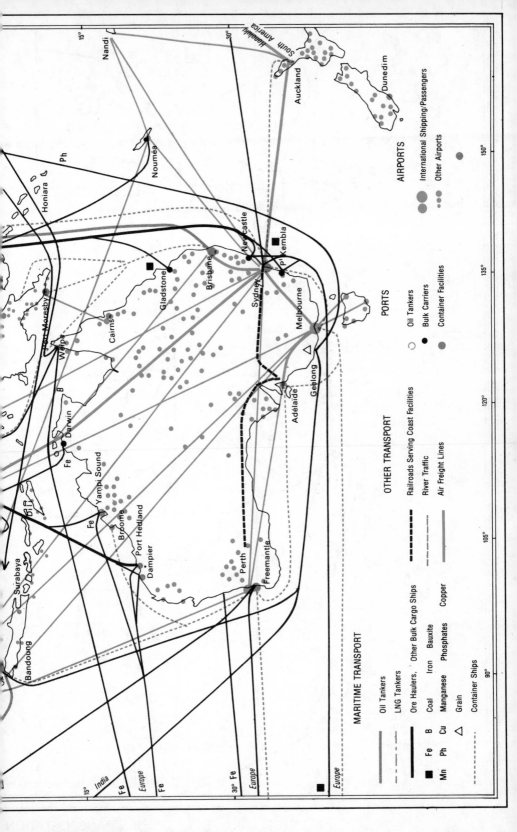

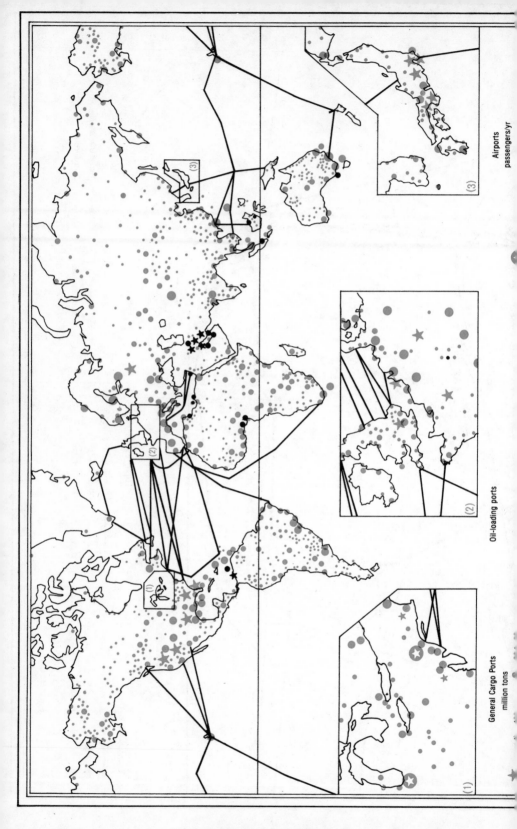

Airports
passengers/yr

Oil-loading ports

General Cargo Ports
million tons

(1)

(2)

(3)

16. PORTS AND AIRPORTS

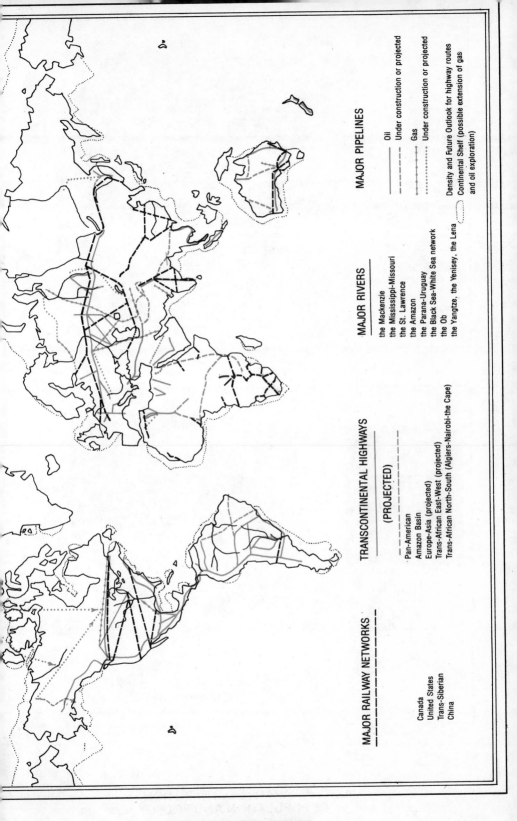

MAJOR RAILWAY NETWORKS

Canada
United States
Trans-Siberian
China

TRANSCONTINENTAL HIGHWAYS

(PROJECTED)

Pan-American
Amazon Basin
Europe-Asia (projected)
Trans-African East-West (projected)
Trans-African North-South (Algiers-Nairobi-the Cape)

MAJOR RIVERS

the Mackenzie
the Mississippi-Missouri
the St. Lawrence
the Amazon
the Parana-Uruguay
the Black Sea-White Sea network
the Ob
the Yangtze, the Yenisey, the Lena

MAJOR PIPELINES

Oil
Under construction or projected
Gas
Under construction or projected
Density and Future Outlook for highway routes
Continental Shelf (possible extension of gas
and oil exploration)

17. OVERLAND TRANSPORT

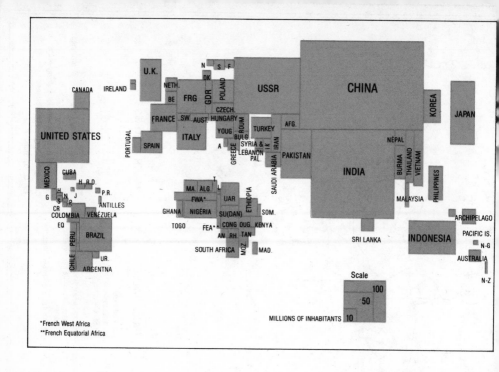

CANADA IRELAND U.K. N S F USSR CHINA KOREA JAPAN

NETH. DK POLAND
BE FRG GDR
FRANCE SW AUST HUNGARY CZECH. ROUM TURKEY AFG.
UNITED STATES PORTUGAL ITALY A YOUG BULG SYRIA & IRAN NEPAL
SPAIN GREECE LEBANON PAL. PAKISTAN BURMA THAILAND VIETNAM PHILIPPINES
MEXICO CUBA SAUDI ARABIA INDIA MALAYSIA
H R.D. MA ALG T ARCHIPELAGO
G H P.R. FWA* UAR ETHIOPIA PACIFIC IS.
S N J GHANA NIGÉRIA SU(DAN) SOM. N-G
CR ANTILLES TOGO SU(DAN) INDONESIA AUSTRALIA
COLOMBIA VENEZUELA FEA** CONG OUG KENYA
EQ TAN SRI LANKA N-Z
PERU BRAZIL AN RH.
CHILE UR. SOUTH AFRICA MOZ. MAD.
ARGENTNA

Scale
100
50
MILLIONS OF INHABITANTS 10

*French West Africa
**French Equatorial Africa

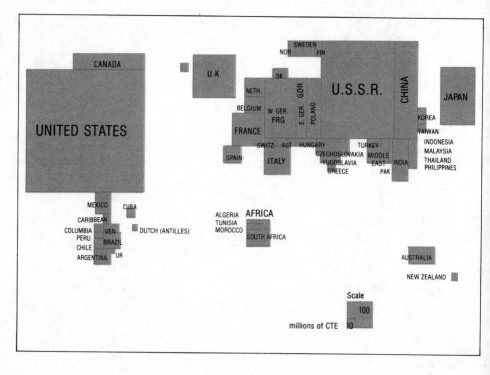

SWEDEN
NOR FIN
CANADA U.K. DK U.S.S.R. CHINA JAPAN
NETH. GDR
BELGIUM W. GER. E. GER. POLAND KOREA
FRG TAIWAN
UNITED STATES FRANCE U.S.S.R. INDONESIA
SWITZ. AUT HUNGARY TURKEY MALAYSIA
SPAIN ITALY CZECHOSLOVAKIA MIDDLE THAILAND
YUGOSLAVIA EAST INDIA PHILIPPINES
GREECE PAK
MEXICO CUBA
CARIBBEAN ALGERIA AFRICA
COLUMBIA VEN DUTCH (ANTILLES) TUNISIA
PERU BRAZIL MOROCCO
CHILE SOUTH AFRICA
ARGENTINA UR. AUSTRALIA
NEW ZEALAND

Scale
100
millions of CTE 10

18. COMPARATIVE DISTRIBUTION
OF POPULATION AND ENERGY

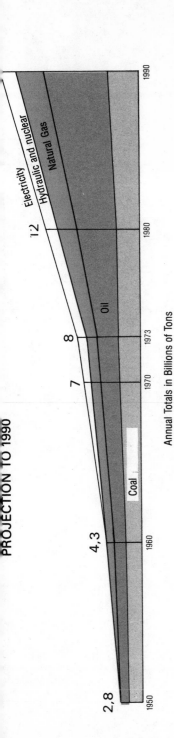

Electricity and nuclear
Hydraulic and nuclear
Natural Gas
Oil
Coal

12
8
7
4,3
2,8

1950 1960 1970 1973 1980 1990

Annual Totals in Billions of Tons

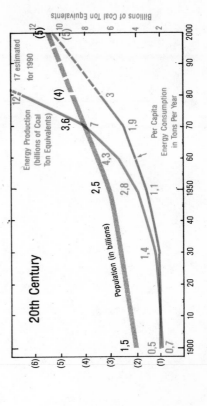

Billions of Coal Ton Equivalents

20th Century

Energy Production
(billions of Coal
Ton Equivalents)

17 estimated
for 1990

12

3,6

7

2,5

4,3

1,9

2,8

Per Capita
Energy Consumption
in Tons Per Year

3

1,1

Population (in billions)

1,4

1,5

0,5

0,7

(6)
(5)
(4)
(3)
(2)
(1)

(5)
(4)
(5)

1900 10 20 30 40 50 60 70 80 90 2000

20. POPULATION-ENERGY CONSUMPTION